RICKY HATTON'S VEGAS TALES

✳ RICKY ✳
HATTON'S ✳
VEGAS TALES

with Justyn Barnes

headline

First published in 2015
by HEADLINE PUBLISHING GROUP

2

Cataloguing in Publication Data is available from the British Library

Hardback ISBN 978 1 4722 2347 0
Trade Paperback ISBN 978 1 4722 3114 7

Typeset in Minion Pro by Avon DataSet Ltd, Bidford-on-Avon, Warwickshire

Printed and bound in Great Britain by Clays Ltd, St Ives plc

MIX
Paper from
responsible sources
FSC® C104740

Headline's policy is to use papers that are natural, renewable and recyclable products
and made from wood grown in well-managed forests and other controlled sources. The
logging and manufacturing processes are expected to conform to the environmental
regulations of the country of origin.

HEADLINE PUBLISHING GROUP
An Hachette UK Company
Carmelite House
50 Victoria Embankment
London EC4Y 0DZ

www.headline.co.uk
www.hachette.co.uk

This book is dedicated to all of my fans for their support in Las Vegas – unparalleled before or since – which made those times so special. Thank you.

ACKNOWLEDGEMENTS

My thanks to Justyn Barnes for his hard work and help in bringing my Vegas memories to life on the page. Also, to my agent Paul Speak for reminding me of some of the madness that went on in Vegas. I'm also hugely grateful to the following people for their contributions: John Angelsea, Marco Antonio Barrera, Joey Blower, Steve Bunce, Kugan Cassius, Ian Darke, Geraldine Davies, Robert Diaz, Jennifer Dooley, David Dunn, Kevin Francis, Noel Gallagher, Matthew Hatton, Thomas Hauser, Dennis Hobson, Oscar De La Hoya, Bernard Jones, Kerry Kayes, Steve Lillis, Glenn McCrory, Will Mellor, David 'The Duck' Owen, Jeff Powell, Mark Robinson, Joe Sharpe and Adam Smith.

Finally, big thanks to Jonathan Taylor and all the team at Headline for backing this project.

Lyrics to *Hi Ho Ricky Fatton* on pages 244–5 are reproduced with the kind permission of Joey Blower.

Punch statistics for my Vegas fights are reproduced with the kind permission of CompuBox, Inc.

FOREWORD

Ricky Hatton was one of the rare fighters who wasn't just a world champion and a boxing superstar, but someone who was just like the fans who paid to see him fight. It wouldn't be out of the ordinary to see Ricky hanging out with his supporters after one of his big fights in Las Vegas, making sure there was no separation between him and the people.

That attitude came from his upbringing in Manchester, and fame never changed him. That's why he was one of the most popular boxers of his era. Of course he was a world-class fighter who beat some of the best in the game and also fought the likes of Floyd Mayweather and Manny Pacquiao, but the reason he was so popular was because he wasn't 'The Hitman' to his fans; he was just Ricky, and watching him fight was like watching one of your friends in the ring.

As the fans always sang during his fights, 'There's only one Ricky Hatton'.

Oscar De La Hoya *Ten-time world boxing champion in six weight divisions and founder of Golden Boy Promotions*
January 2015

CONTENTS

INTRODUCTION

Me, in Las Vegas – what could possibly go wrong?

Well, quite a lot as it happens, but I also had the time of my life when I fought there five times between 2007 and 2009.

In this book, I relive my most memorable moments: from fight negotiations, through trash-talking transatlantic promotional tours, gruelling training camps, bizarre encounters with opponents, fans, A-list celebrities and boxing legends; all the way to fight-week mayhem and the epic post-fight benders that followed.

I've also asked family, friends, journalists and some of the new friends I made in the UK and America during my Vegas journey to give their side of the stories.

Along the way, you'll discover the answers to many of the big questions you might have about my Vegas years . . . and to quite a few more that have probably never crossed your mind.

For example, how did comedian John Bishop help me prepare to fight Floyd Mayweather Jr.?

Why did I get pushed into the Playboy Club in a wheelchair to meet Noel Gallagher?

How did I manage to beat Manny Pacquiao (at darts)?

Why did I blank Brad Pitt?

What caused Team Hatton to have a massive row about biscuits in a Vegas park at 6am?

And how the fuck did a fat little bloke from the Hattersley estate end up topping the bill at the MGM Grand, supported by tens of thousands of travelling Brits?

Yes, it's all here – the good, the bad and the Pretty Boy Floyd. So sit back – and I hope you enjoy the surreal, crazy ride as much as I did.

Ricky Hatton
January 2015

BREAKING AMERICA

DOUGHNUTS AND PRAYERS IN THE BIG APPLE

Boxing fans remember my fights in Boston and Las Vegas at the back end of my career as the time when I tried to 'break America'. They might not realise that I actually broke America many years before, in only my second pro fight . . . it's just that America didn't really notice.

By the time I turned pro, I was quite a student of the game. I'd watched tapes of a lot of the old fights at Madison Square Garden, once the Mecca of boxing in the United States. When my promoter Frank Warren told me I was going to be fighting there on the undercard of the Naseem Hamed–Kevin Kelley show in December 1997, it was a jaw-dropper.

The only downer is that my trainer Billy Graham can't come with me. As with a lot of the big shows in America featuring British fighters, there's also a show in Britain the same night to be screened live on Sky before they switch to the action in New York. On this occasion, it's at Millwall FC's stadium, and one of the top boys in Billy's gym at the time, Ensley Bingham, is fighting Nicky Thurbin for the British light middleweight title, and, of course, Billy has to be there.

So I have to go off to New York on my own the week before the fight.

Once I get out there, I get to know another young British prospect, the Brixton heavyweight Danny Williams, a born-again Christian, who's also on the bill. We're in the same boat because Danny's trainer, Jim McDonnell, is also working a corner back home at the Millwall show. I get to know Danny over the week and he's an absolutely lovely fella.

We train at a good gym near the hotel, and I'm excited to see Iran Barkley there who was involved in wars with two of my childhood heroes, Nigel Benn and Roberto Duran, back in the day.

My opponent is a local Brooklyn fighter called Robert Alvarez, and if you saw us at the weigh-in, you'd have thought it was man against boy. There's me; milky white skin, no tattoos, hardly a hair on my bollocks let alone my chest, and a choirboy basin haircut. Then there's Alvarez, seven years older, hairy-chested as Tom Selleck and covered in tattoos. When Alvarez strips off to get on the scales, I say to Danny: 'I don't know whether to fight him or fucking read him.'

It also turns out he's a welterweight – either that or he's missed the light-welterweight limit by a mile.

I phone Billy up and said: 'This guy's half a stone heavier than me.'

'You're fucking joking.'

'What am I going to do?'

'Well, you're out there now, you'll just have to get on with it.'

Cheers, Bill.

For the fight to go ahead, though, the weights need to be evened up a bit, so the officials tell Alvarez to go for a run to shed a couple of pounds. I get the better end of the deal – I'm told to go eat a few doughnuts. Lovely.

He might be older, bigger and scarier-looking than me, but Alvarez has lost two of his first four fights. I'm already used to sparring with older and high-quality fighters in my gym back home like Ensley, Paul Burke, Andy Holligan and Jawaid 'Too Sleek' Khaliq (great nickname), and doing well against them so I'm not bothered.

In Billy's absence, I have Ernie Fossey, God rest his soul, Frank Warren's matchmaker at the time, in my corner. It's only a four rounder, but I win every round on two of the judges' cards and lose just one on the other.

I'm way down the bill, of course, so the arena is half-empty, but George Foreman who's commentating on the evening's fights for HBO, is impressed. He tells Frank Warren and a couple of people at Sky afterwards that he thinks I have the ability to go all the way.

After my win, I get to sit ringside for the Hamed–Kelley fight among all the A-list Hollywood celebrities. The fight turns out to be the featherweight division's answer to Hagler–Hearns, with six knockdowns before Naz stops him in the fourth round. The atmosphere is amazing.

I'm still buzzing afterwards and fancy going out to see a bit of New York, so I ask Danny, who has also won his fight, if he wants to join me for a beer to celebrate.

'No thanks, Ricky. I'm feeling really tired. I'm just going to go to McDonalds, back to the hotel, say my prayers to thank the Lord for getting me through the fight okay, and go to bed.'

'Alright, Danny. No problem, mate. See you tomorrow.'

So Danny heads off. A few minutes later, I'm standing outside Madison Square Garden on my tod, kitbag over my shoulder, thinking: what am I going to do now?

Just then I hear a Scouse voice from over the road: 'Alright, Ricky lad. What you up to?' Two fellas come over.

'Well, just thinking about going for a pint, but Danny's going to bed . . .'

'Come out on the piss with us, la.'

So I drop my gear off back at the hotel, get changed and off we go.

We had more than a few scoops that night and I certainly enjoyed my first taste of a big fight night in America and big night out afterwards. Little did I know then that a decade later I'd be topping the bill on big shows in Vegas, and instead of looking round for someone to go for a beer with, there would be thousands of people around all up for a party.

LAS VEGAS – MY KIND OF TOWN

It was exciting to fight in Madison Square Garden, but by the time I was getting into my teens, Las Vegas had taken over from New York as the capital city of boxing in the USA and was hosting the biggest fights. Seeing Nigel Benn go over there in 1990 and smash Iran Barkley to bits (see *Ricky's top ten Vegas tear-ups*, page 192) was the one that really fired my ambition to become a pro boxer myself. Watching the TV coverage of the fight, all the excitement surrounding it, seeing the neon lights of the Strip, Vegas just seemed like the place to be. Then I started watching video tapes (younger readers – videos are what we used to watch before YouTube . . .) of the massive Vegas fights of the past. Their boxing events just looked bigger and brighter than anywhere else in the world and that stuck with me. As soon as I won the world title, I wanted to fight there.

Steve Wynn, the billionaire who developed a lot of the major hotels on the Strip, got it right when he said that Las Vegas lets you 'dream with your eyes open'. It's a surreal place and I've learnt some almost unbelievable but true stories about its history.

Looking at the place it is now, it's amazing to think that a hundred years ago, the only people who lived in Vegas was a tribe of native Indians who'd been in the area for centuries and about thirty other settlers.

Vegas is less than 150 miles from Death Valley, one of the hottest places on earth, and the only reason anyone stopped there in the first place is because it has a couple of freshwater springs. A few New Mexican traders stumbled across this little oasis in the desert in 1829 and named it Las Vegas, Spanish for 'the meadows'.

Things changed in 1902 when a very rich and corrupt business-man from Montana called William Clark visited the area for the first time. He'd made his fortune in copper and spent over $300,000 in bribes to get himself elected as a senator. Now he was building a railroad from Los Angeles to Salt Lake City going through Las Vegas. There was hardly anything there then, so Clark set up a company to develop the town. By the time the railroad was completed in 1905, Vegas was well and truly on the map.

Apart from water, though, Vegas had nothing else to offer in the way of resources, so they had to find other ways to bring in people and money. Once the railroad boom was over, in the Twenties, Vegas only survived because people went there for the booze, gambling and prostitution, to which the authorities turned a blind eye. The state of Nevada had always had a bit of an anything-goes attitude and that included prizefighting – at one time it was the only state in America that allowed it.

Las Vegas might easily have become a ghost town, though, if it hadn't been for the US government building the 'Boulder Dam' (the name was later changed to Hoover Dam') nearby. Thousands of jobs were created, millions of dollars were pumped into the area by the government and it was the turning point for Vegas.

At the time 'games of chance' were illegal everywhere else in the States, but as usual Nevada lawmakers were up for anything that would turn a dollar and dished out gambling licences freely. Within a few years, penny slot machines could be found in all the grocery stores and petrol stations around Vegas and casinos sprung up everywhere. This brought in hardcore gamblers from other states and tourists who fancied a flutter on their way to see the Boulder Dam, which was being hyped up as 'the eighth wonder of the world'. Las Vegas was promoted as 'The Gateway to Boulder Dam' and the town's reputation as a scandalous destination was sold as a chance for Americans 'to experience the Old West'.

People started drifting in from Los Angeles, including LAPD vice squad commander Captain Guy McAfee. Weirdly, for a policeman in charge of the vice squad, McAfee was married to a Hollywood madam – he obviously wanted to investigate the sex industry very, very closely. He also owned a few underground gambling dens in LA. By the time the corrupt Captain and his associates came to Vegas, they were experts in running casinos – and they took over most of the local gambling businesses.

The start of the Strip as it is today was the opening of the El Rancho hotel in 1941, three miles south of the centre of Vegas on Highway 91. The hotel for the first time put the casino in the middle of a luxury resort. Even though there were hardly any properties there at the time, Captain McAfee started calling it 'the Strip' hoping that one day it might be Vegas's answer to Sunset Strip in Hollywood.

The Captain might have been wrong 'un, but he was Mother Theresa compared to the next big mover and shaker in Vegas history – Benjamin 'Bugsy' Siegel. Siegel was a mobster from New

York and wasn't someone you wanted to get on the wrong side of. When he wasn't personally carrying out gangland executions, he worked with Syndicate boss Meyer Lansky to manage dodgy businesses in cities across America. Bootlegging, protection rackets, gambling, prostitution, drugs – the Syndicate were into it all.

Vegas was easy meat for the mob and Bugsy lead the way, investing Syndicate money in various casinos and buying the downtown El Cortez hotel outright. It was a perfect arrangement – the old owner of the hotel would act as front man, while cash skimmed off the top was shared out to mob investors.

The look of hotel-casinos up until then had had an old Western theme, but Bugsy told the press he was going to build 'the goddam biggest, fanciest gaming casino and hotel you bastards ever seen in your lives'.

No expense was spared as Siegel tried to impress those 'bastards' by constructing his dream hotel. He named it the Flamingo. It ended up costing around $6 million to build (including bribes), over three times what the Syndicate members expected – and they weren't happy. A lot of rooms still weren't finished when the hotel opened for business in December 1946 and it had to close down again a fortnight later having lost $300,000, meaning Siegel had to go cap in hand to the Syndicate again.

The Flamingo reopened three months later and was making a profit within one month, but Siegel knew he was in trouble. Apart from his mate Lansky, a lot of the top boys in the Syndicate reckoned Siegel had been skimming off some of the money that they'd stuck into the project.

Siegel had the locks changed on the door of his suite at the hotel every week, but in June while sitting in the living room at his girlfriend's house in Beverly Hills, nine shots were fired through the window. Bugsy's right eye was found on the other side of the room from his dead body. Before his body was even cold, another mobster called Gus Greenbaum had taken charge of the Flamingo for the Syndicate.

Bugsy was dead but mob rule of Vegas casinos would continue for years to come and the Flamingo was the start of a new look for Vegas. Stuffed buffalo heads and wagon wheels on the walls were out, and the dazzling neon lights we see today were in.

The Strip was getting busier and busier and its first high-rise hotel, the Riviera, opened in 1955. It wasn't just the serious gamblers and high-rollers coming to Vegas now either, average Joes came too attracted by luxury hotels at a fairly cheap price – the hotels knew the more people they got in, the better. Even if they only bet a few dollars at a time in the slots, it all added up. All the big-name entertainers started to pile into Vegas too – the likes of Frank Sinatra, Bing Crosby, Sammy Davis Jr. and Liberace were being paid up to $50,000 per week even back then in the Fifties.

With money to be made there, it was only a matter of time before boxing joined the party.

Television had really kick-started interest in the sport in the USA – a Willie Pep featherweight title fight in 1944 was actually the first-ever sporting event to be available to watch across America. NBC's Friday-night fights from Madison Square Garden on *The Gillette Cavalcade of Sports* show became massively popular over the next few years. By the late Fifties, boxing in New York and on TV was in decline, though. The quality of fights shown wasn't up to scratch, fights were being fixed by gangsters and viewers were switching off until NBC scrapped the Gillette show in 1960.

Boxing needed a new Mecca and found it in the middle of the desert. The timing was good because the Las Vegas Convention Center had been built and opened in 1959. It was an excellent venue for boxing – eight thousand seats, close to the hotels so their guests could get there and back easily, and with good facilities for TV broadcasts. The game-changer was the first heavyweight title fight to be held in Vegas in July 1963, when Sonny Liston knocked Floyd Patterson down three times and won in the first round.

Hotels were falling over themselves to sponsor title bouts because they could see the amount of extra people – big gamblers and mug punters – which big fights brought to town. With so much money to be made, soon the hotel bosses were thinking, 'Why not stage the fight ourselves?' The president of Caesars Palace, Cliff Perlman, was the guy who really went for it, though. He started off staging fights in the mid-Seventies in the Caesars' indoor tennis arena which could fit 5,000 people, but when Muhammad Ali took on Larry Holmes in 1980, Perlman had a 24,000 temporary arena built in the car park to meet the huge demand for tickets. It proved to be a sad night for boxing, because Ali was a shadow of his great self and took a beating from his old sparring partner, but the event generated massive profits. Money from the fight itself was just the cherry on top; the big bucks were made from the gamblers who packed the casinos in fight week. The million dollars it cost to build the arena and then take it down again was a drop in the ocean and Caesars Palace went on to host the biggest boxing events of the next two decades, ones that I watched growing up and still remember well.

By the time I was in a position to fulfil my dream of fighting there myself, Vegas was the undisputed boxing capital of the world, but things had changed. Caesars Palace wasn't really in the boxing game anymore. One man who worked at Caesars thought I could change that, though, and we did with the help of a promoter from Sheffield.

HOBSON AND SHARPE

Hobson and Sharpe sounds like a TV detective series, but actually they were two of the key people who eventually got me fighting in Vegas – Dennis Hobson and Joe Sharpe.

After my epic win over the great Kostya Tszyu in 2005, I split from my long-time promoter Frank Warren. Frank had done a brilliant job for me throughout my pro career and I really liked him, but sadly our business partnership didn't end well. I'd accepted the purse he'd offered to face Kostya Tszyu because I knew he'd had to pay Kostya to come over to fight in my backyard, but I believed that if I won, I would make the money on my next fights. I did win, and the fight had brilliant viewing figures, but Frank's next offer didn't match my expectations based on our previous conversations.

I don't regret leaving Frank because I think he could have paid me a lot more than he was offering. If he had done, I would have loved to stay with him until he retired. But other promoters put a lot more money on the table. Golden Boy and Main Events in the States made offers, but the Sheffield-based promoter Dennis Hobson offered the most and I decided to go with him.

At the time, Dennis was already looking after the likes of Carl Thompson, David Haye and Clinton Woods, and adding me to his stable of fighters made him as big as any promoter in Britain at the time.

For a while, everybody had been asking, 'Ricky, when are you going to fight in America?' and after a tough fight against Carlos Maussa in Sheffield – my first fight promoted by Dennis – I was scheduled to have my first top-of-the-bill fight Stateside against Juan Lazcano in May 2006.

The Lazcano fight was the chance for me to really make my mark over there. A few of my previous bouts had been aired in America by Showtime, including the Kostya Tszyu battle, and I was already ranked as the world's number one light-welterweight by *The Ring* magazine in the States, so fight fans there knew about me. Lazcano was the first bout in my new three-fight deal with the giant HBO network, though, giving me greater exposure Stateside than ever before and hopefully moving me towards megafights – at the time, Shane Mosley and Oscar De La Hoya were touted as possible opponents.

Then, with just nine weeks to fight night, Lazcano pulled out. I didn't want to lose the exposure on HBO, so we had to find another opponent quick – easier said than done. HBO have an approved list of opponents and there were only two others on there: Vivian Harris, former WBA light-welterweight champion, or Luis Collazo, who had the WBA welterweight belt. Dennis wanted me to fight Vivian Harris at my own weight, but he didn't hold a world title, and I wanted to win more world titles so I insisted on Collazo.

Moving up a weight and going straight into a world title fight was not my brightest idea – most boxers take a couple of warm-up fights to adjust to a new division – and Collazo proved to be a very tough opponent. I struggled to adjust to his southpaw style which I hadn't faced for a while, and to carrying the extra seven pounds. I only just got through a gruelling fight. Although the points win meant I'd become a two-weight world champion, it was far from a convincing performance (apart from convincing me I should move straight back down to light welter again).

Staging the fight in Boston wasn't the best either. That's no disrespect to the Boston people who were very hospitable, and the 6,000 crowd, with plenty of Brits among them, created a good atmosphere. But I was used to filling bigger arenas back home and it wasn't quite how I'd imagined it when, growing up, I'd watched those big fights in America.

Dennis Hobson:

The Boston fight wasn't the most successful promotion because it was last minute. It didn't sell as well. It wasn't a fight I wanted to do. And Don King also represented the German welterweight Oktay Urkal who was the mandatory challenger for Collazo's title, so at the last minute he demanded $100,000 step-aside money for Urkal which we had to cough up.

Urkal himself then asked me for another $50,000 training expenses because he said he went into training camp thinking Ricky would fight him. I said to him, 'No way – you earn more money for not fighting than fighting!' When I bumped into Urkal at an IBF convention a couple of years ago, he asked me again!

On the plus side, I did manage to stitch up Dennis at one of the pre-fight press conferences in Boston.

Dennis will tell you he's not the most natural at speaking at press conferences, and at this one he has to do a speech alongside Don King of all people. When we sit down in front of all the media, I can see he's a bit nervous and that he's made some notes which he puts on the table in front of us. To add to the pressure, he's being filmed for a documentary so he's all mic'd up for that.

Just before we get started, he gets called away from his seat for a minute. While he's gone, I grab his notes and sit on them.

When he gets back, I can see him looking around for them, a look of panic spreading across his face.

'Ricky, where's my notes?'

'What notes?'

'Come on, stop fucking about.'

'I don't know what you're talking about, Den.'

'Come on you little bastard, tell me where my fucking notes are.'

'Den, I don't know what the fuck you're talking about.'

He's completely forgotten he's got a microphone on, so all of this is coming across loud and clear for the documentary crew filming at the side of the room.

I'm not giving an inch, and all the press guys are waiting so Dennis has to get up and start even though his brain's in a jam jar:

'Er, Ladies and gentlemen, um, er, thank you for your attendance today . . .'

I can't let him suffer anymore. 'Looking for these, Den?' I say, waving his notes about.

He shoots me a look, mutters 'you little bastard' under his breath, takes the notes, says, 'Thank you, Ricky . . .' to the audience and cracks on.

That's the kind of relationship we had. We got on because neither of us took ourselves too seriously.

Next up, I wanted to fight Juan Urango. I'd had to vacate my IBF light-welterweight title to move up and fight Collazo, Urango had won it in the meantime, and I wanted my belt back. But it wasn't as simple as that with HBO involved.

Dennis Hobson:

His dad Ray rings me and says: 'Rick wants to fight Urango next.'

'He can't, he's got to fight the mandatory. That's the one HBO want next.'

'But he wants to fight Urango and get his old belt back.'

'Okay, well, I'll see what I can do . . .'

So I get in touch with Leon Margulies, Urango's promoter, and I tie him down to a deal. They're up for it because they were always going to earn more money fighting Rick than they were going to get fighting anyone else. But when I speak to Kerry Davis, one of the main boxing guys at HBO, he says: 'Dennis, you've been in touch with Urango, but Golden Boy have put a deal together for Urango to fight Juan Lazcano.'

'That's going to cause me a problem because Ricky wants to fight him.'

'Golden Boy are saying they've got a contract with him.'

'Well, they haven't because I've done the deal.'

'But we're not going to take that [Ricky vs. Urango] fight. It's not something we want Ricky Hatton involved in.'

So I come up with a plan – create a semi-final for a final. I'd been to Vegas with Ricky for the third Castillo–Corrales fight which never happened because José Luis Castillo didn't make the weight, so I ring up Castillo's promoter, Bob Arum.

'What about this, Bob,' I said. 'Would José-Luis Castillo want to fight Ricky Hatton?'

'Oh fuck, yes, of course he would,' he replies.

'Right, you've got to help us. We've got to create a mini-tournament, a semi-final and a final. You ring HBO and get Castillo on the bill – winners of Ricky's and Castillo's bouts fight each other.'

Bob spoke to HBO and they were happy with that, and that's how Ricky got the Urango fight he wanted in the end.

Then it was a matter of finding a venue in the States, and this is where Joe Sharpe came in. Joe is now 'Vice President of Player Development' at the Cosmopolitan hotel in Vegas where he's in charge of hospitality for their highest-rollers, but at that time he worked in a similar role at Caesars Palace. I'd met Joe at a fight in Vegas. He knew all about me, that my fights drew big crowds in Britain, and he told me that I would be a superstar in Vegas.

Joe Sharpe:

I was absolutely confident that Ricky's success would carry over here because of his demeanour. Bear in mind that with my job I meet easily four hundred people per month – a lot of celebrities, athletes, high-profile people – but Ricky stood out because of his alacrity and eagerness to reciprocate with fans. Also, his style of fighting really complemented the West Coast and Mexican fighters in his division. I could see there were so many fights to be made for him over here. He'd been selling out arenas in the UK and if we could sell just ten per cent of those numbers to British fans, I was sure we'd get the numbers we needed.

Joe had given me his business card and I introduced him to Dennis. Joe also got straight on the phone to HBO and discovered they had a date locked up, January 20th, to broadcast a fight, but didn't have a fight to show yet. It was a weird date between New Year and Super Bowl weekend and Joe liked the opportunity to attract a lot of punters to Vegas – and particularly to Caesars Palace – who would otherwise not have come at that time of year.

Dennis flew out to Vegas to meet Joe and the American promoter Art Pelullo. Art was working with another possible future opponent for me at the time, Acelino Freitas, and the idea was that he'd be our man on the ground over there.

To start with, it seemed like I might end up fighting elsewhere in America though, so Dennis, me, my agent Paul Speak and my mate Simon Hodgkinson go on a trip, criss-crossing the States to look at possible venues.

We go to see Foxwoods Casino in Connecticut. Art has said that they are willing to pay a very big site fee, enough to cover the promotion, but that never happens. If it had, Dennis would have been up for having one fight there, but I wasn't keen. The venue itself is great, but there's the casino and not a lot else. The Boston fight gave us an idea of the size of my fanbase who'd want to come over to watch the fight, and we think five or six thousand Brits might get a bit bored in Connecticut. If they are going to take days off work and spend their hard-earned cash coming over to support me, I want my fans to have a laugh and plenty to do as well as see the fight.

We also go to Atlanta where they have the Philips Arena, Art has said they are also keen to sponsor the fight. We're picked up at the airport by Ebo 'The X-treme Machine' Elder, a lightweight boxer from Georgia, and his father Greg – also his manager – and they take us out for dinner.

Greg has had an amazing life. He tells us that he was a 'tunnel rat', a member of a special US combat unit sent into the tunnels under the Vietnam jungle to go into man-on-man combat with Viet Cong soldiers. The tunnel rats were basically a suicide squad so it's a miracle he survived. Perhaps because of all the horrors he's seen, Greg is a born-again Christian and Ebo is also a believer. They have us all holding hands and saying a prayer before we eat.

The next day, Waymon Harley, president of the Atlanta Boxing Association, shows us around the venue – which is fantastic – and then offers to show us a bit of the local nightlife. Thanks very much, sounds nice.

Ebo comes with us but says he won't come into any bars with us because it's against his religious beliefs. We go on a little bar crawl, with Ebo waiting for us patiently outside each bar, and end up being taken to this dodgy-looking club. At the entrance, we get frisked with a metal detector to see whether we're carrying weapons. It's very dark and dingy inside, with blokes wearing bandanas playing pool and girls pole-dancing. We are the only white people in there and everyone is staring at us as we walk past to the 'VIP area', a shed with a couple of café tables and plastic chairs.

I'm looking around at Speaky and Simon who are clearly thinking the same as me: what the fuck are we doing here?

'What shall we do?' I say.

'I know,' says Dennis. 'Let's get a bottle of vodka and get pissed up!'

I don't need telling twice. We end up having a good laugh mixing with the other punters in the club – I seem to remember Dennis and Simon judging a competition to be a ringcard girl among the pole dancers. When Speaky goes outside to check on Ebo, he finds him sitting happily with a load of blokes cooking burgers over an old 50-gallon oil drum, having a barbecue. It was one of those nights.

A deal with Atlanta never materialised, though, and Joe was getting more and more determined to bring the fight to a Caesars Palace-owned hotel in Vegas. He said to me: 'Look, Ricky, if you're doing those numbers over there there's no reason why we can't do something similar over here.' I think that if the worst came to the worst, he felt he could always offload any unsold tickets to their high-rollers.

The problem was things had changed a lot in the management at Caesars since their heyday when they hosted the biggest fights in Vegas. The guys who grew up in the boxing business in Vegas mostly started at Caesars, but had ended up working at the MGM Grand. The MGM took over as the major boxing venue in the city when they built the MGM Grand Arena specifically for the purpose of hosting boxing and other major events. The same company also owned Mandalay Bay where they built another great arena for boxing.

The new executives at Caesars weren't into boxing so when Joe approached them with the idea of hosting a Ricky Hatton fight, they didn't even know who I was. He was telling them how popular I was in the UK, but they didn't have a clue. Luckily, Joe kept at it and managed to persuade them.

Joe Sharpe:

In the Seventies and Eighties, boxing and Las Vegas went hand in hand. And they fitted perfectly, because boxing gave Las Vegas great exposure and allowed the city to gain a lot of momentum. We didn't have a local sport before and boxing became our local sport. People from all over the country came to watch the likes of Roberto Duran, Sugar Leonard, Hector Camacho, Larry Holmes and Gerry Cooney.

I grew up watching the huge fights at Caesars and was telling the executives in the brand management department that staging a Ricky Hatton fight was a really great opportunity. I eventually persuaded them to do the fight and begged and pleaded with them to take a vested interest in Ricky. They didn't know anything about boxing and they didn't know who Ricky was, so instead they said they'd 'four-wall the deal,' which means they would give up the space to stage the fight at the Paris Las Vegas hotel – which Caesars also owned – and hope to make a return. In six weeks we sold out 5,400 seats in the Paris ballroom. No problem at all.

I organised a meet-and-greet out there for Ricky with some of the boxers and other athletes. Winky Wright and Shane Mosley attended and some top American Football players. They all wanted to be there because they had heard about Ricky or seen his fights. Ricky entertained everybody. He had time for everyone and he was witty. It was like nothing you'd ever seen, because a lot of fighters have no personality. They are intimidated by the fact that they have to fight somebody and prove themselves. Ricky didn't have to prove anything; he had the personality.

He reminded me a bit of Hector Camacho – who was very charismatic – except Camacho had a little cockiness to him, which Ricky hasn't.'

Dennis Hobson:

Ricky was a promoter's dream – he was promoting me to everyone we met in Vegas – 'This is Dennis Hobson, he's done this, he's done that . . .'

Once the fight was made, we held a press conference back home at the Manchester 235 casino. It was around the time the James Bond film Casino Royale *came out, so I got hold of the film poster picture, took off Daniel Craig's head and put Ricky's head on it. Then I borrowed an Aston Martin off a mate of mine, got Ricky to dress up in his tux, so he came driving round the corner to get out in front of the waiting photographers, then as he came out for the press conference, we had the* Casino Royale *theme tune playing. The name's Hatton, Ricky Hatton . . .*

That's how my Vegas adventure began. Six thousand of my fans came across the Atlantic to support me – they had to put more seats out at the Paris to meet British demand – and those who couldn't get a ticket watched the fight on closed-circuit TV. They'd never had more people in and around the hotel at that time of January and my fans were so thirsty, the Paris ran out of beer.

Joe Sharpe:

The Paris executives couldn't believe it. Who was this superstar? Where had he been hiding all this time? And the British media exposure for the hotel was fantastic – I counted over 150 articles published between the time the fight was announced and the time Ricky came over.

The president of the Paris had no clue who Ricky was beforehand, and even though she had a lot of experience, she didn't know how to monetise his popularity because this was something new for Vegas.

Ricky had a team around him who knew how to get his fans here together – ticket, room and access to the after-fight party that Ricky was going to throw. But Caesars didn't realise the value of what they had and didn't have the business acumen to work with Ricky and build something in association with our brand.

Ricky came out to Vegas again after the Urango fight to see the Mayweather–De La Hoya fight and by then, people were really loving him. He was getting a lot of attention that Floyd had never gotten in Las Vegas. He was in Floyd's backyard and after one fight there garnering way more attention than Floyd had ever gotten.

My performance against Urango wasn't my best, but the people of Las Vegas had seen the party atmosphere my fans brought to the town. It wasn't just a fight, it was an event and they couldn't wait for the next one. And because my second Vegas fight against José Luis Castillo was in summer, the Brits came out in even greater numbers – about 10,000 of them.

The original date we were given for the fight was in early June, but the England football team were playing a European Championship qualifier against Estonia at the same time, and a few of them wanted to come out and watch, including Wayne Rooney who I'd asked to carry my belt (see *Wayne Rooney, Celine Dion and Me*, page 171). Dennis made up some excuse why we couldn't do that date – from his point of view as a promoter, he knew that the fight would get loads more back-page headlines with the star footballers coming to watch – and it was agreed to push the fight date back to 23 June.

Dennis wasn't satisfied with just bringing the England players over, he forked out ten grand to fly the team's official supporters band over too to join in the fun. The band, like Dennis, are from Sheffield and are pals of his. The comedian/entertainer Bernie

Clifton plays trombone for them and Den had him in a Union Jack suit marching up and down the Strip 'riding' Oswald the Ostrich as they played.

Dennis Hobson:

The week of the fight, I was sitting by one of the swimming pools at Caesars Palace and they call me up: 'Dennis, we've been barred from every casino on the Strip, what do you want us to do now?'

'Go round again.'

A bit later I can hear them coming over one of the bridges nearby and I get another call.

'Dennis, we've done that, what next?'

'Let me have a look at you – I'm at Caesars Palace by the swimming pools.'

Ten minutes later, they appear, marching round the pools with a conga of Ricky's fans forming behind them: 'De-de-derrr, de-de-de-de, De-de-derr, de-de-de-de . . . walking along, singing a song, walking in a Hatton wonderland.'

A security guy comes up to them: 'Excuse me, sirs. This is the state of Nevada, you have to have a licence to entertain in the state of Nevada – can you tell me who gave you authorisation to perform in Caesars Palace?'

'Dennis Hobson's told us we can do it.'

We didn't have a licence, but we didn't care.

Before the show, they were waiting for me by the elevator and we did a conga around the blackjack tables before we went off to the fight.

This time the fight was staged at the Thomas and Mack Center, but co-hosted by Caesars and the new Wynn Las Vegas hotel owned by

Steve Wynn. Wynn is a billionaire and you don't make all that money without being super-smart, and he totally out-smarted Caesars. He'd seen what had happened at the Urango fight, and he realised that being associated with a Ricky Hatton fight would bring publicity and punters to his new hotel, which hosted my after-fight party.

Joe Sharpe:

Steve Wynn had just opened up the Wynn hotel and the first fight he did was Hatton–Castillo. He knew the value of what Ricky can do. He rolled out the red carpet, showed films of all Ricky's fights on big screens for the high-rollers and got them pumped up to go see the Castillo fight.

Wynn has no problem spending money and Caesars Entertainment didn't know what they were doing, they just thought they were getting a discount not paying for the whole thing. They didn't see the bigger picture at all. It's not just me saying this; it's obvious.

When Wynn rolled out the red carpet, he knew the exposure his new hotel was going to get and took all the high-rollers from Caesars and took their database. He was taking business away from Caesars, easy.

Even after the second fight, the Caesars execs still didn't realise the value of what they had. I was thinking we could milk this for the next five years, because Ricky was that kind of superstar and there were so many great fights out there for him. We had an option for another fight but Caesars just didn't move quick enough. I was tearing my hair out.

Even though Caesars didn't continue to host my fights, I've kept in touch with Joe ever since. Every time I'm out in Vegas, I'll look him up and he's organised some incredible nights out for me, my friends and family over the years. I'll always be grateful to Joe for his help in achieving my dream of fighting in Vegas.

The same goes for Dennis. As Frank Warren had done building my career in England, Dennis did a great job in establishing me in America. He made sure I was paid well and he looked after my interests. He was also a right good laugh to be around. Dennis was the type who'd be in the Galleria bar at Caesars Palace in fight week having a drink and singing with my fans and you don't see many promoters do that.

We used to have play-fights, and one time we were in the back of a limo having a scrap. I got hold of one his shoes and chucked it out of the window onto the freeway. Den had to hobble to his next meeting at a casino wearing one shoe, while Speaky went back out in the car to try and find the other one.

Another time in the build-up to the Urango fight, I finished my training session at the Top Rank gym, and Den got in the ring and did three rounds with one of his staff, 'Spud'. Spud used to be in the army and he'd been calling Den out for weeks, so they had a little spar (for the record, Den got the better of it).

When I was out shopping in Vegas before that fight, I saw a life-size mannequin of a butler, with a tea-towel over his arm and a serving plate, which I quite fancied for my house. But when I asked how much it was, I was told ten or fifteen thousand dollars, so I thought, I'm not paying that.

When we had the first press conference of fight week, though, I'm sitting there and they bring out the butler and present it to me. Den had been told that I liked it and had gone to the shop, got a discount and bought it for me as gift.

I know Dennis was very upset when I went with Golden Boy to promote my third Vegas fight with Floyd Mayweather. It was not how I would have wanted it to end, but we had a lot of fun along the way and I still value his friendship.

Dennis Hobson:

They were great times and it was just a shame they were cut short. In my view, I helped to get him in position to fight Floyd Mayweather – Rick did the fighting, I did the manoeuvring. So many other people want to take the credit for that, but I think that I did a fantastic job for him after he left Frank Warren. Sky wanted him to go with Barry Hearn, but he went with me. I'd done all the hard work in America and I deserved to be involved.

I've never had a wrong word with Ricky himself, though. For me as a promoter, you don't usually get the bond I had with Ricky. We were more like pals. I always tried to go that extra mile for Ricky, because we had such fun.

In my office now I've still got the Urango and Collazo posters up on the wall and the ponchos we made for Rick and Castillo. Even though we didn't talk for a while because of what happened, I never took them down from my wall. I could have got bitter about it, but life's too short. I'm proud of being part of that time in his career.

We had very special times together. Money comes and goes, but those memories are priceless and will remain with me forever.

VEGAS, HERE WE COME . . .

FROM FATTON TO FIT'UN

If I could turn the clock back, the one thing I would change in my boxing career would be to look after myself a bit better between fights. There's no doubt that blowing up like I did shortened my career. However, I think it was also one of the reasons the Americans took to me during my Vegas years. They were fascinated by the idea of this Guinness-drinking, sausage-eating English bloke who fights against the best in the world in between binges. They were like, 'This can't be right. Who is this guy?' It added to my everyman appeal. They could see I wasn't a red-carpet merchant, I was just a wise-cracking scallywag off the streets who was very good at what I did. The American press absolutely loved it, because they didn't have any fighters over there like that.

So although it wasn't the right approach – and I would never recommend to any other fighter that they let their weight go up so much between fights – it worked for me in terms of gaining fans at home and in the States.

Also, you have to bear in mind that there's a physical and a mental side to boxing. It's not just about conditioning and, personally, I needed that release between the fight and the next training camp. My logic at the time was that if I trained my nuts off for twelve weeks to win a world title, but couldn't then have a break, eating and drinking what I liked, what was I doing it all for?

It's about what makes your mind right. It know it sounds daft, but after my fights finished, if I didn't have those three or four weeks where I could blow my brains out, I wouldn't feel comfortable going back into training camp.

People would say, that's no way to prepare. I'm sure critics would also say that you shouldn't eat 1,000 McDonalds chicken nuggets in ten days when you're a sprinter trying to win the Olympics, but Usain Bolt admits he did that at Beijing 2008 and he broke three world records. Watch the *24/7* TV series showing the build-up to my fight with Floyd Mayweather Jr. (for my fights against Floyd and Manny Pacquiao, I had an HBO film crew following me, throughout the build-up, for the *24/7* series. Over the years, these documentary or 'reality TV' shows have become an important part of getting the public excited for major Pay-Per-View fights), and you'll see him eating sweets while in training for our fight – that used to really piss me off because I struggled to lose every ounce. If I so much as looked at a sweet during a training camp I'd put on weight. Every nutritionist will tell you that sweets make you think you have more energy than you actually have – they are 'empty calories' – but Floyd's the best in the world. Everyone's body reacts differently. It's about what works for you overall.

My long-time trainer Billy Graham once said about me: 'He's under pressure being who he is, so he's got to let off some steam somehow . . . but, Jesus, he lets off a lot of steam!'

Billy understood me because we are very similar characters and we became very close over the years. For our sins, we used to go for a pint or six together when I was out of training – not every night, because we'd need a break from each other, but we'd have the odd night out every now and then.

As good a trainer as Billy was, if he'd told me he didn't want me going out, to be in bed by seven o'clock, don't do this, don't do that, we wouldn't have lasted five minutes working together. Instead, he used to say to me: 'Listen Rick, I don't mind you having a drink as long as those twelve weeks before a fight, you don't touch a drop. You've got to do it right.' I always stuck to that, without fail.

It doesn't matter how many parties I went to, how many beers I supped, how many Chinese takeaways I ate, the thing I enjoyed best was my training, my boxing and having my hand raised in front of thousands of cheering fans – that's the biggest addiction I could ever have, and nothing came close. The reason that I had a nice lifestyle, was because of what I did in that ring, and if I didn't prepare right, everything else went out the window. I always knew that.

Perhaps what people don't realise was how dedicated I was. When I was having three fights a year and doing a twelve-week training camp for each one, that didn't actually leave me much time off for drinking and partying. The thing is with me is that I was all or nothing. When I was training, I went for it a hundred per cent, and when I had time off to eat, drink and be merry, I didn't hold back either. Like my brother Matthew, who boxed on all my Vegas shows; we both put on weight easily if we're not careful, so that post-fight partying meant it wasn't unusual for me to blow up to forty pounds above my fighting weight between bouts.

So, yes I definitely could have looked after my body better and that might have prolonged my career. However, you don't win four world titles at two weights without dedication and, in a funny way, my binges between fights meant I had to be even more dedicated.

Matthew Hatton:

Both myself and Ricky liked to enjoy ourselves between fights – maybe a bit too much – but when it came to preparation everything was done correctly, Ricky was as dedicated as they come. You don't get to the level he got to if you're on the pop 24/7.

One of Ricky's main assets was his engine. His fitness in his heyday was second to none. The amount of work that is involved in top-level boxing, that's required for twelve-round title fights is phenomenal, but he was a ferocious trainer. I set my standards for the boxers I train now by the way Ricky used to train and it's very hard to find anyone who can match that. He was a phenomenally hard worker and his fitness was incredible.

If anything, Billy had to hold me back. We trained hard every weekday, and I also went running at the weekends, even though Billy would have been happy for me just to rest. He didn't believe in what he called 'old-school bollocks' where coaches get their fighters up at the crack of dawn and make them eat raw eggs. He thought sleep was very important for a fighter and our daily sessions started at 12.30pm.

In the *24/7* series, they showed Floyd going to the gym at 2am for a run on the treadmill. He apparently pulled this nightshift five or six times a week because he felt it gave him a psychological edge. His manager Leonard Ellerbe was sitting there watching him, trying to stay awake, then afterwards at half three in the morning, Floyd had a barber in to give him a haircut. Each to their own, but Billy and the rest of my team would have told me to piss off if I'd said I wanted them to come to the gym to watch me jog at 2am.

To me, as long as you put the hours in, it doesn't matter when you do them. Because Floyd ran in the early hours, it meant he didn't start his boxing training till 5pm, so it wasn't like he was doing more training than I was.

I did twelve-week rather than eight-week training camps because I knew I had to shift more weight than other fighters. No one was more dedicated than me when it was time to train. Because I'd let myself go, I knew I had to do everything by the book – there was no room for error. Because I was bringing off so much weight, if I didn't do it correctly, I would be a shadow of myself. It says it all that I only once missed weight once in my entire career – before a WBU title fight against John Bailey, and that was only by a couple of ounces because my scales were calibrated slightly differently to the scales at the weigh-in.

In the year and a bit training for the Urango, Castillo and Mayweather fights, in total I shifted approximately nine stone, not far off the equivalent of one whole prime-condition Ricky Hatton. For the Mayweather fight, Team Hatton's official behind-the-scenes photographer in the Vegas years, Mark Robinson (who became a good friend of mine), took photos of my body every week or so from the start of training camp for the Mayweather fight right up to fight week. The change in my physique was amazing.

So how did I go from Ricky Fatton to fit'un, in fighting shape to take on the best in Vegas? As well as hard, traditional boxing training, it was also down to weight training and nutrition.

Losing weight and maximising strength was crucial and I was very fortunate to have had an exceptional strength and nutrition coach in Kerry Kayes on my team to help me do that.

Kerry is a former British bodybuilding champion and he went on to run CNP, a very successful sports nutrition company. I was introduced to him by Billy Graham. Kerry had known Billy's brother Joe for about fifteen years. I never knew Joe personally, but he was a professional strength coach – he'd even held a couple of world records for strength feats himself. When Billy was a pro boxer, Joe was always telling him that bodybuilders were experts at gaining and losing weight. By the time that Billy became a trainer, Joe was advising him on different methods adapted from body-building training to use with his fighters. These were very different from traditional methods and Billy got plenty of stick for taking them up, because years ago most boxing trainers would tell you not to touch weights. Billy had a very modern approach to coaching and was a firm believer in using weights to generate more power in your punches, so even before I met Kerry I was lifting weights with Billy as part of my training. Billy and Kerry were pioneers in bringing that to boxing.

In around 1997 Billy started talking to Kerry about working with his boxers, including one young prospect he had who was just turning pro – me. Three or four years later, Billy moved his gym, the Phoenix Camp, into Kerry's gym (Betta Bodies in Denton, Manchester) and that's when Kerry started working with me day-in day-out.

By then I was WBU world champion – if I remember rightly, it was just after I beat Tony Pep to win the title – and unbeaten in twenty-odd fights, so Kerry didn't try to change everything overnight. I knew he was very well respected in the bodybuilding trade, but it takes time to build trust in the new methods, so he changed the strength and nutrition side of my fight preparation bit by bit. Each time he changed something I felt the benefits, so I was happy to go along with him; after four or five fights I was doing it all his way.

Kerry explained that he wasn't trying to turn me into a bodybuilder. Bodybuilders have an unbelievably low body-fat ratio when they are competing – a percentage in single figures – because it's a visual thing and it's all about muscle definition. At a bodybuilding contest, the bodybuilders themselves might be the unhealthiest people in the room.

Basically, there are two types of fat: outer body fat, and visceral fat which protects important internal organs like the liver. A bodybuilder wants to reduce both to a minimum, but they aren't getting hit. A boxer needs to keep their body fat ratio around twelve to fifteen per cent, because any lower and you're losing visceral fat. Fat is also a reserve of energy, and if you're doing twelve rounds of championship boxing, you need it.

To get the right balance, Kerry taught me how to eat right. Between fights I'd be living off takeaways, so just by cutting them out and swapping, say, a McDonalds meal, that has about 1,500 mostly empty calories, for a 'clean' meal of chicken breast, rice and veg, I'd be eating a 1,000-odd fewer calories and getting better nutrition. On top of that, Kerry not only told me the right nutritional supplements to take and when to take them, but he also could supply them all through his own company.

Before he came along I would go about losing weight in a very basic way, and wasn't taking any sort of protein drinks to help keep my strength up while I dieted.

I was eating pasta, jacket potatoes, but I didn't really know what I was doing; with Kerry, it became a lot more scientific. We followed the bodybuilders' principle of 'eat small and often' to make sure I had plenty of energy and kept my metabolism going to shift the weight. Instead of having three big meals, he advised me to eat six small ones because it's easier to burn them off. The supplements were also really important for reducing my food intake. The ones I was taking contained forty-odd grams of protein per 270 calories, and you'd need to eat 1,000 calories of normal food to get that amount.

The late trainer and matchmaker, Dean Powell, God rest his soul, described Kerry as 'a pioneer of nutrition in boxing' and that's spot on. Kerry's advice made such a difference to my preparation.

Kerry never used to babysit me, check I was eating what I was supposed to. He didn't need to, because I knew how important it was and after a couple of fights it became second nature. Kerry did make adjustments for my fight with Floyd, which was made at welterweight, so I could afford to put on a bit more muscle. Muscle weighs more than body fat, and you don't want a ten-stone fighter carrying an extra seven pounds of body fat. I had to add muscle, but without becoming muscle-bound. Kerry had me taking a supplement called 'Creatine E2' which drives straight into the muscle and gives you more energy and power to help with that. When you're used to fighting at ten stone, an extra seven pounds feels like a lot extra to carry – when I fought Luis Collazo, my only previous outing at welterweight, I had struggled, so we looked for a middle ground for the Floyd fight. I actually weighed in at ten stone five, a couple of pounds under the limit, and I felt really good at that weight.

When my training camp shifted from Manchester to Vegas, it was important to get the right food to maintain the diet. The first time I fought out there against Urango, we ate at the hotel's all-you-can-eat buffet; only, in my and Matthew's case, it was more a case of 'all you can't eat'. We just had to stick to the healthy stuff, and that worked fine.

For my Castillo bout, Team Hatton moved into a house away from the Strip, and we hired a personal chef called Rick. Rick was an older fella, a lovely guy who had been a chef for a lot of celebrities, and stayed with us for the last four Vegas fights. A brilliant cook, his role became more and more important the longer I spent in Vegas before fights. When you are three or four weeks out from a fight, that's the hardest part of training camp and it's vital that you have good food.

The food Rick prepared for us was immaculate, but he did make Matthew and me laugh every time he came in because he wore a really dodgy syrup. We'd be sitting round the table waiting for our tea, watching Rick working away. He'd lean over the stove, and his wig would slip a bit. Matthew would be nudging me, going, 'Hope that doesn't end up on my steak!'

The only problem I did have in Vegas food-wise didn't come until after the weigh-in, and that was getting my traditional breakfast on the morning of the fight. When I was fighting in Manchester, I'd always head straight to The Butty Box café in Hyde with my brother and have their £3.80 'Mega Breakfast'. The morning of the Urango fight I was like, 'Right, let's go and get a full English.'

I reckon the casinos won't have what I want, and that a diner could be my best bet so we drive out to find one off the Strip. I've starved myself for weeks so I can't wait, but when I get the menu it's all 'egg and bacon', 'sausage and egg' or 'pancakes with maple syrup'. I end up having to buy four breakfasts and piece my full English together, taking bits from each plate. It's good, but no Butty Box and ends up costing a lot more than £3.80. Luckily, I did eventually discover the Crown & Anchor, an English-style pub in Vegas, where they serve a decent full English on one plate.

As soon as I got back in the gym to start any training camp, I was always dead keen to start boxing again, but Billy had other ideas.

'Come on, Billy, get the pads on,' I'd say.

'There's no way you're hitting the pads while you're that size, you tosser.'

So the first few sessions, I'd spend most of my time on the treadmill, the step machine or cross trainer, and hitting the heavy bag to lose the lard.

After a few rounds on the bag, I'd be sweating buckets, so I'd take my shirt off. With my gut hanging out and my tits wobbling all over the show, it was quite a sight. 'Put your shirt back on – have you no shame?' Billy would say, but I didn't care. I'm probably the least vain person you'll meet.

The most extreme part of training for making weight was the first two weeks. I used to just hammer the cardio work and I got really strict with my diet, eating mostly protein and practically no carbs. Billy and Kerry's view was that it was best to break the camel's back so that when it came to the real intensive work on the pads, weights and sparring I could afford to start eating carbs again.

Before the Floyd Mayweather fight, my diet (plus light jogging and weight training) began during the five-city promotional tour and by the time I got back, I'd lost ten pounds, which was a good start.

I'd usually aim to get a stone off in the first fortnight and that would leave two more to shift. The next fortnight, I'd lose another eight pounds, so with eight weeks to go I'd have around a stone and four pounds to shed – where everyone else would normally be from the start. I had three wardrobes at home – one with clothes for when I was out of training, one for when I had a few weeks under my belt and one for when I was at my fighting weight. When I could fit into the clothes in wardrobe two, I knew I was getting somewhere.

A great cardio exercise Billy swore by – and one I still use with the fighters I train at my gym today – is jumping the bar. It's as simple as it sounds, but it's brutal. It involves a long steel bar on adjustable supports at either end so you can alter the height. I'd usually have it at about three-and-half-feet high. Then you put both hands on the bar and use the strength in your arms, chest and shoulders to flip your legs up and over from one side of the bar to the other.

I didn't jump the bar in the first few weeks of camp because I was too heavy. I did try it once in my 'Fatton' state, but I've always had problems with my Achilles tendons from playing football and I could feel them creaking, so after that I waited till I'd got my weight down a bit.

One set was a minute of jumping the bar (at least forty jumps per minute), then a minute of non-stop punching on the heavy bag, then a minute's rest and repeat. I'd build that up until I was doing fifteen sets. It's a killer, but great for building up strength and stamina. I never saw a bar like it in American gyms, but if you've got a bar at your gym, give it a go and see how many sets you can do. Or just head straight to the bar for drink – it's a lot easier.

In the third week of camp, Billy would finally allow me to get in the ring and do some light pad work, just to find my range and get my rhythm going.

Then in week four, Billy would bring out the body-belt, heavy padding which he strapped round his body so he looked like the Michelin man. I could chase him around the ring relentlessly battering him to the body, mixing in punches to the hand pads held at head height. At the time, I wasn't aware of any other trainer who used the body-belt – although I believe it was an innovation brought in by another legendary Mancunian boxing trainer, Phil Martin, who Billy once worked with – and it was one of the reasons I wanted Billy to train me in the first place when I turned pro. It just suited my boxing style perfectly. A lot of trainers use some version of the body-belt now, and perhaps me being the spotlight and using it as such a key part of my training did help to popularise it.

From week four through ten of training, we'd work on the body-belt five days a week, gradually increasing the number of rounds from four to six to eight to ten and then twelve. On my last big workout, the Friday a week before the fight, I'd do fifteen rounds.

We'd kept that same routine for years, from winning my first pro belts right up to my last fight with Billy as my trainer. Billy always used to do twelve rounds with all his other fighters – Ensley Bingham, Carl Thompson . . . they all did twelve – but me being the way I was, I always wanted to do more than the next guy. I said to him: 'If they do twelve, I want to do fifteen, so I've got three extra in the bag.'

If someone had done eighteen rounds, I would have wanted to do twenty. That was my mentality – I might have let myself go between training camps, but when I was on it, I wanted to do more than anyone else.

Doing fifteen rounds on the body belt is unbelievably gruelling, but, psychologically, it felt great to get through it. It put the finishing touch to all the hard work, proved I was fit and then for the last week, the training tapered down to preserve energy for fight night. The only time I didn't do my fifteen rounds for a championship fight was actually in Vegas, before the Juan Urango fight for reasons I'll explain later (see *Facing the Iron Twin*, page 82).

Apart from the bodybuilder's diet and the body-belt, another aspect of my training that was quite different from most fighters at the time was the use of weight training. Again, it really suited my style of fighting. My game was to get in close, to maul, and push my opponent to the side to get in body shots.

Kerry always said that, pound for pound, he'd never known anyone as naturally physically strong as me; that if I hadn't been a boxer, I could have been a powerlifter. My stocky physique was ideal for that. I have what they call 'short levers' – short arms, short legs – which meant I had great leverage and less distance to lift the weights from A to B.

'If I was training you to be a bodybuilder or powerlifter, it would be frightening what you could lift,' he told me. 'But I don't want you lifting too much because of the risk of injuries. There's no point me killing you with the weights and your boxing goes to shit.'

I did weights four days a week:

Monday: quads and calves

Tuesday: chest and biceps

Thursday: back and hamstrings

Friday: shoulders and biceps

The workouts would only last for a quarter of an hour, because I'd do them after my boxing training with Billy, but Kerry pushed me really hard in that time.

He always made me lift weights 'to failure' of the muscle, so the last repetition of the last set on each exercise should be a real struggle. The only way you can train a body to get stronger over time is to train to failure. Kerry said I was very good at judging exactly how far I could push it without injuring myself.

If I'd been training as a powerlifter, he would have chosen a weight that I could only do one or two repetitions with, but we'd use a lower weight for eight to ten reps per set. Any less than eight reps, injury is more likely.

I was still lifting very heavy weights though. For instance, my best physical attribute was the strength of my legs; I had massive legs for a welterweight. On the leg press, where you sit down on an angled seat starting with your knees up by your chest and then push your legs out straight, I was doing sets of ten reps lifting 1,050 pounds, around seven times my body weight. HBO's *24/7* documentary crew filmed me doing that in training for the Floyd fight, and they worked out that in one weights workout, I lifted a total of thirty-eight tonnes.

Kerry will tell you that there are too many strength and conditioning coaches now who think they're more important than the boxing trainer and he knew that was bollocks. What's the point of you destroying the boxer in the strength and conditioning sessions to the point that he's got nothing left for his boxing training? Weight training alone is not going to make you punch harder. If you punch with just your arm, you can lift all the weights in the world, but you don't get the power; and if you get too muscle-bound, you can lose your speed. I was able to keep my flexibility, punch with everything behind it – my arm, shoulder, legs, everything. With me lifting such heavy weights, as long as my technique was right, the power would go on the end of every punch. I was never the most explosive puncher in the world, but I punched with leverage and definitely became a more powerful puncher through weight training.

All the work Kerry did with me was designed specifically to improve my strength for boxing and support Billy's training. He would say, 'Right, Billy, what do you want me to do?' and adjust accordingly.

He knew that with the majority of boxing training – running, circuits, hitting the pads and bag etc – you're unlikely to get injured. The only ways a boxer is really likely to get injured in training is sparring or weight training. Kerry was always confident in what he was doing, but that was always his big fear at the back of his mind.

Kerry Kayes:

If I was training Wayne Rooney and he got injured, Man United would still play their next match, but if I'd injured Ricky Hatton a month before the Mayweather fight and it had to be called off, it would have cost tens of millions. No pressure, then . . .

As well as keeping the reps higher on each exercise, there were certain exercises we avoided completely. Heavy deadlifts, bent-over rowing, clean and jerks – which are standard exercises for powerlifters – were out. We tended to use weight machines more than free weights, because they are safer. As a strength coach, Kerry must have felt like he had one hand tied behind his back sometimes, but he got the balance right. He pushed me hard, but he was always balancing gain and risk.

The benefit of all those years of weight training was shown in my best-ever performance, against Kostya Tszyu. He had a reputation as a real powerhouse, blasting out everyone in a couple of rounds. I wasn't as powerful as Kostya in the sense of punching power, but I was able to bully him around the ring because of that strong foundation. No one thought I was going to beat Kostya, let alone beat him in that manner. He'd never been bullied before, but my natural physical strength and Kerry's training gave me the edge, especially in the later rounds.

It also stood me in good stead when I fought in Vegas against the freakishly strong Juan Urango, who I just about matched for strength, and José Luis Castillo, who was also known for his physical strength, but I felt I was much stronger than him.

The mixture of heavy weight training and working the body belt alongside normal boxing training – sparring, circuits etc – was ideal for me because a lot of my game was up close, leaning on my opponent, pushing and shoving to open them up for my body shots. It's not for everyone, though.

Now I'm a trainer, I do a fair bit of weight training with Zhanat Zhakiyanov, my champion bantamweight from Kazakhstan, because he's quite stocky. With the three young Upton brothers – Paulie, Sonny and Anthony – it's more resistance and pad work because they like to box from distance. You've got to train each fighter to what their strengths and weaknesses are. You don't have someone who's six-feet-tall and nine stone hitting the body belt.

Billy Graham is the best trainer I ever worked with, and my only criticism of him is that he trained everyone the same way. It was bang on for me, but that doesn't mean it's right for everyone else. My job now is to try and even improve on what Billy did, as good as he was. That's no disrespect to him, but you always have to look at ways to advance. If people didn't do that in sport, then records would never be broken. You might succeed or fail, but you've always got to try and improve.

Kerry and I worked together all the way up until my split with Billy after the Juan Lazcano fight. Kerry and Billy had always been a team and he didn't feel he could continue in the circumstances, which I understood. We parted ways amicably and Kerry told me I knew what I was doing now anyway, and that his phone was on twenty-four hours a day if I ever needed to call for advice. Of course, me being a stubborn sod, I never did – but we still get on fine and whenever I see Kerry I'll go over and give him a hug.

He says his only regret was that he wasn't around to help in the build-up to the Manny Pacquiao fight, when I felt that I was over-trained by my new trainer Floyd Mayweather Sr. Kerry was in Vegas for that fight, because he was working the corners for our Matthew and another Manchester boxer Joe Murray on the under-card. He hadn't been around my training camp, though, but could tell it had all gone wrong for me at the weigh-in.

Before that, when people asked him how he thought I was going to get on, he had told them the downside was that I didn't like fighting southpaws, but the upside was that I would be too big and strong for Manny. Then he saw me strip down to get on the scales.

Kerry Kayes:

I earn my living looking at physiques, and I was shocked at his lack of muscle. Ricky's advantage over Pacquiao should have been his strength and he didn't look strong. The harder you train, the more important nutrition becomes, and I wish I'd been there in that camp because perhaps I could have done something to counteract the over-training.

Kerry never asked me for a penny of payment in all the years he worked with me. He felt being part of the team was good promotion for his company, whose name I wore on my gear at my fights. But also he just really enjoyed being involved. Looking back now, Kerry describes being in the corner for my Vegas fights as 'a fairy tale' for him.

Kerry Kayes:

I was sixty years old, married with four kids, a millionaire, drove a Bentley – I wanted for nothing in life, but being part of those Vegas fights was something else. There were thirty-five thousand people going over to the Mayweather fight and they were there to see Ricky, and only Ricky. But I was with Billy Graham in the corner, so I had the second or third best seat in the house. I thought, it's crazy, this – I'm off a council estate, how the fuck have I got here? I kind of felt important, that my mum and dad would be proud of me.

But, as daft as it sounds, for all the glitz of Vegas, for me the most fun was the half-an-hour drive to the gym, the gym and the half an hour travelling back to the apartment. It was like being kids again, back at school messing around, but getting the work done. Those two or three hours we spent together were the most enjoyable.

BISCUITGATE

Living in Vegas in the last weeks before a big fight, you do miss some of the simple comforts of home. So my team were well pleased when we found a shop well off the Strip that sold British goods; we could stock up on a few favourite things – proper tea bags, HP Sauce, McVities digestives, Holland's pies, Cadbury's chocolate and the like. The only problem was that me and our Matthew couldn't touch most of it as we were trying to bring our weight down before our fights. That never stopped Paul Speak and the other boys from getting stuck in.

We didn't mind seeing them stuffing themselves a few weeks before the fight, when we could still eat a reasonable amount. But the last week or two, when we're eating naff all, it could cause a bit of tension.

A friend of my assistant trainer Lee Beard called Val (who sadly passed away in 2014) had helped out around the gym in Manchester during the training camp, and as a reward I'd invited him to join the team out in Vegas. But ever since we got to Vegas, there was a running joke that Val was nicking Paul's food.

We've got Rick the chef preparing all our meals at the house we're staying in and he always makes plenty of food, but it's not enough for Val who's got a big appetite to say the least. One time we're all shopping at the local outlet mall and we've arranged to meet back at the minibus at five to go back to the apartment for dinner. The rest of us spend our time looking for bargain designer clothes and stuff, but when we're walking back to the minibus, we find Val chowing down on a massive pizza. He's having another dinner before dinner.

Meanwhile, Paul's food supplies at the apartment are mysteriously getting lower. Speaky likes his food, so he's getting more and more agitated. But every time he challenges Val, Val blankly denies stealing anything, which gets Paul even more annoyed.

'Eh, you've been nicking my pies, you.'

'I never.'

'You've been going into my digestives.'

'I haven't touched yer fucking biscuits.'

And so it goes on.

Meanwhile, Floyd Mayweather Sr. is beasting me in training. It's not quite as tough as it got before the Pacquiao disaster, but still takes a lot out of you when you're not eating as much as normal. Twice a week, Floyd would take me running up Mount Charleston, northwest of downtown Vegas, and the highest point near the city, and it was gruelling to say the least.

This particular morning, though, Matthew and I are just doing our normal early-morning run round the lake at the local park. Speaky drives us down there in the minibus with Val and Lee Beard. When we get there, we all hop out and Matthew and me are doing a few stretches to wake ourselves up. We're three days from a fight, on the weight, and 'looking forward' to a six-mile run followed by a very small breakfast.

Just then, Paul says to Val: 'Listen you, you've been at my digestives.'

'No, I haven't.'

Here we go.

'Yes, you have. I folded the packet down and marked it where the biscuits were up to and left it in the cupboard. You've had four more biscuits out of it.'

I can't listen to this shit anymore.

'Will youse two shut the fuck up! You're on about food. We're starving here and you're going on about who's nicked the McVities. Shut up now or I'll throw you in that fucking lake.'

'But, Rick, I paid for them biscuits,' replies Paul.

Matthew chips in: 'Paul, shut the fuck up – you've been told once.'

I'm training for a world-title fight, it's half six in the morning and we're standing around in a deserted park arguing about biscuits.

Looking back on it, it was a farcical scene, but at the time we were all genuinely fuming – Matt and me because we were so hungry, Speaky because Val was nicking his stuff and wouldn't admit it . . . and Val because he'd been rumbled.

BASHING THE BISHOP

When I do my after-dinner speeches, unsurprisingly, they normally take place in a hotel function room, bar or club. But on one occasion in 2006 a firm of lawyers invited me to their annual do in their office, to talk about my career.

There's about a hundred people there and as it's about to start, I introduce myself to a bloke sitting next to me at the front of the room.

'Alright, Ricky,' he replies in a Scouse accent.

'What are you doing here?'

'I'm the comedian – John Bishop.'

I've never heard of John before – he's only recently quit his job as a rep for a pharmaceutical company to become a full-time comic.

He does a good set that has the lawyers laughing, but to be honest, it's not my cup of tea. I've been brought up on old-school comedians like Mick Miller, Frank Carson and my good friend Bernard Manning – all quickfire gag merchants whereas John is more of a storyteller.

It would be another few months – when I signed to fight Floyd Mayweather – before I got to really appreciate John's comedy. A TV production company were looking for different ways to promote the bout, and Floyd was appearing in the *Dancing with the Stars*, the American version of *Strictly Come Dancing*, at the time. That seemed ripe for a piss-take so the idea came together to make a sketch with a comedian.

'We're thinking of using a guy called John Bishop.'

'Oh, I know him . . .'

Our short film starts with a caption across a black screen: 'To better understand the mindset of his opponent . . . Ricky Hatton decides to integrate dance lessons into his training routine,' with me doing the voiceover: 'Floyd has said that dancing will help him

46

prepare for the fight. So I think I might try a few dancing lessons, although I might be wasting my time, cos I can't see how it's going to help for boxing preparation . . .'

The screen cuts to me looking at a flyer about dance lessons with the 'Celebrity Dance Judge; Bruto Schlong – as seen on TV', and the voiceover continues:

'. . . I even asked my missus, "How do you think this will relate to boxing?" and even she hasn't a clue.'

The next thing, John aka 'Bruto' wearing a suit and a silk scarf, bounces up the steps to meet me at the door of Billy Graham's Phoenix Gym. He's talking in a ridiculously camp, part-Italian, part-Eastern European, part-Scouse accent:

'Dahhhhlings, dahlings, come, we have verk to do . . . Come, come, come!'

I'm like, 'How you doing? Y'alright?'

Cut to us two in the boxing ring.

'So what dance moves are there for going backwards,' I ask, 'Because my opponent Floyd goes backwards all the time.'

'Floyyyd? I have a very good friend called Floyyyd,' replies Bruto. 'But backwards is not for you dahling. Backwards is, 'ow you say in England? Girly – the girlies go backwards. What you've got to do is move close . . . then away . . . then close, again . . .'

'But my opponent, Floyd, he goes back . . .'

I start following John – I mean Bruto – as he minces around the ring, shaking his hips and giving it the 'showbiz hands', before striking a very camp pose in the corner.

'That's exactly how he moves,' I say, trying to keep a straight face, and ignore the other lads in the gym watching who are creasing up at the scene.

Next Bruto is doing all sorts of supposed dance moves: 'The rumba, the rumba . . . the salsa, dahling . . .' stepping in close to me and then darting away.

'You need your man to come to you, come to you, dahling . . . then move away . . . then come to you again . . . then take him, dahling, take him!'

It's very similar to a normal session on the body bag with Billy, really.

Bruto is getting right into it now, waving his arms around like a deranged ballet instructor, talking absolute bollocks: 'You have to dream, dahling. You have live the dream. You have to feel the space, you have to *own* the space.'

'Right, then,' I say, 'shall we get some gloves on now and do some proper moves?'

Bruto thinks for second: 'Okay!'

Cut to me doing a bit of shadow boxing in the corner, checking out my form in the mirror. The bell rings.

I turn round and march across the ring to meet my dancing opponent, who's still wearing his silk scarf and suit: 'Come on then!'

But Bruto is more interested in admiring my moves than getting into a war: 'Oh you cha-cha-cha, you can foxtrot, dahling . . . you can live, you can dream, you can flow . . .' he says, before swishing his jacket over my head as if I was a bull. 'You can even do the matador, my dear!'

I duck under the jacket, turn round and say: 'I've always just done this . . .' and throw a right-hander that looks like it lands flush on the chin.

Poor Bruto falls to the canvas. He lifts his head briefly, looking around dazed and confused: 'Dahling . . . ? Floyyyd?', before collapsing supposedly unconscious while we all piss ourselves laughing.

Thankfully, Bruto has since recovered from that brutal KO to become a comedy superstar capable of filling the O2.

LADIES AND GENTLEMAN, IT'S FLOYD JOY MAYWEATHER SENIOR . . .

After my split with Billy Graham, I chose Floyd Mayweather Sr. to replace him and he went on to train me for my last two Vegas fights against Paulie Malignaggi and Manny Pacquiao.

He had an impressive track record in boxing and a colourful life story to say the least. As well as coaching his son, he'd trained world champions like Chad Dawson, Joan Guzmán, Oscar De La Hoya and women's world champ Laila Ali, Muhammad Ali's daughter. He was once a top-ten-ranked welterweight; his biggest fight was against Sugar Ray Leonard in September 1978. A few months later, the brother of Little Floyd's mother pointed a gun at his head. He held up the then one-year-old Floyd Jr. in front of him reasoning that the fella wouldn't shoot a baby. Instead he blasted Floyd Sr. in the leg. I've seen the scars and he was very lucky not to lose his leg, but after five operations, he was back in the ring within a year.

Floyd did time in the early Nineties for drug-dealing, and by the time he got released from jail, his brother Roger was established as Floyd Jr.'s trainer. Floyd Jr. stuck with Uncle Roger and then fell out with his dad big time, kicking him out of his house. After that they didn't speak to each other for long spells and it was only in 2013, that they fully patched things up and Floyd Jr. re-employed his dad as his trainer. Whether they'll still be working together by the time you read this book is another matter though.

There's no doubt that Floyd Sr. was the man who taught his son to fight. Senior himself was known for his shoulder-rolling defensive technique during his career, and you can see that with Junior. Floyd Sr. once told the journalist Donald McRae: 'Sometimes he looks almost as good as his daddy.' But the truth is that his son has taken boxing defence to another level.

Funnily enough, I benefited a little bit from their feud in the build-up to my fight with Floyd Jr., because of Floyd Sr.'s relationship with Oscar De la Hoya. He probably would have been in Oscar's corner for his fight with Floyd Jr. in May a few months before our bout, but reportedly asked for a $2 million fee. In the end, Oscar hired Freddie Roach instead. Roger Mayweather was in jail at the time for domestic assault, and for a while Senior and Junior buried the hatchet, but when Little Floyd chose to have Roger back as his trainer after his release from prison the relationship between dad and son became frosty again. Floyd Sr. must have been hurt by that decision and he was happy to tell Oscar, the co-promoter of my fight, where he thought his son was vulnerable.

A week or so before the fight, Oscar came down to the gym in Vegas and passed on the advice.

'I was talking to Senior the other day,' he says. 'He was saying that when he goes like this [he stands very side-on and puts his left shoulder high up by his chin, Floyd-style], he's wide open to a left to the body. And you're great at body shots.'

It makes sense to me.

'If he gives me the shoulder, change the angle – hook, hook, finish straight,' I reply.

Oscar himself had only lost to Floyd Jr. on a split decision, and I think that if he'd boxed the last six rounds the way he boxed the first six, where he tried to make Floyd work and pushed him back, I think he would have won the fight. It wasn't a case of Floyd taking the bull by the horns and winning the fight, it was as much that Oscar lost it.

He tells me: 'Never forget about your jab, keep using it. When I fought Floyd, in the fifth, sixth, seventh rounds, when I was using my jab, I had an easy time. He's vulnerable against the jab, he's doesn't know how to block them. Start everything with the jab and use pressure in a smart way.'

Oscar believed he had shown the blueprint for how to beat Floyd Jr., and that performance combined with the advice from Floyd Sr. gave me even more belief. I was confident that I could keep up the aggressive attack for the whole distance. In an interview with *24/7* that day, Oscar tells them: 'Ricky has all this information now and he can take it, learn from it and execute his perfect game plan. I believe he will do that.'

Of course, as I discovered in the ring, it was easier said than done against a lightning-quick defensive genius like Floyd Jr. Oscar was right about starting everything with the jab, because if you threw the hooks first he'd twist and turn quickly and take them on the shoulders, or pull away to take the sting out of the punches. It was better to throw a straight punch first, try to knock his head back and then bring in the hooks.

When I split from Billy, trainer Lee Beard, who had done a lot of work with Floyd Sr. in the States, recommended I go to see him and find out what he was all about. My partner Jennifer and me happened to be going to Vegas on holiday soon after, so I took the opportunity to meet him.

Jen and me had hired a luxury poolside cabana at the MGM Grand that day, complete with private patio, daybed, flatscreen telly and personal waiter service. As we're sitting there by the pool in the morning, I say to Jen: 'I'm just going to nip and see this Floyd Mayweather. I'll only be an hour.' I ended up staying out with Floyd at the gym he was working at the rest of the day, leaving Jen on her own – she isn't best pleased when I get back.

He was entertaining, I liked his ideas on boxing and we clicked. I liked the fact that he was a totally different trainer to Billy. I could have gone with a lot of trainers who were more attack-minded, but how much could I learn from them at that stage of my career? Floyd was a more defensive coach, working on speed and catching punches. I wanted someone who'd teach me something I'd never been shown before and could add something to my game.

Things started off well with Floyd. In training for the Malignaggi bout, I felt I was learning new things from him, and people who came to watch me train said they could see the difference. It's a bit like when a new manager comes in at a football club – the new man wants to make his mark, and the players find an extra gear. In my case, I was keen to learn from Floyd. It gave me a fresh outlook and an extra spring in my step.

With Floyd, the body-belt and weight training were out in favour of sparring and pads. He also stood over me as I did every bit of training – which was slightly different to Billy who, over the years, left me to get on with certain aspects. We were together for so long it all became second nature, but perhaps over time you can lose a little bit of intensity working on your own. At that point in my career it helped to have Floyd stand over me and push me even harder.

Billy probably wouldn't admit it but I think he had lost that little bit of appetite by the end. Fair enough, he was suffering a lot of pain with his hands and arms, which meant he couldn't do the pads every day, but he could have compensated in other ways. With Floyd, whenever I was hitting the bag, or even skipping, he'd be right there watching. Towards the end of my time with Billy, he might be sat in his office smoking. When I'm in the gym training my lads now, I watch them hit the bag, because they can still make mistakes. I'm looking to see that they are maintaining their technique as they get more tired, and executing the moves we've been working on with the pads and in sparring.

It was all fast-forward and no pause button with Floyd, though. He was totally against me doing my usual drinking and eating fast food between training camps. After the Malignaggi fight, I said I needed to have a rest and unwind, but he wanted me to stay in the gym.

It did make me laugh when he came over to train me in

Manchester before the Pacquiao fight, though, because he'd be shuffling out to KFC every day to eat.

'Got to have my chicken, man . . .'

That did make me chuckle, thinking, 'You're telling me how to live and you're going to KFC every day!'

I was used to training very, very hard, but with Billy I'd alternate between hard days and easier days – push your body and let it rest. That stood me in good stead throughout my career and it's how I train my fighters now, but with Floyd, after a month to get my weight down, I'd spar most days for the five weeks up to the week of the fight. It was always 100 miles per hour, and bloody knackering. The last training session before the Malignaggi fight, I was thinking, 'This is killing me now,' like I'd overcooked it. I just about got away with it against Paulie, but it was a warning sign of problems to come against Manny.

I did really like Floyd. He was so different to me, he's a unique character; I found him comical at times. He loved reciting his poems. He's been coming up with little rhymes since way back when, like this one before his bout with Sugar Ray in '78:

> *The Ray is young, he must be taught.*
> *This 'Joy' will turn his Sugar to salt.*

Unfortunately for Floyd, Sugar proved just too sweet for him in the ring, knocking him down twice and stopped him in ten rounds.

With the 'poet laureate of boxing', as he's known, in my corner, I didn't need to do any trash-talking – Floyd did it all for me. For a press conference before the Malignaggi fight, he reworded a couple of his poems just for the occasion:

> *The man you meet if you wanna go to sleep*
> *He's back, it's amazing, ain't no jive, the Hitman comes alive.*

Continuing,

when Hitman breaks your jaw, you'll be sucking on soup.

And:

He's the man with the man who's gonna make the plan,
To put Paulie on his pants.

Paulie was a bit pissed off: 'Man, you should have wrote children's poems – what you doing in boxing?'

Floyd is also a talented artist – if you ask him, he'll tell you he's the best American artist that ever lived. When we're in training for the Pacquiao fight, he invites everyone over to his place for a barbecue, and shows us his paintings of Elvis Presley, Muhammad Ali standing over Sonny Liston in the ring and Bruce Lee. They're really impressive. He also shows off his lairy clothes – Floyd likes to dress up loud and proud, but some of his shirts would've won first prize at the New Inn's famous 'Shit Shirt' competition. I'm taking a call as he's pulling out the suits from his wardrobe and I have to ask him to turn his suits down because I can't hear the phone.

For all his talents, Floyd isn't the most organised bloke in the world. At the start of the Pacquiao press tour, he rocks up at Vegas airport in his suit, no luggage, and says to me: 'What time do we get back?

'What do you mean get back tonight – we're staying overnight.'

'You're fuckin' shitting me, man. I haven't even got a fuckin' toothbrush.'

Floyd doesn't like heights or flying either. When we flew from Vegas to Los Angeles, it's only an hour, so we're travelling in a tiny little plane. When we take off he's gripping the armrests and looking a bit green: 'Oh my God, man, get me down!'

I think it took a while for Floyd to get my sense of humour. I'd be messing around, dropping my shorts and pulling up my pants so they looked like a G-string, wiggling my arse at him, and he looked at me like I was crazy: 'Goddam, what's he doin' – he's wearing girls' underwear, man . . .'

He didn't seem to mind me taking the piss out of him a bit though – although maybe sometimes he didn't realise that's what I was doing.

Of course, we were never going to have as close a relationship as Billy and me had, because we had been mates as much as trainer and fighter, but Floyd liked a laugh and we got on really well. More important, my performance in the Malignaggi fight was encouraging. After the defeat by Floyd Jr. and so-so display against Juan Lazcano, I felt like I was back on form, learning new skills from Floyd and couldn't wait for my next training camp.

But the preparation for the Pacquiao camp proved to be a disaster.

I spent four weeks in Vegas prior to the Malignaggi fight, but I extended that to six weeks for Manny. Floyd came over to Manchester to train me for Pacquiao as he had for Malignaggi.

The omens weren't good when Floyd put the pads on for the first time and got into an orthodox stance.

'Floyd, what you doing? He's a southpaw . . .'

'Nah, man. We'll spar southpaw, we'll do the pads orthodox.'

I didn't see the point of doing the pads orthodox when I was going to be sparring against southpaws and, more importantly, facing Manny Pacquiao, one of the best southpaws in history. For me, pads is preparation for sparring, and then sparring is preparation for the fight – it's all linked. That's why I ended up doing extra sessions back at my apartment with Lee Beard, who would do southpaw pads with me.

Now I'm a trainer, I do southpaw pads with all my fighters if they are going up against a left-hander, because I wouldn't want anyone to feel like I felt in the build-up to that Pacquiao fight. It takes a bit of practice to get good when you've always fought orthodox, but you've got to do it. Floyd's poems wouldn't have rhymed so well if he'd said 'I'm the best, better than all the rest . . . but I can't do southpaw pads.'

He could have done, if he pulled his finger out of his arse and actually tried to.

While he was offering me the wrong kind of padwork, he was also over-training me – there were just no easy days. By the time I got out to Vegas, my weight was down much lower than it usually was at that stage.

As I got nearer to the fight I'd say to Floyd: 'I'm fucked here, I'm knackered.'

'Nah, nah, man,' he'd reply. 'I'm the best at this. I know what I'm doing.'

Floyd has a real old-school attitude to training – the more you do, the fitter you get. He seemed to forget that I'd prepared for twenty-odd championship fights before. He wasn't the only one who knew how to do it. My work-rate and stamina had always been second to none.

Floyd is a showman, he loves playing to the cameras and he always seemed to work me harder when the *24/7* crew were filming our sessions. Watch the shows and you'll see him, right up to the fight, absolutely hammering my body with the medicine ball. When you're down to ten stone four, not much meat left on you, that could break your ribs.

Robert Diaz – matchmaker for Golden Boy Promotions (see *The Manchester Mexican*, page 182, to find out how Robert and I first met) who promoted the fight – well remembers the problems of that Pacquiao camp.

Robert Diaz:

Here's what I saw: Ricky felt that his prior trainer wasn't giving him the full attention, so he goes to a new trainer who's giving him too much. But Ricky doesn't want to be the guy who says that's enough. I could see Floyd destroying him on the medicine ball, and a couple of times, I kid you not, I said: 'Ricky, you got a call, it's a very important interview.' I had no one on the line. I wanted him to say, 'Stop, time-out', but Ricky was having none of it. He looked at me like, 'You've got to be kidding me.'

I said to Lee Beard, 'Hey, you brought this guy [Floyd] in, you better go take care of your fighter.' Lee said, 'No, no, I'll end up fighting with him if I do it now.'

Eventually, I pulled Ricky and said we've got to do the medical for the licensing. I went with him and Paul Speak. I said to Rick: 'What's wrong? You're not the same.' I could see that he was really down, he was bummed. 'Rick, listen to your body, you need a break. This guy's killing you.'

It's now fight week. The weight's under control. And Floyd tells him to do ten miles on Mount Charleston. It's good to do mountains at the beginning of training for your strength, but in fight week? I said: 'Ricky, this is crazy. You've never done that. Is there a problem with the weight?' He said, 'No.' So I said, 'Then do your regular 30-40 minutes on a flat surface.' But he did what he was told.

Floyd also had this thing about me running in army-style hiking boots rather than trainers. Look at the pictures of Muhammad Ali back in the day – that's what he used to wear – and I'd do the same when I was doing my training runs. My brother did too, to start with, but soon said, 'Fuck that, these boots are wearing me down,' and switched back to running in trainers. Matthew's a bit different to me and I wish I'd had a bit more of his mentality, but instead I stuck with the boots despite the blisters.

Floyd started training me for Pacquiao in Manchester. By the time I got out to Vegas, my weight was lower than it normally would be at that stage after six weeks' training. With three weeks to go I was pretty much on weight, but Floyd never put the brakes on. A couple of press guys who visited the camp around that time and saw that I was already in fighting shape asked me if I felt I'd peaked too soon. Of course, I said no, but as the fight got nearer, I said to Lee Beard, 'I've got nothing left here. I feel drained.'

There is a stubborn side to me that if someone challenges me to do something, I'll do it, so I did it Floyd's way. That ate me up after the fight. In hindsight, I should have said: 'Floyd, I don't care what you say. No one knows my body better than me – I've trained for God knows how many title fights. If I don't have a rest, I won't have a punch in me when I get in that ring. I'm having a fucking rest.'

If I'd been in my normal fighting shape, I think the only chance Manny had would have been to nail me early as I was coming in, like he did. If he hadn't have got me out of there in six rounds, I believe my work-rate and intensity would have rumbled him. As it was, for the only time in my career, I walked to the ring, thinking: I'm going to get beat here.

Floyd has a different opinion of all of this, reckoning that I followed Lee Beard's gameplan: 'You can't learn from two different trainers . . . it's confusing,' he has said since. 'My thing is that I think it was a ball of confusion. I think Ricky Hatton was scared more than anything . . . Of course I like to win. When I win, everybody wins. But at the end of the day, everything is on him . . . He made the decision to have Lee Beard train him a second time in the evening. It wasn't me overtraining him or Lee Beard over-training him, it was him overtraining himself.'

Absolute rubbish. Scared of what? I think everyone who knows me will tell you I've never been afraid of any opponent. The only reason I did extra training with Lee was because Floyd couldn't do southpaw pads. Simple as that.

After I got beat by Manny, Floyd just went back to the dressing room, zipped up his zoot suit and scurried away sharpish. It was a sad ending because I liked Floyd in many ways. He's a character and, apart from the issue of not doing southpaw pads, he was an excellent boxing coach – I learnt a lot from him and use a lot of his methods with my fighters nowadays, but I wasn't happy with the way he prepared me for the Pacquiao fight. I'm not saying I would have beaten Manny Pacquiao, but if I was on my normal game I think it was a 50–50 fight. One thing is for certain – Manny didn't beat me at my best.

Paul Speak:

The training camp before the Pacquiao fight was the worst experience I've ever had in my time with Rick. The worst part for me was seeing people's egos. It's a very dangerous sport for egos to get in the way.

THE BEST (AND WORST) OF SPARS

Good-quality sparring is crucial before any fight, and even more so when you are fighting at world-class level. Of course, it's not just about sparring against really good fighters, they also need to have a similar style to the opponent you are going to face. When you start fighting the likes of Floyd Mayweather, that gets very difficult because there's no one as good as him – so all you can do is look for sparring partners that each test some of the skills that you are going to need.

It can be a bit hit and miss. Sometimes sparring partners turn up and they box like absolute world-beaters. Other times you do one spar, and have to say sorry and send them home if they are not up to scratch. Before the Castillo fight, one guy got injured in the last session, which comes with the territory, but even he seemed to have a good time overall. When I was sparring I didn't usually hit with full power, but still with a fair bit of force. A lot of people do tap-tap sparring, but I don't like that because it's not realistic. To tap someone, it means it's a little bit slower, so you've got to put a bit of weight behind it without taking liberties.

Until I went to Boston to fight Luis Collazo in 2006, all my fights bar four – three in America (New York at Madison Square Garden, Atlantic City and Detroit) and one in Germany (Oberhausen) – had taken place in the UK, so I'd usually spar against British fighters. But for the big Vegas fights I spent more and more time out there training beforehand so I needed to find good American and Mexican fighters. That's where my connection with Robert Diaz paid off. Robert, who sent a couple of people over to Manchester to spar before the Juan Lazcano fight as well as organising sparring for my last four Vegas fights, tells me that everyone he sent across always thanked him later. I didn't just beat them up and send them home. They were paid very well, put up in nice hotels and when they went back they'd say we'd taken them to play darts or to see a 'soccer' match (I always like to recruit new fans for Manchester City . . .). Robert was very good at picking the right sparring partners for the job in hand. For instance, for Paulie Malignaggi, he brought me a couple of lads who did nothing but jab and move, move, run, hit and hold. He wanted them to frustrate me, so that when it came to the actual fight, I could deal with Paulie's tactics. That worked out perfectly. Previously, for Castillo, it was the totally opposite approach. Most of the sparring partners involved were Mexican, because we didn't want anyone who was going to run and jab. We needed people who were going to be on top of me all the time. Robert also brought in American Steve Forbes, the former IBF super featherweight champion, for that fight to give me some top-quality sparring. Billy Graham got Forbes to work me over on the inside, using his elbows and sharp little uppercuts. Forbes didn't have the punching power that we expected from Castillo, but he had faster hands, so it was like facing Castillo on fast-forward which was great preparation.

Looking back, probably the best sparring session I did (not just for Vegas fights – *ever*) was before the Castillo fight. Robert had brought in Mexican Alfredo Angulo. Angulo was twenty-four years old at the time, an unbeaten light middleweight prospect who would go on to win the WBO world title in that division a couple of years later. He was chosen because he was aggressive like Castillo, but he was a lot bigger than me. When he turns up, Robert goes: 'Oh, you're sparring this kid today.'

I look across and think, fucking hell – you're joking.

Robert Diaz:

Before they start sparring, Alfredo asks me what I want him to do. I tell him: 'I need Ricky to work, to sweat and make weight.' He says, 'Okay, no problem.' As a young, up-and-coming fighter, he could have been tempted to try to impress his promoter, make a name for himself, especially considering he was much bigger physically, but he's a nice, humble kid. And he gives Ricky a really good workout. Proper Mexican-style in-fighting. All the while, he's encouraging him: 'C'mon Ricky. Work, work. Hit me, hit me.'

The next session a couple of days later Alfredo is back again. Another of my sparring partners Anthony Salcido missed the previous session with a 'major headache' (I can't help thinking I might have been responsible for causing that . . .), so Robert asks Alfredo: 'Do you mind doing your sparring session and two extra rounds?'

Alfredo's up for it, so off we go.

This time, I put in six razor-sharp rounds of sparring with him. Bang, bang, bang – picking him off. Absolutely as good as I can box.

Afterwards, Alfredo looks like he wants to kill me because I've boxed so well. He wants to carry on and get his own back.

Billy Graham is like: 'No, no, just six rounds, mate. Finished now.'

Alfredo says: 'I come back Wednesday, I come back Wednesday.'

I'm thinking, no way. I can see the way this is going to go – we want good sparring, we don't want wars. I've already proved I'm in top form ready for Castillo

Fast-forward to the build-up to the Manny Pacquiao fight and it was a case of from the sublime to the horrendous. Robert Diaz has told me he can recall which day he first turned up for sparring, a Wednesday. It was a memorable day for all the wrong reasons.

Robert comes along with three sparring partners for me. He's seen me train many times before, and he knows that while I train really hard, I usually find time to enjoy myself – doing a moonie, squirting water at someone or whatever – but Floyd Mayweather Sr. is working me into the ground, and our relationship is getting more and more strained.

Robert Diaz:

Ricky is unrecognisable from the fighter I've seen in previous training camps. Something's not right. He looks tired, can't get any sort of rhythm going and the sparring partners are getting the better of him. He's supposed to be doing six rounds – two rounds with each guy – but halfway through Floyd tells him: 'You're going to do eight now.'

It doesn't get any better in the two extra rounds, and at the end of the session, rather than say, 'You had a bad day, forget about it,' Floyd tells Ricky in front of everyone: 'You looked horrible, you're going to do another eight rounds tomorrow.'

Normally, you have a day off between spars, so I butt in and say: 'You mean Friday, right Floyd?'

'No, Thursday and Friday – another eight each.' This is a couple of weeks before the fight. Before his last sparring session I did something I never had before. I felt he had to. I came in with three sparring partners – Marvin Quintero, Cornelius Lock and another guy – and gather them round in the corner of the gym while Ricky is getting gloved up. 'Guys,' I say. 'This is the last day of sparring. I need Ricky to come out mentally feeling great, because that's our only shot now. So I want you guys to hold back a little.'

Of course, I don't know what Robert has said so I go in there and, sure enough, I have my best few rounds of the camp in Vegas, not realising that my sparring partners are going a bit easier than normal.

I know Robert was just looking out for me, because things were going so badly I needed some kind of mental boost before stepping in the ring to fight Pac Man. It worked, because at the end of the session, I said a couple of times: 'That was my best sparring, I'm ready.' I was trying to convince myself as much as anything.

Robert wasn't convinced though; he was really worried for me.

Robert Diaz:

I told my wife on the night of the fight, 'As soon as Ricky gets in the ring, I want to get out of the arena, I don't want to witness the fight.' I didn't expect a quick KO like happened, but at least it was quick, and there were no long-lasting effects. I was envisaging a bloodbath, because I'd seen him. He was over-trained; the training camp was more about Floyd than Ricky.

'REALITY TV' AND REALITY

Having a camera crew following me around, like I did for the *24/7* series, was nothing new to me by this time. From very early in my career, my promoter Frank Warren and Sky Sports worked hard to build my profile, and a big part of that was filming me away from the ring, before and after fights. I'd often get a visit from Adam Smith, now Sky Sports' Executive Producer of Boxing and co-presenter of the popular *Ringside* show. Then, Adam was just a young reporter and he spent a lot of time visiting fighters at their training camps, so he'd often turn up with a camera crew.

Adam Smith:

Talking with the Sky Sports boys about those days, Ricky was just the best possible person to work with. The access to boxers is always good, but the access to Ricky was something else. He allowed us to do pretty much anything, bar letting us go to the loo with him. Sometimes the cameraman would actually say, 'Ricky, I'm going to stop filming now,' but he'd reply, 'Whatever you want' – he just didn't mind us being around.

I remember on the day of one of his big fights, we pitched up at his house in the morning and Ricky was driving away. He winds down his window: 'Just going down the shop, lads. Let yourselves in and put the kettle on,' and chucks his keys out of the window to us.

Filming him training, driving to fights in his old banger, going to tea at his parents' house, playing darts at the New Inn, the traditional 'Shit Shirt' competition at the pub the day after the fight . . . we covered it all. You could see there were no airs and graces, and everyone got ribbed, including Ricky. It was always good fun being around him and we had such a laugh.

He let us film him exactly as he was. It didn't matter if he had his ridiculous slippers on or his Elvis hat. It was amazing insight into a fighter's life, in and out of the ring, for our viewers – reality TV before reality shows came in.

For Sky, who covered all my Vegas fights except the Castillo one (shown on Setanta), and for HBO, the chemistry of my fight against Mayweather was brilliant. Both unbeaten fighters, one was the down-to-earth guy, the other was the flash, arrogant bloke that no one really liked. The stuff they both did in the countdown to the fight really captured the imagination and helped to sell the fight.

On the *24/7* show, they didn't have to try too hard to show the difference in our personalities and lifestyles. You'd have Floyd saying, 'You see me – 250 on the wrist, 300,000 on the pinky, 600,000 on the neck,' then cut to me taking the piss out of him: 'Look at me ring, look at me chain, look at me tailor-made suit worth $3,000 – who gives a shit?' The producers didn't need say to me, 'Floyd said this, what do you say to that?' We did watch the episodes as and when they were broadcast so sometimes something he'd said might stick in my head and I'd say something back, but the producers didn't have to manufacture a clash of personalities, because there couldn't have been a bigger contrast.

If you watch reality TV these days, like *The Only Way is Essex* and *Geordie Shore,* there does seem to be a level of staging scenes – apparently, they call them 'augmented reality' shows. That wasn't the case with *24/7* series on my fights, but the producers did offer up ideas of things we could do.

For example, towards the end of my Mayweather training camp, they asked if they could film me going to the fridge in the kitchen, as if I was getting a snack in the middle of the night. I wasn't up for that – when you're a boxer close to a fight, training hard and watching your weight, it's not a good look to be sneaking down to the kitchen for a Scooby Snack. The idea behind it was that I was supposed to be restless thinking about the fight, and as I opened the fridge, they were going to create some sort of vision of Floyd fighting in the light from it. I was, like: 'Fucking hell, that's a bridge too far.'

Another time, they said to me, 'You like karaoke singalong back in England, don't you Ricky?'

'Oh yes, love it.'

'Well, why don't we take you out to a bar tonight and film you on the karaoke.'

'I'm fighting in two weeks – I normally do karaoke sixteen weeks before the fight when I'm pissed out of my head!'

I know they were just trying to think of different things to make the shows interesting, but preparing for the fight was always priority.

I didn't mind them filming anything I was doing anyway, though. For instance, Matthew and me would go down to the Crown and Anchor pub. It's as British a pub as you'll find in America and we'd go down there to watch the football back home and play darts, so the film crew could come down there with us.

In 2014, Floyd Jr. got in trouble with the Nevada State Athletic Commission (NSAC) for some content of the *All Access* reality series, Showtime's answer to HBO's *24/7,* in the build-up to his rematch with Marcos Maidana at the MGM Grand Garden Arena. One episode, which aired a few days before the fight, showed two amateur boxers at his gym apparently fighting for thirty-one minutes straight with no breaks while Floyd watched. 'The dog house – the rules are you fight 'til whoever quits,' Floyd said on camera. 'Guys fight to the death. It's not right, but it's dog house rules.'

One of the boxers involved was a lad called Donovan Cameron from England. He was training with another Manchester trainer, Bob Shannon, and came to my gym the year before to spar with one of my lads, Sergey Rabchenko. He looked a good young boxer.

In the show, you see Cameron give Sharif Rahman – the son of former world heavyweight boxing champion, Hasim Rahman – a pasting in what is supposed to be a sparring session. Sharif's older brother, Hasim Rahman Jr., then arrives at the gym and challenges the smaller Cameron to take him. Cash bets are shown being placed on who's going to win and the two boxers appear to fight continuously for half an hour, with Floyd and co cheering them on, until Cameron can't go on. The episode also had scenes of Floyd at his mansion with a load of girls rolling and smoking joints.

At the NSAC hearing, Floyd claimed that both the 'dog fight' and spliff-smoking scenes were actually staged to help sell his fight with Maidana. He is the executive producer of the series and talked about, being 'able to edit and chop footage the way we want'. He claimed that although he himself spars fifteen-minute rounds without a break, Rahman Jr. and Cameron actually took breaks during their 'dog fight'. Going back on his 'fight to the death' comment on the show, he said: 'I'm not going to let anyone get hurt.' Floyd's attorney said the scenes of gambling were all staged for the reality show, too.

Floyd, who doesn't drink or smoke, also told the five-man panel he was against drug use and wouldn't be around second-hand marijuana smoke because it can show up in drug tests for the fight: 'It wasn't real marijuana,' he said. 'It's all about entertainment.'

The Commission of course was most interested in the issue of health and safety of fighters at his gym and they pointed out that he wasn't licensed to have amateurs sparring there and would be liable if they got injured. Generally, though, they seemed satisfied with Floyd's explanation.

The Rahman brothers thought differently and later launched legal action against Floyd, Mayweather Promotions and Showtime alleging battery, tortuous assault, false imprisonment, negligence and defamation among other charges. According to the suit: 'Defendant Mayweather knowingly misrepresented facts while testifying before the Nevada State Athletic Commission.' It alleges among other things that when an onlooker told Sharif to leave the ring, Floyd responded by telling Cameron and others that 'if Sharif left the ring, to beat his ass outside the ring,' which made Sharif fear for his safety and continue to fight.

Floyd denies all charges and at the time of writing the case is waiting to be heard.

In all my years in boxing, I've never seen anything like that – 30-minute rounds, betting on who's going win. Never. If it did happen as the Rahman brothers say it did, then that's very dangerous. If it was all staged for entertainment as Floyd claims, I'm not sure that's good for the image of boxing either. It's a hard enough sport without pretending that lads are fighting to the death in the gym.

Although the series I appeared in for my two mega fights was called *24/7*, the camera crew weren't there every minute of every day and there were things that were kept private. The shows were televised before the fight so we could watch what the other was doing, so you had to be a bit sensible about it. For instance, when Floyd sparred fourteen rounds at his gym with Carlos Baldomir, one of his former opponents and ex-welterweight world champion, HBO weren't allowed to film it. They'd brought Baldomir to emulate my style of boxing, so Floyd's team didn't want that shown in case it gave away some tactics. All you saw was Floyd kneeling on the floor with his head over a bucket when they'd finished.

I don't know whether, in theory, I could have had any say in what they showed in the episodes that were broadcast, but neither me or my dad or Speaky ever asked them not to show anything they actually filmed. The only thing I didn't always allow them to film in the first place was, like Floyd, most of my sparring sessions.

Viewers of the *24/7* series covering the build-up to my Pacquiao fight wouldn't have known quite how badly things were going for me, though. They didn't see me get knocked on my arse in sparring two weeks before the fight by a featherweight, Cornelius Lock, then sitting on the ring apron with a towel over my head crying and inconsolable. They didn't see my dad and others, with a couple of weeks to go, seriously talking about pulling me out of the fight.

Kugan Cassius (*my 'bodyguard' for the Pacquiao fight – see page 79*):

I was out with Lee Beard about two weeks before the fight, and he said to me: 'What do you think of Ricky at the moment?'

I'd never seen sparring at that level before, and I'd made a conscious effort throughout the camp not to comment on boxing matters. But I had seen people getting the better of Ricky. To be fair, he was sparring with the likes of Cuban Erislandy Lara who I didn't know at the time, but went on to win a world light middleweight title, so they were no mugs, but he'd had very few good sparring sessions.

'D'you know what,' Lee continued. 'I know Ricky and he's not ready for this fight. He's going to get knocked out. He's not injured, but if I could have my way, I'd pull him out.'

Of course, the financial implications of pulling out would have been huge and it wasn't an option in my mind because I wasn't injured, and there were thousands of fans who had forked out a lot of money to fly over and support me.

My last sparring session was filmed for *24/7* and I performed well, partly because I finally bit the bullet and insisted on three days off beforehand – which turned out to be too little, too late – and partly because, unbeknown to me at the time, the sparring partners had been instructed to go easy. Watching the show, my fans would have thought I was ready to go.

The *24/7* viewers did get a flavour of my trainer Floyd Sr.'s timekeeping, or lack of it, though. On a few occasions, I'd be sat there waiting for an hour, hour and a half for him for turn up and it really pissed me off. When you're paying someone hundreds of thousands of dollars to train you for a world title fight, the least you can expect is for them to turn up on time. But Floyd would just breeze in late, no explanation or apology. You'd have thought he was the star. I've never looked at myself as a star, but I was the one fighting the top of the bill at the MGM Grand, and his job was to prepare me.

One of the strangest moments was when *24/7* filmed us all round at Floyd's house. My dad, young Sam Cantwell (the son of my mate Mickey Cantwell, the former British flyweight champion, who came out to stay with us and train), Matthew, Speaky, Kugan and me are sitting with Floyd on the sofas in the kitchen-lounge area to watch a preview of the latest episode of *24/7* on the telly. None of us have seen it before, so it's like the people on *Gogglebox* being filmed watching themselves on *Gogglebox*.

We're all having a laugh at first as they show me warming up on Mount Charleston and Floyd bigging me up: 'This is a real racehorse, right here. Freddie 'The Joke Coach' Roach gotta a mule, but this is an Italian Stallion right here.'

But later they show me waiting around at the gym, with my hands bandaged up ready to train. Cut to Floyd who is cruising around in his car and then into a Drive-Thru to buy a burrito.

I'm watching this thinking: are you fucking kidding me?, and for a second or two there's an awkward silence around the room which I break by making a joke of it, saying, 'So that's where you were?' Floyd doesn't seem to be embarrassed at all.

People have asked me why I didn't have a go at him there and then, but for me, by that point in time, it was just a case of add it to the list.

When I talk now about how things went wrong in my preparation for that fight, people can't say I'm making it up, because a lot of it was shown on telly. Viewers could see it with their own eyes, and the bits that weren't immediately obvious at the time are if you watch the shows again and read between the lines.

So, yes, there is a difference between 'reality TV' and reality, but those *24/7* series were brilliant for building the excitement for the Mayweather and Pacquiao fights and did give boxing fans a good insight into the preparation that went into them.

DARTS WITH THE DUCK

There's a mate of mine called David Owen, but everyone knows him as 'The Duck' – he's quite famous round our way. We call him The Duck because he laughs like a duck quacking – Wwwaccck, wwwwacck, wwwwacck. Really loud, too – you can hear it from Vegas.

When he used to live with his mum, I once phoned up and said:

'Is Dave there?'

'Dave?'

'Yeah, Dave – have I got the right number?'

'Oh, you mean The Duck?'

Even his mum only knows him by his nickname.

The Duck's a bit older than me – I've known him since I was about ten and he was in his late teens. He's from the same Hattersley council estate and used to be a regular in the New Inn pub when my dad was the landlord. He says that while he was playing darts upstairs, all he could hear was me downstairs in the basement leathering the heavy bag. When I wasn't training, I'd come upstairs, sneak up and give him a little tickle as he was about to throw a dart to put him off. I've played darts with him for years ever since and still see him all the time.

He came to my fight in Boston and all five Vegas fights with a group of my mates, and pretty much everyone involved in the Vegas events got to know him. I gave him and the rest of the lads 'Team Hatton' T-shirts, and although they didn't have official credentials, the management and security people got to know them and gave them access to the weigh-in, press conferences and all that. They were treated like part of the team, and I wouldn't have had it any other way.

The only people in Vegas who didn't seem to know who The Duck was were a couple of bouncers at a nightclub in the New York-New York hotel.

The Duck suffers from spina bifida which means he is a little bit hunched over – I always joke that he irons his shirts with a wok. These doormen wouldn't let him in along with the other boys – and it seemed to be because of his disability. A couple of the lads went into the club, including another mate of mine, Bernard Jones and they find the place is packed with my fans. They immediately put the word round: 'The bouncers aren't

letting The Duck in – put your drinks down and let's all fuck off.'
To a man they do – all walk out, leaving the place deserted.

The Duck's a massive Manchester United fan (I don't hold that
against him), so when he was in my dressing room before the
Mayweather fight, he was gobsmacked to see David Beckham in
there too. He couldn't take his eyes off him and he told me later
that he was even more amazed when Becks came up to me and
said, 'Thanks for letting me come in here today.' To The Duck, I'm
just his mate, so it was unbelievable to him that one of his football
heroes was thanking me for allowing him in the dressing room – it
was surreal for me, too, to be honest.

The most legendary Duck incident came about four weeks out
from the Mayweather fight and the film crew from *24/7* were over
from America and following me. They wanted to compare how me
and Floyd were preparing for the fight, but also our lifestyles away
from the gym.

'So what do you do when you're not training, Ricky?

'I play darts with The Duck.'

'The Duck?'

'Yeah, he's my mate.'

'Er, okay . . . can we come along and film you playing darts?'

'No problem.'

'Are a few of your mates from the pub going to watch you fight
in Vegas?'

'The majority of them are, I think. The Duck definitely is.'

The *24/7* fellas come down and film us playing darts one evening
at the Clarkes Arms in Hyde. When we've finished our game, they
decide they want to interview The Duck. He's had a few drinks, by
this time, and he's not shy at the best of times.

First question: 'So you're going to Vegas, then?'

'Oh absolutely, I'll be there. I've known Ricky since day
one, been to every single fight of his. Went to the his first two

in Vegas and now he's gonna whup Mayweather . . . is this interview going to be on the TV in America?'

'Er, yes, it is.'

'Well, listen girls. My name is David 'The Duck' Owen – I'm over in four weeks' time and this is what's coming for ya . . .'

With that he whips down his trousers and pants in one movement – the whole lot – and there is The Duck's 'little Duck' out for all to see. He's waving his hands above his head, thrusting his hips and shouting: 'C'mon baby!'

The jaws of the film crew hit the floor, their eyes hypnotised by The Duck, naked from the waist down, gyrating in front of them.

Now, I should point out here for those of you who haven't met him, that The Duck's got a big belly and – I'm sure he won't mind me saying as he wanted to show it to all of America – he's also got a little penis.

So it's quite a sight. It's a bit like driving past the scene of a car crash – horrible, but impossible to take your eyes off. Meanwhile, we're all pissing ourselves.

It's not the first time I've seen him pull this stunt. He previously exposed little Duck to the TV presenter Helen Chamberlain. We were at the world championship darts in Purfleet, Essex, which she was presenting on Sky, when we went up to say hello.

'Who's this fella?' says The Duck, pointing to the bloke with her.

'This is my boyfriend . . .'

'What are you doing hanging around with a guy like that,' replies The Duck. 'You want a proper man like this,' and promptly drops his strides.

Helen looks at me: 'Who. Is. This?'

'It's The Duck.'

To be fair you could be arrested for that sort of thing, but luckily Helen's got a good sense of humour and just thought it was hysterical.

Chatting to one of the *24/7* fellas later, I ask how the other crew are getting on following Floyd over in Vegas.

'I just spoke to one of the guys and he said Floyd's always late so they're having to wait around a lot. He asked what we're doing, so I'm telling him, "We've been to watch the football, Man City, we've been to the pub to play darts, and a guy just got his cock and balls out during an interview!" He was, like, "Whaaaat?"'

When the show aired, The Duck was looking out for his moment in the spotlight, but, funnily enough, it hadn't made the final cut.

'They never showed my interview,' he complained, next time I saw him.

'You got your dick out!'

He couldn't understand why that might be a problem.

Mind you, since The Duck learned that the *24/7* series won an Emmy award in America, he likes to claim that he's won an Emmy anyway.

THE 'BODYGUARD'

During an interview before my fight with Floyd, I offered him a bit of advice: 'The fans make you, so don't shield yourself away from them. I don't need five bouncers pushing people away from me. That's why I've got 33,000 fans wanting to come and watch me and he's got thirty-three.'

I never wanted a bodyguard during my career even at the height of my success. I've always enjoyed meeting people and I was flattered that they spent their time and money coming to support me, so why would I want to shut them off?

However, the attention I got during fight week of that Floyd fight was overwhelming, beyond anything I could have imagined. It was wonderful, but a couple of times it did get a bit hairy, not because there was any trouble, but just because of the sheer number of people who came out to cheer me on.

For my next mega fight against Manny Pacquiao, who had his own army of fans, I realised that I might need a bit of extra help – not really a bodyguard, so much as a marshal to keep a bit of order at the bigger events. Also, it would be good to get someone who could help take the load off Paul Speak. In the run-up to the previous Vegas fights, Speaky had always been mad busy, but I'd also relied on him to drive me around, so we could get the new guy to do that and save him one job.

The thing is I didn't want a normal bodyguard, and it needed to be someone I'd get on with and have a laugh with – I was planning to spend six weeks in Vegas before this fight, longer than ever before. I thought of Kugan Cassius.

Boxers and boxing fans today will know Kugan from the iFL TV video channel he co-founded. Kugan goes around the gyms talking to the fighters, their trainers, family and friends, and films all the pre- and post-fight press conferences. I don't know what you'd call his job exactly – a video journalist, maybe? – but his interviewing style is certainly a bit different to traditional boxing journalism. He's likely to start an interview with me by saying: 'How you doing Ricky, you fat bastard?'

He's certainly not shy. I saw an interview he did with Tyson Fury where he was wearing a sweatshirt with 'CASSIUS BY KUGAN CASSIUS FOR KUGAN CASSIUS FOR KUGAN BY KUGAN CASSIUS IN COLLABORATION WITH KUGAN CASSIUS FOR KUGAN BY KUGAN CASSIUS' written on the front. Must have made it himself.

He's a funny lad and gets away with taking the piss out of the boxers he interviews because he doesn't mind having the piss ripped out of him too. iFL TV has been great for boxing, because they go to all the gyms, cover all the shows large and small, the top fighters and the up-and-comers, and Kugan himself has built up a big personal following.

I first met Kugan in 2008 when my Hatton Promotions company were co-promoting a boxing show in Bristol with the former women's world champion, Jane Couch. Back then, Kugan was a boxing fan, but he wasn't really involved in boxing at all. He'd been trying his hand at acting since leaving university, and he'd met Jane on a film set. Jane asked him to tag along with me on the night, just make sure I was looked after, and we clicked. I thought he was a right laugh.

I bumped into him a couple more times in the next few months and when the bodyguard question came up a month or so before I left for Vegas, his name popped into my head. Kugan was a big unit so at least he'd look the part even if he wasn't a professional minder. Anyway, he couldn't do a worse job than one of Floyd's bodyguards did during his pre-fight tour of Britain – he was a man mountain, the biggest bloke I've seen in my life, but when someone threw a plastic bottle at Floyd on the stage outside Manchester Town Hall, this fella ducked and the bottle flew past him and hit Floyd on the head.

I sent Kugan a text explaining that I wanted him to come out to Vegas for a six-week camp and what I wanted him to do.

Kugan Cassius:

I was in a kebab shop with my then girlfriend when I received this text from Ricky out of the blue. It was a really long text. I was totally surprised. My missus told me she thought it was a great opportunity and I had to go, so I texted him back and said I was up for it.

So a few weeks later, off we went – me, Paul Speak, my lawyer Gareth Williams and my new 'bodyguard', Kugan Cassius.

One of Kugan's first jobs was to walk up the red carpet with me and the likes of Mark Wahlberg and Mickey Rourke at an event in LA to promote the fight. After that it was down to the less glamorous business of waking me up and driving me to Sunset Park for my early-morning run in Vegas and ferrying me back and forth to the gym. Every evening, he'd check if I needed anything and he'd drive me downtown if I fancied going out.

Kugan had a funny relationship with my trainer Floyd Mayweather Sr. They got on well, but no matter how many times he told Floyd his name, Floyd kept forgetting it. Floyd ended up referring to him as 'the big Paki' (even though Kugan had also told him that his parents are from Sri Lanka).

At the start of fight week, sorting out the accreditation, Speaky comes in and says: 'Batista is going to walk Manny Pacquiao out. Do you want 'The Undertaker' to walk you in?'

For those of you not familiar with the names, Batista and The Undertaker (real names: Dave and Mark) are superstar American wrestlers. Both are giants so I think about it for a second, glance at Kugan and say: 'No it's alright, I'll just stick with the big Paki.'

Everyone falls about laughing.

Kugan Cassius:

I see Floyd Sr. every now and then when I'm in America these days filming for iFL TV. I still have to re-introduce myself to Floyd and remind him that we know each other. Last year I showed him photos from the camp to jog his memory. 'Ah, you've lost weight,' said Floyd. 'You used to be fat and now you're a little bit fat.'

Kugan was carrying a lot of extra timber back then. He obviously liked his food so I was quite impressed that he kept me company by only eating the same amount as I did at meal-times and not drinking a drop of alcohol for the entire camp. Kugan's not a big drinker so that part wasn't hard, but some were suspicious about his eating habits. Despite supposedly living off the strict diet of a light welterweight boxer in training, Kugan's big belly didn't seem to be getting any smaller as the weeks passed by. Young Sam Cantwell, who joined us out there, said to Kugan: 'There's no way you're just eating this.' Kugan swore at the time he was, but he's since admitted that once we were all tucked up asleep in bed, he was slipping out for Scooby Snacks.

In terms of being a minder, Kugan had it pretty easy. I spent most of my time at a private gym which was pretty inaccessible, so no one really turned up there except for press and TV crews every now and then. Come fight week, my fans were as good as gold as always, so it was more a matter of marshalling duties than being a minder.

Kugan Cassius:

I've covered a fair few Floyd Mayweather Red Carpet MGM Arrivals for iFL TV since, but nothing comes close to that Pacquiao experience. Pulling up in a limo at the back of MGM and then walking into blinding flashlights and packed crowds singing 'There's only one Ricky Hatton'.

I still rate doing the ringwalk with Ricky as one of the top two moments of my life. A few months before, I'd been messing around with him at a boxing show in Bristol, and then I found myself in the ring in Vegas before a top-of-the-bill fight, with the likes of Bernard Hopkins and Oscar De La Hoya. I was in such a daze that it was only when everyone started clearing out of the ring that I realised I didn't have a clue where my seat was.

Before I could have a look round to find it, the bell went for the first round. All I could do was crouch by the ring apron near my cornermen. I ended up watching the entire fight – for as long as it lasted – with my chin on the canvas. The only way I could have been closer was if I'd been in the ring with him.

It was only really after the fight that Kugan actually had to do a bit of proper bodyguarding. I was taken to hospital in an ambulance for a check-up after the knockout. Kugan was following in the car behind with a couple of security guys from America who helped out at the MGM on the night. We were on the freeway in traffic, and unbeknown to me two blokes jumped out of their cars, ran up to the ambulance, and held up their cameras to film through the windows. Kugan and the other guys had to jump out and chase them off. One of the photographers was shouting, 'I'm going to put this on YouTube, man' as he ran away. (I've yet to see that exciting footage of me having a lie-down on the internet.)

The next day, Kugan comes to see me and Jennifer. He's got his bags packed and he's just come to say goodbye before he catches his flight home. I'm devastated about losing, but planning to stay a few more days in Vegas and drink a lot of beer to numb the pain. Jen, who probably knows I'm about to go on a huge bender, is just as keen as I am that he stays on with me.

Kugan Cassius:

I'd had an almighty row on the phone with my girlfriend the week before, so when I rang her to explain Ricky wanted me to stay on, she wasn't best pleased, but said, 'Oh well, it's only one more week . . .'

That was when I really earned my money, because Ricky was out every night on the piss! He was a nightmare, not because he caused any trouble, but he never wanted the party to end. He was the happy chap who wanted to be with everybody.

When we all finally did fly back to England, Kugan brought with him his own lasting memento of his time as my sort-of-bodyguard. He had a 'Team Hatton' T-shirt and wherever we had been in America, he got people he met to sign it for him. By the end he had 30-odd signatures on there – everyone from Mickey Rourke and Oscar De La Hoya to Sugar Shane Mosley and Tom Jones had signed it. It's framed and hanging in his living room at home now.

What didn't last was his relationship with his girlfriend – they split up a month after the fight, although Kugan assures me the timing of the break-up was purely coincidental.

SECTION III

MEET THE OPPONENTS

FACING THE IRON TWIN

In January 2007, when I first fought in Vegas, just as Vegas wasn't ready for the Hatton army of fans, me and my team weren't quite ready for Vegas. It's fair to say we had a few teething problems.

All my training in England had gone well. Christmas was put on a backburner for me and for our Matthew who was fighting on the undercard. I was even in the gym sparring on Christmas morning. Getting punched in the face is not the way I normally liked to spend my Christmas, but those are the sacrifices that make the victories all the sweeter later.

By the time we fly out to Vegas ten days before the fight I'm in tip-top shape. I've also been awarded the MBE in the New Year's Honours list, which gave me another boost.

Even though it's deep midwinter in England, for some reason I have it in my head that it's going to be hot out in Vegas. It always has been when I've been out there before, so I've packed up my suitcase with T-shirts, vest and shorts. Of course, as I discover, Vegas in January is colder than Manchester if anything, and that year it was like the Antarctic. So cold that we see a waterfall outside a hotel on the Strip that is frozen solid. None of the clothes I've brought with me are any use for going out and about, so one of the first jobs is to find the nearest outlet shopping mall and buy woolly hats, jumpers and fleeces.

We're staying at Caesars Palace and Joe Sharpe has arranged to put me up in a fantastic suite there. The only problem is the air-conditioning. A lot of visitors to Vegas who aren't used to the air-con can find it blocks up your nose and I'm no different. That, combined with the freezing weather, meant within a couple of days I've got the flu. I'm unable to do my normal fifteen rounds on the body-belt – Billy can see I'm knackered after twelve and decides to cut it short there.

I'm forced to take a couple of days' off training to try and shake off the flu bug. I'm not good at sitting around though, so after a while cooped up at the hotel, I decide to wrap up in my new winter gear and go for stroll with the boys. We see the Las Vegas Convention Center, once the biggest boxing venue in town. But as we get closer we discover it's hosting a very different event today – a porn convention. Suddenly, being indoors seems like a better idea and we spend a couple of hours wandering around this massive exhibition hall among some of the world's biggest female porn stars. Obviously, I didn't recognise any of them . . .

The other thing we haven't really thought about before arriving in Vegas is transport to get to the gym or around town. We're always dependent on people outside the team to drive us so we do end up hanging around quite a bit.

I train at the promoter Bob Arum's Top Rank gym, which is a big, old-school gym – two rings, a few punch bags and that was that. Basic, but everything we need. The thing we haven't bargained for is that it's open to everybody – if you turn up and pay your subs, you can use the gym. Great if you're just coming in to keep fit, but not ideal when you're training for a big fight.

One time we're in there, both rings are in use, and a couple of fellas in one of them are messing about, not doing much.

'Can we use the ring?' I say.

'No, we're using it.'

'It's Ricky Hatton,' says Billy. 'He's fighting for a world title in a few days' time.'

'Don't give a fuck, man.'

So we just have to wait our turn.

The other problem with an open gym is that anyone from my opponent's camp can just wander in. Another day, Paul Speak spots a couple of blokes hanging around in the corner of the gym watching me closely, so he goes over.

Speaky says: 'Where are you from? Are you from the Urango camp'

They don't even try to deny it.

'On yer bike. Come on, get out.'

Speaky dealt with all the shit jobs like that, bless him – he had thirty years in the police force before he started working with me so he could handle it.

After training back home, I'd often go for a massage but we don't have a clue where to find a sports masseur in Vegas. Driving back from the gym, one of the boys sees a massage parlour out the window, so we pull up. They're advertising $10 massages, which seems very reasonable, so Speaky and I go in to investigate.

'Do you do a proper massage,' he says to the girl at reception.

'Yes, yes, we look after you . . .'

Looking round the place, it looks a bit seedy and we both start to suspect I might get more than I bargained for. I need a sports massage to recover from training, not a 'happy finish', so we make our excuses and leave.

Despite all of these little problems, I was still confident of beating

Juan Urango. He came into our fight unbeaten in eighteen bouts, with just one draw. He also had excellent amateur pedigree, even beating Miguel Cotto in the unpaid ranks – and Cotto was being talked about as a future opponent for me at the time. He was nicknamed the 'Iron Twin' because he fancied himself as a Mike Tyson wannabe. He had a come-forward style, squaring up, all hooks, no jab, but from the fights I'd seen on video he wasn't anywhere near as fast as me or Tyson. Urango was a southpaw, but not the tricky kind. He was good if you stayed right in front of him, but I thought I'd be too quick and too smart for him. Urango described himself as a 'good boxer, a good puncher, a good athlete' – I just felt I was a little bit better than him in all three departments. It was one of those fights where I could either make it hard or easy for myself – as long as the red mist didn't set in and I wasn't drawn into a scrap, I'd have my old IBF light welterweight title back.

Urango is from a poor background in the Colombian country-side, and had only moved to Florida four years before in search of a better life for his family. He is a Christian and he spoke a lot about his faith in the pre-fight interviews and press conferences. He thanked God for giving him the opportunity to come to live in the United States and when asked whether he expected to knock me out, he said: 'It's about what God wants. If the knockout comes, it comes. I'm ready to fight.'

He came across as a really nice, humble guy, but he was confident and I wasn't underestimating him.

He looked pretty thickset, but he was wearing a jacket in the press conference so I couldn't really tell what his physique was like. It's only when he strips down at the weigh-in that I see he really is a mini-Tyson. He looks huge for a light-welter – broad shoulders, muscles popping out everywhere. The place is jam-packed with my fans and they're all chanting, 'Who are ya? Who are ya?' as he steps up to the scales.

I turn to Billy and say, 'He'll never make ten stone'.

He gets on and the MC announces: 'Juan Urango weighs in at ten stone exactly!'

Fucking hell, he's done it. His bones must be made out of fibreglass. Massive guy. After the making the weight, Urango holds his arms out wide and shouts: 'Praise Jesus!'

'He's not going to fuckin' help ya!' shouts a Scouser in the crowd. I pissed myself laughing at that one.

After the weigh-in, I'm taken into a room to choose the gloves I'm going to wear on fight night.

As most people do in title fights, I used to wear Cleto Reyes boxing gloves, but as I was sponsored by Lonsdale we'd put the Lonsdale logo on them. But when we'd got to Vegas we'd been told that Urango and me must fight in ten-ounce gloves rather than the usual eight-ounce gloves. Normally, you only go to ten-ounce gloves when you get up to welterweight, but a new regulation had been introduced in Nevada following the tragic death of American lightweight Leavander Johnson after his world title fight with Jesús Chávez in Vegas in 2005.

The problem is we hadn't bought any ten-ounce gloves with us. The guy from Lonsdale, Dave Jarman, got hold of a couple of pairs of Everlast gloves out there for me to try on. They fitted fine, but you are required to have three or four pairs for a title fight, so he has to order a couple more pairs from England.

I hadn't thought any more about it until the weigh-in, and after surviving on small rations for weeks in the build-up to the fight, choosing gloves is not high on my priority list. I'm starving bleeding hungry and all I want to do is get some food in me. When I'm showed into a small, dark room with all the gloves lined up I just pick the first pair, put them on briefly, and hand them over to the officials. They sign them and keep them until it's time to glove up to make sure there's no tampering with them. Job done, it's away to the serious business of trying to find a decent full English breakfast in Vegas.

Come fight night, I get my hands bandaged in the dressing room, stick the gloves on, hit the pads and warm up as normal. The gloves are strung tight and bandaged up, but they feel a bit roomier than normal round the fist. I'm focused on the fight ahead so I don't pay it much attention.

I get in there against Urango, pummelling away at him for twelve rounds, without ever really threatening to knock him out. Fair enough, because he's a built like The Incredible Hulk and I've still got the flu, so I'm coughing up all sorts of crap during the fight.

It's only a few weeks later when I'm about to get my gloves from the fight framed that I think: 'Bloody hell, these things are massive.'

Turns out that the extra gloves I was sent from England were 10 ounces as requested, but they'd sent the larger fitting for people with bigger hands. If you look at the photos from that fight, you can see I'm wearing these big pillows on my hands.

I'd got my first Vegas win under my belt, and learned a few valuable lessons for the future:

1. January in Vegas is very, very, very cold.
2. Don't stay in a hotel before a fight; rent an apartment.
3. Hire a minibus and make Speaky the designated driver.
4. Train at a gym where you can get in the ring whenever you like, and spies from your opponent's camp can't just wander in.
5. $10 masseurs are not sports physiotherapists.
6. Don't wear pillows in a world title fight.
7. Jesus won't help you to beat me, even if you are built like Tyson.

WHEN (MATTHEW) HATTON MET CASTILLO

To publicise my second Vegas fight against José Luis Castillo, part of the deal was that I'd attend a press conference in Vegas and he'd do the same in Manchester. So, about fifteen weeks out from the fight, he spent a couple of days over on this side of the pond with his promoter Bob Arum. My agent Paul Speak made sure they were well looked after while they were in town.

In the evening following the press conference, Speaky phones me up.

'Where are you?' he says.

'I'm just out in Manchester, having a drink.'

'Oh, well, I'm at Lounge 10 [a restaurant], having a meal with Bob and José. Do you want to come down and say hello?'

'Yeah, no problem . . . I've had a few scoops though.'

'Don't worry, they're having a few too.'

So I head down there and join them for dinner. I know Bob quite well but I'd only met Castillo briefly, at the day's presser and previously when he fought on the undercard of my fight with Urango. He doesn't speak much English so conversation is a bit limited, but he seems alright and we're all having a friendly drink together.

Then my phone rings. It's our Matthew.

'Alright, Rick. Where are ya? Are y'out?'

He sounds a bit merry, to say the least.

'Yeah – I'm having a drink with Bob Arum and Castillo at the Lounge 10.'

'Right, I'll be there in half an hour.'

Half an hour later, Matthew rocks up . . . or rather falls through the door – he's blind drunk. He wobbles over to our table and sits down next to me: 'Alright, lads.'

Bob says: 'So Matthew – have you been to Las Vegas before?'

(Obviously, Bob hadn't noticed Matthew's fight on the Urango undercard.)

'Yeah, I've been to Vegas before,' replies Matt. 'We went over to watch that fight, didn't we, Rick. But it got cancelled. Some dickhead didn't make the weight. What was his name, Rick? That fat bastard . . . ?'

Oh God – he's talking about Castillo's world title fight against Diego Corrales the previous June, which had to be aborted at the last minute because Castillo was miles over the 135-pound lightweight limit.

Castillo weighed in four times in a two-hour period, and the nearest he got was 139.5 pounds. Corrales gave up a $1.3 million purse rather than go ahead with the fight at a higher weight, saying it was too dangerous.

At the time, Bob, who's been a boxing promoter for over forty years, said he couldn't ever remember a fight being cancelled like that. 'I'm mortified and embarrassed . . . it's a disgrace.'

It was supposed to be the deciding match of a classic series as they'd fought twice before in Vegas, with one win each (the first fight was one of the greatest fights I've ever seen). What made it worse was that Castillo hadn't made the weight for the second fight either, tipping the scales at 138.5 pounds. That time, Corrales agreed to go ahead with the bout and got sparked by a big left hook from Castillo in the fourth round of a spectacular fight. He wasn't going to make the same mistake again. Castillo had failed to make the lightweight limit for his previous fight against Rolando Reyes too (that fight had went ahead with both boxers weighing in at a 'catchweight' of 138 pounds), so he wasn't really a 'fat bastard', he had just outgrown the division. Even Bob (once he'd calmed down) admitted that Castillo had done everything he could to make the weight, but just couldn't physically do it anymore.

Not that our Matthew is aware of any of this. I need to stop him . . . but he's still rattling on:

'Who was it, Rick? Five pounds overweight he was, the fucking idiot.'

Bob's laughing along, thinking he's winding them up. José is smiling too – hopefully not understanding anything. But I know Matthew's serious – he hasn't got a clue that José Luis Castillo is the name he's looking for.

Paul's looking at me as if to say, 'Do something!' I'm trying to subtly get Matthew's attention, pointing behind my ear in José's direction, saying under my breath, 'Matthew, it's him, it's him . . .', but he's on a roll.

'D'you remember, Rick, we paid all that money to go over there, and he didn't make the weight. The fat fucker . . .'

I just want the ground to swallow me up. All I can do is keep pointing and whispering.

Finally, the penny drops with Matthew, and he immediately tries to backtrack. But in his pickled state, it doesn't sound very convincing: 'Oh right, well, yeah, er, y'know, it's really hard making weight, innit . . .'

Luckily, José's English is not so good that he understands that Matt's been talking about him, and Bob sees the funny side so doesn't let on. Otherwise, we might have seen a Castillo versus (Matthew) Hatton fight right there and then.

In an interview before the actual bout, I did warn that our fight would be called off too if Castillo didn't get down to 140 pounds, saying: 'For all the great fights he has been in, and the reputation he has built for being such a great fighter, if he doesn't make the weight, he'll only be remembered for what he did on the scales.'

There was never any real danger of that happening, though. We were fighting in a higher division (he had been banned from ever signing another contract to fight under the light-welter limit) and

Castillo simply couldn't afford not to fight. Because the third fight with Corrales was called off, Castillo missed out on his $1 million purse, but still had to pay his own training expenses. He'd also been slapped with a total of $250,000 in fines by Nevada State Athletic Commission and suspended for the rest of the year for turning up overweight for two fights with Corrales, and still owed $100,000. He had to cough up the remainder out of his $500,000 purse for fighting me beforehand or the Commission weren't going to let him in the ring.

On top of that, the estate of Diego Corrales, who had tragically died in a motorcycle accident the previous month, was suing him for his failure to make weight in fights and trying to get his purse for our fight and his previous one on the Urango bill 'attached' to go towards paying Corrales's family.

Bob Arum estimated Castillo's legal fees for dealing with all of this added up to another quarter of a million dollars, and the suspension meant he'd had months off without being allowed to fight and earn money to start paying all these debts off. He'd even had to borrow money from Bob.

To make matters worse, he had suffered a terrible personal tragedy recently, when one of his eight brothers and sisters, Cesar, died of a brain injury. Cesar always used to carry his championship belts into the ring and José dedicated our fight to his late little brother.

The late, great trainer Emmanuel Steward also said before the fight that Castillo desperately wanted to beat me to be considered one of the all-time great Mexican boxers, up there with Julio César Chávez, Érik Morales, Marco Antonio Barrera and co. Although Castillo had mixed it with the best, he'd lost his biggest matches with Floyd Mayweather (albeit, the first one very controversially) and the first and most memorable Corrales fight, so he was still looking for that career-defining fight.

Altogether, he had huge motivation to fight me and to beat me. 'I let a lot of people down,' he said in fight week. 'I'm just glad I'm getting this opportunity to make it up to them. It was a huge hit financially, but I just hope to get some big fights before I retire and get well rewarded. It will be a war when I fight Hatton.'

Unfortunately for him, I was in great shape and in no mood to let him win our war.

When I'm interviewed by HBO's Max Kellerman immediately after the fight, I have José's former opponent Diego Corrales on my mind. At the pre-fight press conference, my promoter Dennis Hobson had arranged for a bouquet of flowers, which I presented to his widow Michelle, and when Max mentions Corrales, I take the opportunity to dedicate my performance to his memory and to Michelle who is standing nearby in the ring and give her a hug.

Another person in my thoughts after the victory is Floyd Mayweather Jr. and Max tees me up to send a message to him.

'You've now done something in this fight that Floyd Mayweather failed to accomplish against Castillo in his first fight,' he says. 'Beat him convincingly and do it in a fan-friendly, exciting fashion. Do you have anything to say to Floyd Mayweather or about a potential fight with Floyd Mayweather?'

'Well, you saw this fight tonight . . . what was it? Round four. I think you saw more action in these four rounds than you saw value for money in Floyd's whole career. I'll just leave it at that.'

My fans liked that one, and I find out later that Floyd took the bait. Apparently, he was sitting watching the fight with his manager Leonard Ellerbe, and when he heard me say that, he turned to Ellerbe and said: 'Make the fuckin' fight.'

COME FLY WITH ME, FLOYD, LET'S FLY, LET'S FLY AWAY . . .

Over the years, I'd got used to doing plenty of media stuff to promote my fights, but the Floyd Mayweather fight was another level from the start. Instead of doing one press conference in America and one in England, as we had to announce the Castillo bout, we went on a five-day, five-city media tour, from Los Angeles to Michigan to New York and then flying back across the pond to London and finishing back home in Manchester.

From day one, it felt like I was really part of a Las Vegas mega-fight, just like those I'd read about and seen footage of involving Muhammad Ali, Mike Tyson, Sugar Ray Leonard and co when the fighters toured America to stir up interest for the fight. From day one, at the red-carpet event at Universal Studios CityWalk in Hollywood, Floyd set out to do everything he could to get under my skin and show that he was the main man.

When we have our first head-to-head at CityWalk, he's calling me towards him, saying all sorts of shit. 'C'mon give me some of that face-to-face action . . . You know you're facing the best, right? You willing to die?'

I hadn't expected anything different since I first bumped into him in Las Vegas two years before at the second Jermain Taylor–Bernard Hopkins fight. Our seats were in the same row and when Floyd arrived, he had to walk past me to get to his seat, so I stood up to let him past, said, 'Hi Floyd, how are you doing?' and put my hand out. He wouldn't shake my hand, and just hurried past muttering something along the lines of: 'Let's get it on; I'll knock you out.'

He was trying to intimidate me, but Floyd really didn't intimidate me at all. It wasn't exactly facing off against Mike Tyson. To be honest, I've met a lot scarier people on the Hattersley estate.

As I tell the press during the tour: 'I was never someone to get right in your face, try and intimidate you like that. But I knew it was coming. "I'm going to beat you like a bitch, butt-fuck you." Basic stuff like that. It was nonsense, really. I found it quite amusing. Floyd's not exactly intimidating-looking with his nice suits and his bling. He doesn't make me want to run down the street to get away.'

Floyd has his way and I have my way. I don't take it personally because he says the same things about his opponent every time he fights. Besides, nothing that either of us says matters. It's only about what happens when we fight. But where do you draw the line between selling tickets and looking for an edge and disrespecting the sport? What's the point of being the best fighter in the world if everyone thinks you're a dickhead?

Floyd's tendency to behave like a dick was seen again after that first official press conference, when me and my team stop off at a restaurant for a meal before heading off to Michigan. The press guys are all dotted around the restaurant too.

Floyd comes in just as the bill arrives.

'Hi Ricky, how're you doing, man? Is that the bill? I'll get this, man.'

He starts lobbing hundred dollar bills on the table.

'Is that all I'm worth, Floyd?'

'Oh you want some more . . . have some more then . . .'

I start collecting them up. Six hundred dollars. Very nice.

'How much is that bill,' I say to the waitress.

'Two hundred and fifty dollars, Mr Hatton.'

So I hand over the two fifty and a good tip and pocket the rest.

All the press are laughing, but Floyd isn't. He thought he was being a smart arse, but ends up just looking an arse.

The next day we visit the school Floyd went to as a kid, in Grand Rapids, Michigan. He's a hero to them, of course so I'm the pantomime bad guy for the day with all the children booing me and cheering Floyd.

It does make me laugh how they introduce him: 'Welcome back to Floyd who's done so much for boxing, he's been a world champion for ten years and he's brought out his own sauce . . .'

What? Apparently, to add to his boxing achievements, Floyd is now selling his answer to HP Sauce.

Then Floyd himself gets up and makes a speech. 'I hope to be an example to all the kids here,' he says. 'If you work hard, stay away from drugs, stay away from drink, and dedicate yourself, you could be like me. You could be a world champion too, you could have your own sauce too. You could be a rapper . . .'

I'm thinking, are you taking the piss, Floyd? You could be a rapper and have your own sauce?! Not you could be a doctor or lawyer or the president. God knows what the teachers make of his advice.

Golden Boy have laid on a fancy private jet each for us for the whole tour, so we can get around quickly from place to place. I happen to arrive at the Michigan airport just before Floyd, so our plane is the first to take off.

Oscar De La Hoya, Richard Schaefer who was the CEO of Golden Boy at the time, Robert Diaz, Kerry Kayes, Billy Graham, my dad, Paul Speak are all making the trip with me. It's an unbelievably luxurious plane – plenty of space to stretch out and the crew even includes a chef who cooks us all steaks to order in-flight.

A few minutes into the journey, we're chatting away, having a drink, when I see the door of the cockpit open and the pilot gestures for me to come forward.

So I get up and go down to see him.

'Hey, Ricky, listen to this idiot.'

'You what?'

'Listen . . .'

He turns on the speaker and over the radio, I can hear Floyd arguing with the pilot in his plane behind: 'I'm not letting that muthafucka get there before me – fuckin' overtake them!'

'We can't do that, sir.'

'Overtake the muthafucka – I'm the champ, I got to get to New York first. I'll pay you whatever you want. C'mon, overtake him, c'mon.'

'Sir, we can't overtake anyone. We're 30,000 feet in the air. We'll lose our jobs.'

It's hilarious. Floyd really is the stuff legends are made of. He thinks it's *Wacky Races* up here. Luckily, the pilot behind doesn't listen to Floyd, and we all make it to New York in one piece.

The presser in New York is held at the Rockefeller Plaza, and I tell the press there: 'Floyd is the best. That's why I want to fight him. It would be easy for me to stay in the comfort zone in my own weight division in my own backyard in England. But I fancy the challenge.'

The pattern of the tour Stateside was generally Floyd dishing out the insults, putting me down, and me laughing, taking the mickey and getting in a few little jabs in return.

He'd say: 'Ricky took this fight because he's getting older and losing his edge. Look at how scarred up his face is and how beat up he is. He knew he was going to lose soon. That's why he wants to fight me. If you lose to the best, there's little shame; but if you lose to a nobody, you're washed up. Ricky Hatton should be appreciative just to be sharing the ring with me.'

I'd say: 'Floyd's life is a lot like his fights; all show, no substance. With Floyd, it's all about what his watch is and what jewellery he's wearing. His watch is bigger than my world title belt. He makes a Christmas tree look gritty. What man gets up on stage and goes on about his suit and his rings and his watches? Financially, I've done fantastically well. I have a nice home, two good cars, and I can go on holiday whenever I want. But I don't flash my money. I think to do that belittles people.'

While I'd expected all the abuse from him on stage, what did surprise me was how he continued bad-mouthing me when there were no press around. I said to him at one point: 'Alright pal, there's no cameras here, no TV, what are you trying to prove?' There's one thing selling tickets and putting bums on seats but you've got to have a little bit of respect for your opponent, surely.

But just as boxing styles make fights, opponents with totally opposite personalities help to sell a fight. Here you had not only the best pound-for-pound fighter in the world against the most exciting pound-for-pound fighter in the world, but two characters who couldn't be more different. The American media lapped it up.

Over in London at the O2 Arena, Floyd turns up at the presser wearing over $2 million-worth of diamonds and carrying a few of his world title belts. He is as dismissive as ever of me, too, telling Sky Sports: 'He's gotta go home and watch tapes of me, I'm going to go home and dance with the stars . . . I gotta watch out for his head butts and his holding – that's all I've gotta do. Actually, he should go on *Dancing with the Stars,* since he likes to slow-dance so much.'

He obviously hasn't watched me fight very closely if he thinks I hit and hold.

At the head to head, he tries to stare me down and I just smile back: 'You're not going to kiss me, are you?'

I mostly kept my powder dry, knowing that I'd have the last word back on my home turf in Manchester. By then, I was getting a bit sick of Floyd slagging me off and was ready to let him have it. So were my fans. Despite torrential rain, five thousand of them turn up outside the Town Hall to watch the press conference on big screens. Quite a few get inside the hall too along with the journalists, including a band who strike up 'Walking in a Hatton Wonderland' as I stand up on stage to speak. As they play, Floyd stands up next to me, dancing and pretending to conduct the band. I just let him get on with it, and look at him smiling.

When the band stops, he sits down next to me, sticks his feet on the table and I begin: 'Thank you for that reception. I'm sure the crowd would like to agree with me that if he dances like that on *Dancing with the Stars*, he's got fucking no chance, has he?'

The fans cheer, the band start playing again and Floyd claps and smiles thinly.

'Thank you all for coming,' I continue. 'We've had a long tour, very tiring and it's nice to come back and see my friends, my family . . . Floyd, will you stop touching my dick, you poof . . .'

I've my wallet in my trouser pocket, and Floyd is messing around touching my leg pretending to try and nick it.

'He's been talking about my arse all week – kicking my arse, whupping my arse . . .'

Floyd is still smiling.

'No, it's great to be back. Sorry, I've not brought the weather with me. I've missed my six-year-old son for a week, but I haven't missed him quite as much as you might think, because I've had the fortune of spending the week with another fucking six-year-old.'

As laughter fills the room, I look across at Floyd who now is stoney-faced. Another person who isn't looking too happy is the Sky Sports cameraman who, I notice out the corner of my eye, is waving his arms about, saying: 'Ricky, we're live, stop swearing!'

Oh ffff . . . I wasn't told beforehand that it was being shown live.

Realising it's about nine hours before the watershed, I cut out the effing and blinding and spend a few minutes offering a few thank yous, but I can't resist a couple more little digs at Floyd before I finish: 'Floyd's been aggressive towards me all week. I think he's been trying to get under my skin and wanting to look in my eyes and see a little bit of fear. I only have one message . . .'

I turn to Floyd who looks straight back at me: 'You're pissing in the wind, son. I ain't scared of you.'

He laughs his head off, very over the top, but hopefully deep down he's getting the message.

'Floyd's gonna run away all night. He says he isn't, but he is. I know I'm going to have to be fast on my feet to catch him, so I've got two wonderful sparring partners coming in – Forrest Gump and Carl Lewis . . . And he can run, but sooner or later his back's going to hit the ropes. When he does, I'll get him. See you December 8th, Floyd.'

With that, I sit down to cheers and the band starts playing again.

After the press conference, we all troop outside onto the stage in front of the crowd. I feel an unbelievable sense of pride that so many people have turned out for me. We're all standing under umbrellas on the stage, but most of the spectators are getting soaked to the skin. Floyd swaggers up onto the stage surrounded by his enormous bodyguards, the boos and chants ring out with 'Who are ya?' It's like a derby-game atmosphere that Floyd tries to stoke up further by putting on a Manchester United shirt and clowning around. A few of my previous opponents have worn a United shirt as a wind-up, so I just think, oh, that's original. I don't think any Reds who also support me are suddenly going to start backing Floyd because he's pretending to be United fan for the day.

Adam Smith from Sky goes over to him: 'Floyd Mayweather, welcome to the lions' den . . .'

Floyd grabs the mic: 'Welcome to the lions' den? I am the lion. I'm the king of the jungle. This is called Manchester Mayweather.'

'There was talk that you weren't going to come out and face this crowd,' says Adam. 'What do you think of them, Floyd?'

'I ain't scare of nuthin'. I love Manchester.'

He doesn't love it so much when the crowd start singing 'Who the fucking hell are you?' though, and he responds by giving them the finger with both hands.

It's a bit different from a few school kids booing me in Michigan, and Floyd, for all his previous world championship fights, can't have experienced anything like it.

In the end we don't have the usual face-off, because Floyd decides he's not a Man United fan anymore, rips of the shirt, lobs it into the crowd and storms off.

The MC introduces the Lord Mayor of Manchester who's here to present me with a certificate for being a good ambassador for the city.

'I've just seen another boxer going off the stage,' says the mayor. 'Have you upset him? He's not very happy at all . . .'

Meanwhile, apparently, Floyd is standing at an upstairs window in the Town Hall, dancing around and flicking the middle finger at my fans below.

Later, I get a call from Robert Diaz at Golden Boy who is on the train with Floyd back to London to catch their flight home. He says that Floyd is still furious, ranting and raving about me disrespecting him. That makes me laugh, because he's done nothing but disrespect me the whole week. The thing is I came away from the tour, feeling more confident. To me, all the brashness covered up his insecurities, and the way he reacted in Manchester to me and five thousand Mancs giving him a taste of his own medicine only made me more confident.

HAIR TODAY, GONE TOMORROW . . .

When you're in the ring fighting at the top level, there's all sorts of dangers you have to be aware of. But one thing I never had to worry about during my career, though, was getting smacked in the eye by my own hair.

While I was no stranger to wearing flashy shorts, my haircut was always a pretty straightforward short-back-and-sides. There was never much point having a fancy haircut with the people I had around me in my camp. After one training session in Vegas, I came out of the shower after washing my hair. I dry and comb it all nice and neat in front of the mirror, plonk my floppy hat on and then we all pile into the minibus back to the apartment. Kerry Kayes is smiling away next to me, but I don't know why – must be delighted with my training. It's only when we get back and I try to take my hat off to find my hair half-glued to my head that I discover the bastard has smothered the inside of my hat with Vaseline.

So, no, I've never bothered with flashy haircuts. Unlike one of my Vegas opponents, Paulie Malignaggi. During his career, he's had all sorts of hairdos – hedgehog spikes, Mohicans, cornrows, shaved-in designs – and all the colours of the rainbow – red, orange, blond highlights, the lot. The maddest of the lot was when he came over to fight at the City of Manchester Stadium on the undercard of my fight against Juan Lazcano.

He comes into the ring wearing a mask, which he takes off to reveal these long dreadlock extensions pulled back in a ponytail (one journalist wrote that he looked like 'the love child of Milli Vanilli and Medusa'). Aside from looking a bit shit, the other problem is that Paulie has never actually sparred with these braids in, and he's up against Lovemore N'Dou who keeps putting him in headlocks which makes them come loose. Normally, between rounds, your cornermen are trying to give you advice, put Vaseline on your face and keep you cool with the magic sponge. But in Paulie's corner, it's more like backstage at a fashion show as they're spending most of their time trying to sort out his hair.

To make matters worse, he breaks his right hand in the second round. So he's boxing almost one-handed having to avoid N'Dou's punches while his own braids are whirling round and slapping him in the eye.

After eight rounds, his trainer finally loses patience and orders his cutman to hack off the fake braids. When the cutman was asked to work Paulie's corner, he probably wasn't chosen for his haircutting skills, but his handiwork leaves Paulie seeing clearly enough to go on and nick a split-decision win.

It must be one of the only fights in history where a boxer has lost at least two rounds due to being hit by his own hair, and the first time a boxer has ever been given a haircut during a world championship bout.

Paulie's promoter Lou DiBella has a great line on the whole hair farce afterwards: 'I love Paulie,' he says, 'But sometimes he's an idiot.'

What Lou and a relieved Paulie don't know is that by this time Paul Speak has got hold of his hair extensions. Speaky saw them lying on the ring apron near his seat and, for reasons best known to himself, decided to grab them from under the noses of Paulie's cornermen.

He keeps the hair safe at his house, and when I sign up to fight Paulie next in Vegas, we think it'd be nice to give them back to him. We get them beautifully framed along with some action photos of his fight in Manchester, and at the pre-fight press conference in Manchester, I present them to Paulie. He's genuinely thrilled – loves it. Sadly, though, Paulie and the framed hair are only reunited for a few hours. He's staying at the local hotel and someone nicks it that night.

Months later, on the day of the fight in Vegas, HBO have me in for the normal pre-fight interview with Larry Merchant. 'I hope he's got his hair cut this time,' I joke. 'Last time he had to cut his dreadlocks off. I mean, who wears dreadlocks these days anyway?'

I look round and there's Lennox Lewis standing there, with his dreads all tied up. Lennox shakes his head and shoots me a look, pretending to be annoyed.

Even though it was stolen, Paulie doesn't forget my hairy gift. After our fight, he presents me with a great gift in return. He obviously learnt a bit about Manchester City on his visit to England, because when he later saw a beer called 'Blue Moon' on his travels he thought of me and bought me a few bottles. Cheers, Paulie.

THE BATTLE OF EAST AND WEST ... AT THE NEW INN

Both Paulie and Floyd talked a lot of 'smack' – as they say in the States – to hype up our fights. The promotion for my fight with Manny Pacquiao made for a nice change after that. The fight was billed as 'The Battle of East and West', but Manny is always respectful to opponents, so our media tour, from Manchester and London to New York and Los Angeles, was much friendlier than the Floyd Mayweather circus a year and a half before.

Manny might not give the journalists funny one-liners to put in their articles, but he's very professional in everything he does. Apparently when he was on the train up from London, where his plane landed from the States, he was practising his speech for our first press conference to make sure he got it word-perfect. Also, his rags-to-riches life story and the incredible support he gets from his Filipino countrymen gives the press pack plenty to write about.

I thought I had a lot of fans, but the Philippines has a population of about a hundred million people and everyone of them knows Manny. When he returned home after beating Oscar De La Hoya in the fight before ours, there were hundreds of thousands lining the streets to welcome him home. He's worshipped like a God over there.

The story goes that Manny ran away from home as child after his father ate the family's pet dog. He had times where he was homeless, slept on the street and had just one meal a day, so he had a very tough start in life. Although he's made millions in his boxing career, he's never forgotten that and there are many reports of him donating huge amounts of money to help Filipinos who are in the situation he once was.

In all my dealings with him, he came across as a nice fella and I could relate to his attitude. I felt that I was fighting not just for myself, but for the people of Manchester and Britain and I had their backing. Manny had the same relationship with the people of the Philippines. 'I know that millions of people are praying for me, and that gives me strength,' he said before our bout. 'It inspires me to fight hard, stay strong, and remember all of the people of my country trying to achieve better for themselves. My fight is not only for me, but also for my country. Every fight I dedicate to my country.'

In the build-up to our fight, there was no animosity between the two of us, just mutual respect, which is how it should be. We left all the bad-mouthing to our coaches (see *Trainer vs. trainer*, page 106).

The previous year, Manny had named his new-born daughter Queen Elizabeth in tribute to our Queen, but he'd never been here before. Coming over here for the tour was a dream come true for him and he got a great reception. Before our press call at the Imperial War Museum in London, Manny goes to Mass at Westminster Cathedral. Hundreds are waiting for him outside and hundreds more turn up at a local hotel for a meet-and-greet afterwards.

When we go to the Trafford Centre in Manchester, he's absolutely mobbed. I didn't realise there are so many Filipinos in Manchester, but there are 5,000-odd people there and plenty among them cheering for him. Even Manny is amazed. 'I did not expect it because this is Ricky's home town where I know he is loved,' he tells the press. 'I appreciate my supporters coming to see me.'

The best part of the whole tour is having a game of darts with Manny at the New Inn. Manny challenged me to a game and, originally, the plan was to go to the Rovers Return 'pub' on the *Coronation Street* set, but at the last minute we diverted to my local instead.

I get there first, so I'm waiting there with the camera crews, photographers and regulars for Manny to arrive. I'm dressed casually in my jeans and T-shirt, having a drink (non-alcoholic, because I'm already in training), when the doors to the pub open. Manny walks in, beautifully dressed, suited and booted. For a second the whole pub goes quiet and all eyes on him. It's like an old-time Western, when the fastest gunslinger in town walks into the saloon bar. Except we're in a pub on the Hattersley estate.

'Alright, Manny – how you doing? Do you need to borrow some darts?'

'No, I have brought my own weapons,' he replies, and whips out a very smart darts case from his inside pocket.

'O-kaaay . . .'

Manny is a nice guy, but, like me, when it comes to sports he's very, very competitive. When he's not boxing, he likes to play various other sports such as basketball, pool and darts and he takes them seriously. I find out later that when he got to his hotel the previous night, he put up a dartboard in his room and practised for a few hours. A few weeks later, after a day's sparring for our fight, he sponsors and plays in a $30,000 'Pacmania' darts tournament in LA.

But our challenge match is over just one leg of 501 up, so it's whoever starts fastest will win.

We have darts commentator John Gwynne dressed in a tux to

introduce us and act as referee: 'Welcome the challenger from the Philippines, it's the Pac Man – Manny Pacquiiiaaaaooo! . . . And here from Manchester, it's the Ricky 'The Hitman' Hattonnnnnn!'

With home advantage and drawing on all my experience of playing darts in the Hyde & District League every Thursday night since I was about twenty, I throw a decent fifteen-darter finishing on double two to emerge victorious in the Darts Battle of East and West.

'That's the only thing he's going to win,' says his trainer, Freddie Roach, loud enough to hear. (He proved to be right, but at least I beat Manny at something.)

It's a good laugh, and afterwards, I present Manny with a Manchester City away shirt with 'Pacman 1' printed on the back, telling him that City 'are the best football team in the world'.

We also get my trainer Floyd Mayweather Sr. and Freddie Roach to throw the arrows in a special challenge match – first to hit the bullseye wins. They're both crap, and after fifteen darts each, none of which are close to the bullseye, it has to be called off as a draw. It won't be the last time these two will clash in the run-up to the fight, though.

TRAINER VS. TRAINER

As well as my own rivalry with my opponents, in the build-up to my two biggest Vegas fights there was a fair bit of needle between our coaches.

The Floyd Mayweather Jr. fight pitted Billy 'The Preacher' Graham on my side against Floyd's Uncle Roger. Like me, Billy wasn't one for trash-talking opponents, but he had a good line in deadpan put-downs for trash-talkers, and the Mayweathers with all their brash comments were ripe for some of that. 'They can be nasty or they can be nice,' said Billy in the build-up. 'I'd prefer them to be nice, but I don't give a fuck if they're nasty.'

And it was pretty clear from the start that Roger wasn't going to be nice: 'I know what kind of fighter Ricky Hatton is,' he said. 'He's the kind of fighter who's going to get the same kind of whupping the rest of the muthafuckers got.'

Billy was with me for most of the pre-fight promotion events, and he heard all the stuff that Roger and Floyd Jr. were coming out with to try and intimidate us, but he wasn't bothered in the slightest.

'I think some of these Americans think we come from fuckin' Buckingham Palace,' Billy said at the time. 'If Floyd walked round where I come from with that fur coat and all that bling, he'd be stripped naked in two minutes. He wouldn't last a night. He'd be naked and skint in some alley somewhere. That's where I come from. He's wasting his fuckin' breath, to be honest with you. I think he wants to be like Muhammad Ali, but he's missing the point. He just makes himself sound like a prick.'

When talking about Floyd as a boxer, Billy was always very respectful, though. He'd talk about his breathtaking hand speed, fantastic defence and how he was rightfully regarded as the best pound-for-pound boxer in the world. He only really bit back when Roger and Floyd dismissed me as 'one-dimensional'. Then Billy would talk up my own ability – 'fantastic peripheral vision, balance and reflexes; amazing strength and ferocity; an incredible boxing brain; the most skilful pressure fighter on the planet.'

'Hatton can put on all the pressure he wants,' said Roger. 'Can he outbox Floyd? Do he have more skill than Floyd? The only thing he can do is pressure Floyd. But other than that, he can't do shit. He ain't nothing but a high-profile club fighter.'

That sort of stuff didn't annoy us – we were happy that they seemed to be underestimating me because we believed I had the perfect style to beat Floyd.

'They think that Ricky's one-dimensional?' Billy said a few

weeks before the fight. 'Fuckin' one-dimensional? Let them think that. I hope they still think that on the night when they walk into the ring, because then they're going to get an almighty shock.'

In the final press conference before the fight, Uncle Roger does offer some advice on how to beat Floyd. 'I'm telling you the best way to deal with my nephew,' he says. 'You gotta use a stick. That's a fishing pole. If you get in there with a fishing pole, you may stand a chance. But if you ain't got no fishing pole and you come in there with your face, I ain't going to tell what'll happen. Because he's too crafty, too slick. He can do it all.'

I'm up next to speak: 'After listening to Roger, I can't believe it's not 10–1 or 20–1. This little, fat, beer-drinking Englishman who's fought no one, been over-protected, fought a load of has-beens, and yet the betting's so close. Personally, I think you've got nowt to worry about Floyd, I think you'll be alright.'

Unfortunately, I'd left my fishing rod at home, and Floyd was alright on the night. Afterwards, Billy goes up to Roger to offer his hand and say congratulations. 'I told you he was going to get fucking whupped,' is Roger's response.

Charming.

The battle between the trainers got even more intense before the Pacquiao fight, though, because it matched up my new trainer Floyd Mayweather Sr. against Freddie Roach.

Floyd's approach to training was totally different to Billy's, and he was damning about Billy's methods, especially Billy's use of the body-belt.

'What can you learn from hitting a pillow?' Floyd had said before my fight with Malignaggi. 'That is what you punch when you're in a bad mood, not when you prepare for the best fighters . . . if I had trained Ricky Hatton to fight my son, you would have seen a completely different fight. Ricky was taught nothing for that fight and had no corner.'

I was very uneasy to hear him saying stuff like that because Billy had been a great trainer for me and he had never said anything negative about Floyd's skills as a trainer, other than that he didn't think he was the right trainer for me. But that's Floyd – he thinks he's the best trainer of all time and he doesn't show a lot of respect for rivals. Not even Freddie Roach, who was then regarded as the best trainer in world for his work with Manny and other fighters.

Freddie had been training Pacquiao for eight years. Manny was already world-class when they started working together, but Freddie had helped to take him to a whole new level as he moved up through the weights, winning world titles all the way. Despite his achievements, Floyd was dismissive: 'Don't ever compare us. Freddie Roach is in the Hall of Fame. He should be in the Hall of Shame. We're going to whip Pacquiao's ass, because I got the best fighter and because I'm the best trainer.'

Freddie doesn't normally get drawn into a war of words with opposition trainers, but Floyd got under his skin and he gave some back, saying: 'As long as Floyd is in Hatton's corner, I have absolutely no concerns. Floyd training Hatton for this fight is our biggest advantage.'

He also had a good line about my nickname – 'Ricky's "Hitman" tag is accurate, because on May 2nd, Hatton is going to get hit, man, and a lot.'

As the fight got nearer, though, Freddie decided to step back from the trash-talking. He said later that Manny had told him to be a gentleman, not get involved and he'd take care of business on the night. Floyd kept going though. After seeing Floyd on *24/7* going to a drive-in to buy burrito when he should have been at the gym, when Floyd went into his 'joke coach Roach' routine, I did think, 'Shut the fuck up – you've got some front.' Manny must have been rubbing his hands watching that – Freddie Roach was in the gym on time every day working with him, and my coach was leaving me sitting around while he got a bloody Mexican takeaway.

Because Manny Pacquiao and I were very respectful of each other in the build-up to the fight, the producers of HBO's *24/7* series focused more and more on the Floyd vs. Freddie angle. So much so that they do an extra 'Overtime' show on hbo.com in fight week where presenter Jim Lampley interviews them both in the ring at the MGM Garden Arena and introduces them as 'the two stars of the show'.

It doesn't take long in the interview for the tensions between the two to come to the surface again. Jim asks: 'When the fight is over, do you go back to being friends?'

'We've never been friends,' says Freddie. 'He disrespects me everyday, calls me "cockroach" – why would I be his friend? He's so disrespectful.'

Floyd smiles and says: 'I'm having fun with this, Freddie. It's just selling the fight.'

'No, the thing is you think it's the Floyd show – it's not, it's the Ricky Hatton–Pacquiao show. Give the fighters some credit.'

Freddie jokes about Floyd showing off his muscles on *24/7*. 'You can't do anything about that, because you ain't got none!' replies Floyd.

Then Freddie gets a dig in about Oscar De La Hoya replacing Floyd Sr. with Freddie as his coach before Oscar's fight against Floyd Jr.

'He fired you for me.'

'You know why?' says Floyd who's getting a bit annoyed.

'Because I'm better than you,' says Freddie with a laugh.

'No, because he paid you less than I asked him for.'

'I wish you could see my cheque . . .'

'You got three hundred thousand . . .'

'Seven-fifty – I got 750 . . .'

'I was looking for two million!'

Jim has to try and wrap the show up with Floyd pointing his finger across him towards Freddie: 'I'd knock you out, bam!'

'Who cares?' says Freddie. 'Ten thousand years ago – you're an old man.'

'You're an old man – you're older than me right now.'

'I know I'm old!'

They keep the cameras rolling as Floyd jabbers on at Freddie by the ropes: 'I want to tell you something, Freddie – you're too soft.'

'Too soft for what?'

'You're going to be soft that night.'

'What has that got to do with it? When Pacquiao gets up there and fights, I sit down, I don't have to be fucking hard. Jesus Christ – the only time I've got to be hard is when I'm with a girl.'

THE MAIN EVENT

FROM KINGSWAY LEISURE CENTRE TO THE MGM GRAND

I had great support from the British boxing press and TV guys throughout my career. Quite a few of the lads covered my fights from my first pro fight all the way to Vegas. Some even earlier than that, and no one earlier than the legendary Steve 'Big Daddy' Bunce. Buncey has been covering boxing at all levels for thirty years and he followed me all the way up through the amateur ranks from winning junior titles to senior titles. He was working for the *Daily Telegraph* back then, and mentioned me in the paper a few times, making them the first national newspaper by a few years to run stories on me.

One of his biggest stories surrounded the world junior championships in Havana, Cuba, where I won the bronze medal, but got robbed in the semi-final against a Russian lad. I was so upset that I chucked my medal in a drawer and didn't look at it for years. It was only a few years into my pro career that I took it out, got it framed and displayed it in my games room. I dominated that semi-final, but got a scandalous decision against me – they were using computer scoring and one judge had me losing by sixteen points. It turned out there was all sorts of dodgy business going on.

Steve Bunce:

I ran that story quite heavily in the Telegraph *and it had legs. The Eastern Bloc countries were very powerful at that time inside AIBA, the International Boxing Association who ran the sport, and Ricky was one of several Western boxers who got terrible decisions out there.*

It came to light that officials were receiving $1,000 bungs to influence their judging. The British official was given one of these bungs and reported it. There was an inquiry and several people were banned for life. It got worse for the official who allegedly gave the bung to the British judge – he was later found tortured and killed at his flat in Moscow when a toaster was dropped into his bath.

Ricky was an exciting fighter from the start – he had a very pleasing style and a great run of results in the amateurs, until he got stitched up in Cuba. I wrote a piece on Billy Graham's gym when Ricky would have only been around sixteen and he was in there with 'Gypsy' John Fury, Tyson Fury's father. In that piece I wrote about Billy introducing me to Ricky, one his young prospects.

Sky's Adam Smith and Glenn McCrory, the former world cruiser-weight champ, also remember seeing me training at Billy's.

Adam Smith:

I went to Billy's gym in the days of Steve 'The Viking' Foster, Ensley Bingham, Paul Burke etc. There were all those guys around and Billy Graham took me to a corner and said: 'Watch this kid hit the bag – he hits like a mule – he's going to be unbelievable.' There was this boy with spiky blond hair, pale white skin – I guess he was about seventeen – and I remember thinking, he really does hit hard for his age.

Glenn McCrory:

I knew of Ricky very early on. When he was getting ready to turn pro, going down to Billy Graham's gym and Billy saying he was the next big thing. You could tell. I've been around that many fighters, you can tell when you see a kid's balance and movement. He reminded me of a Mexican fighter. He had that great balance, nice little slips to the side, that upper body movement – very slight movements, but just enough to get out of the way. I couldn't see then whether he could take a punch on the chin, but I could tell he had that something extra to go a long way.

Kevin Francis, who's been covering boxing and all sorts of other sports for the *Daily Star* for over thirty years, remembers my first-ever pro fight well. That was on the undercard of Robin Reid's world super middleweight title defence against Hacine Cherifi at Kingsway Leisure Centre in Widnes way back in 1997.

Kevin Francis:

Ricky put Colin McAuley away in a round. That was the first sign of his body-punching. There's not many fighters you see in their first pro bout and think, wow, this guy's got it, but I did with Ricky. Steve Lillis was sitting with me and we both said the same. When I got home I told my wife I'd seen a kid who looked really good.

Kevin and Steve, who was writing for *The Sport* back then and is now a great pundit on BoxNation, were among the few that stayed on to watch the fight. Adam Smith was there too and would have done, but Robin Reid collapsed in his dressing room with heat exhaustion and was rushed to hospital, so Adam went with him to cover that story. Robin was okay, but I couldn't get in the ring until the medics returned well after midnight and Sky didn't even record the bout.

Adam recalls my twelfth fight, on Naseem Hamed's undercard at the Royal Albert Hall, as the one which really showed my potential.

Adam Smith:

He blew away the lorry driver journeyman Brian Coleman – stopped him inside a couple of rounds with body shots. Coleman was very durable, went on to have 170-odd fights, and everyone thought, no one does that to Coleman, other fighters have trouble with him. He takes them the distance.

Very early on he looked like he was going places, but I remember him driving me to one of his early fights in his old banger. I was talking to him about Naz's fleet of cars, and he said: 'You know what, Adam. I'm never going to change who I am.'

And he hasn't – he's always been one of the people. He still knocks around with the same friends from his estate.

What was great that a lot of the press guys have become friends over the years, and in the build-up to the Kostya Tszyu fight, I was delighted when Adam invited me to his wedding, which was happening a week later. Adam will tell you that back at the hotel after that war with Kostya, I was too exhausted even to have a Guinness – a first for me after a fight. But I saw him the next day at the 'Shit Shirt' party down the pub and assured him I'd be there for his wedding.

Adam Smith:

Ricky was going away on holiday and I thought he'll never make it. A week later, I'm waiting at the altar for my bride and I look round and there he is sitting right at the back. I thought, wow, he's made it. I appreciated him making the effort so much. That typifies him – a real genuine guy.

It was unfortunate for Adam and Glenn McCrory that they never actually got to Vegas in person to see my fights. Glenn had been co-commentator alongside Ian Darke when I won the world title, but by the time I went to Vegas, Sky had changed things around, making Jim Watt co-commentator with Glenn back in the studio in Britain. As my Vegas fights were in the middle of the night British time, there would be an undercard show back home to give viewers plenty of action beforehand to keep them awake and Glenn would be covering the British leg. Meanwhile, Adam would be at the venue commentating on a load of British and Commonwealth fights. For the Mayweather fight, after doing all the build-up with me in the training camp, he was on duty at a Frank Maloney show (younger readers will know Frank as Kellie) at Wigan Leisure Centre, and had to watch my fight on the big screen.

Adam Smith:

You do the best you can as a pro commentating on the British leg, but I'd seen the coverage of the Mayweather weigh-in and I did wish I was out there in Vegas. I'd been to Vegas loads of times for fights, but I'm very jealous of those who went to that one. I covered the spit and sawdust of Ricky's preparation for four of his five Vegas fights – apart from Castillo, which was on Setanta – from start to finish so was probably closer to him than any other journalist, but I just didn't get to go to the actual fights because I was here commentating in Barnsley and Wigan!

Steve Bunce, who's covered more than fifty major Vegas boxing shows during his career, reckons I came to America – and Las Vegas in particular – at just the right time.

Steve Bunce:

The American boxing scene around that time had gone a bit cold. They hadn't had any big heavyweight action for a few years – the big fights had been a decade earlier. We're talking about 2007 and the Bowe–Holyfield trilogy had ended in 1995, it had been six years since Lennox Lewis had fought in Vegas. So we were left with various guys we were trying to build. Let's get this right, Floyd Mayweather was a star then, but he wasn't the superstar he is now.

People hadn't warmed to him – to this day, a lot of people don't really like Mayweather.

Ricky came to town and for a start the American press had instant access. They liked him, he could talk well, he was funny, they got his jokes (once he explained them). He fought like a Mexican, he was aggressive, he was nasty in the ring. What wasn't to like?

He just came at a time when Vegas boxing needed somebody, and they instantly warmed to him. The casino operators loved him because he arrived with thousands and thousands of mug punters who didn't have a clue about gambling. All they knew was how to spend – and they spent every penny they had.

The British newspaper boys would usually fly out to Vegas the week before the fight, and Speaky would arrange for me to do a sit-down interview with them all on the Monday at the venue. We knew they'd flown 5,000 miles to cover the fight and needed plenty of stories to keep their editors and readers happy, so I was always ready to do that.

Steve Lillis:

Before the Mayweather fight, Ricky and Speaky turned up at the MGM, each carrying a case of beer for us to drink while we were interviewing him – six days before the biggest fight of his life.

Steve, incidentally, is a big fan of punk music – every year he goes to the UK punk rock festival in Blackpool – and when I introduced him to Noel Gallagher at the Malignaggi fight they ended up having a good chinwag about it.

The *Daily Mail*'s Jeff Powell has been a journalist for almost half a century and he's another writer who followed my career closely. Jeff's interviewed all the greats of boxing in his time and he had the honour of being the only British journalist invited to Muhammad Ali's seventieth birthday party. One thing he remembers about me in Vegas is how they'd see me out and about during fight week.

Jeff Powell:

Normally, at those big fights, you only see the fighters when they come to staged events or scheduled press sessions. With Ricky, you'd see him wandering round the hotel, chatting to people, entertaining people with his one-liners. The man-of-the-people thing Ricky had was unusual for American fans and they liked that very much.

Fight week did always drag a bit for me. All the hard training was done, and I just wanted to get in there and do the business, so there was a lot of time to kill (and to not eat). That's why I'd sometimes go for a wander around the casinos and it was nice to bump into the press lads and have a chat.

Early in the week before the Malignaggi fight I was having a late-night wander around the MGM when I spotted Kevin Francis in the ground-floor bar, so I tapped him on the shoulder and joined him. We ended up sitting there for three-quarters of an hour – him a bit pissed and having a nightcap, me with a cup of coffee – chatting football, Man City . . . anything but boxing.

I've always got on well with Kevin, but he's been the victim of a few of my pranks over the years. In Boston before the Collazo fight, it was Billy Graham's fiftieth birthday and I presented Billy with a birthday cake in the ring. Then I called Kevin over, asking him to take the cake so we could start training, but shoved it right in his face. Then in Vegas, I was running round the ring, took a big mouthful of water from my bottle and spat it all over him. Quite a few journalists got 'baptised' by me if they came down to the gym.

Because of the time difference to back home, a lot of the media guys had to keep very odd hours while they were out in Vegas for my fights. Steve Bunce, for instance, would be available 24/7 to do radio reports. The more appearances Buncey made, the more money he earned, so he'd just grab two or three hours' sleep when he could. That meant he'd find himself downstairs at the MGM any time of the day and night and he'd see all sorts.

Steve Bunce:

On the Thursday before the Mayweather fight, I was called to a meeting at about three or four in the morning and in the same bar there was a group of about forty or fifty blokes who were the leaders of the different hooligan groups associated with Premier League clubs. The Football Intelligence Unit would have been frothing at the mouth. They were all sitting around, very calm, casual and relaxed, chatting to each other. I ended up sitting there for about an hour with them, because I knew several of them. They'd declared an amnesty and were all working together on ticket touting at the fight. That was very bizarre – a gathering of Premier League football's top boys.

Buncey was so inspired by his experiences at my Mayweather fight that he even based the plot of his novel, *The Fixer*, on it. The book is a thriller telling the story of Ray Lester, a boxing fixer who makes fights happen. One day a girl turns up at his door and asks for his help finding her dad, a Vegas crooner called Eddie Lights. Ray flies over to Vegas along with 35,000 other Brits on their way to see my fight with Mayweather, and gets caught up in a murderous plot.

Steve Bunce:

The original draft of my novel had Mayweather fighting Castillo in their 2002 rematch, but it takes a long time to get published, so it morphed – I got rid of Castillo and brought in Ricky. It wasn't the original idea, but it suited the purpose perfectly.

I write about in the book how every time Ray comes out of the lift, he hears the same chorus: 'Walking in a Hatton Wonderland'. That's how it was. When the fight was over, I headed back to my room at the MGM to work on my report, and as I got into the lift to go to my room at midnight, the fans were singing 'Hatton Wonderland'. When I came down at 5am, they were still singing 'Hatton Wonderland', when I came back from the press room at the MGM Grand an hour later at 6am they were still singing it. And the next time I came down, after having a few hours' sleep, they were still singing it!

For Buncey and a lot of the other members of the British press pack, their lasting memories of my Vegas years are centred on the fans.

Steve Bunce:

It's an interesting thing about Vegas that there's not a lot of fun there. People might laugh at that statement, but all the things that are fun in Vegas cost you a fortune. You go to the bar at the MGM now, buy two bottles of beer, give the guy twenty dollars and there's no change. Then if you want to go to Studio 54, it's $125 to get in on a Tuesday night . . . and you can't get in! We're meant to be having fun because we're in Vegas, but where's the fun in that?

When the Ricky Hatton fight was in town, it was just fun.

His Mayweather fight wasn't the best I've seen by any stretch of the imagination, or the best outcome, but it has to be the best event. It was different in the sense that there was a massive collective will for Ricky to win among the travelling fans. They weren't stupid, they knew he was up against it, but they were willing him to do it.

It was a very good time to go to Vegas. There were 35,000 people there and about 35 women among them. The men could all go home with a gift for their wives and girlfriends. There wasn't a man on my plane home who didn't have a box of Ugg boots, which were in fashion then and, at the Vegas outlet stores, were half the price of back home.

Steve Lillis:

I first went to Vegas in 1992 for the Evander Holyfield–Larry Holmes fight, but I've never seen anything like Mayweather–Hatton in my life. There were people checking in at the MGM Grand and just wheeling their suitcase into the bar next to reception – not even bothering to drop their stuff off at their rooms first – and then staying there for ten, twelve hours.

My wife came out for the fight – she was in the Fashion Show mall, and she overheard two women in the shoe shop talking about how they were buying up all the shoes because they'd had a record-breaking week. My wife turned around and realised they were prostitutes. Even the hookers were talking about how much money Ricky's fans had brought in that week.

Jeff Powell:

The week of the Mayweather fight, one head barman at the MGM told me: 'Ricky's following is unbelievable – it's first time in the history of the MGM Grand that we've been drunk out of beer!' The Hatton fans were very well welcome and well-received – they didn't cause any aggro of note. Las Vegas loved Ricky, no question about it.

Kevin Francis:

I've been to the MGM loads of times to see fights and the thing about the place is that the pervading sound when you get out of the lift on the ground floor is normally the bleeps of fruit machines. But whenever Ricky Hatton fought there, from Wednesday onwards when the fans started arriving, the pervading sound was people singing 'There's only one Ricky Hatton'. It was a constant reminder to me how far he'd come since his pro debut in Widnes.

Ian Darke:

I was around Jim Watt for those fights, and it's the only time in my career that I ever got an idea of what it's like to be an A-list celebrity. The British fans had all seen us on the TV, so everyone wanted to stop us and ask how we thought the fight was going to go. By the end, we realised that they didn't hear what we really thought what was going to happen in the fight, they just wanted to hear us say that Ricky was going to win. Sometimes we shortened the conversation and just said, 'Yeah, he's in great shape, we think he's going to do it.'

Of course, I didn't always win out there, but when the press guys go out to Vegas, people still talk to them about those times. Kevin has been back a few times since for Amir Khan fights and the bartenders ask him, 'How's Ricky doing?' When Steve checked in at the MGM Grand in September 2014 for Mayweather–Maidana II, the receptionist saw he had the special media room rate and the first question was, 'Ah, you're from Britain – do you know that guy, Ricky Hatton?'

Steve Lillis:

You talk about Britons who've made it big in Vegas like Tom Jones, Elton John and Engelbert Humperdinck . . . you can add Ricky to the list – he could take his one-man show there.

'WHO DID YA COME TO SEE?'

Headlining shows back in Manchester at the M.E.N. Arena in front of 22,000 people had prepared me well for Vegas where even the MGM Garden Arena – the biggest venue – holds a maximum of 16,800. I was well accustomed to fighting in front of big crowds at the actual fights, but the weigh-ins for the fights were like nothing I'd ever experienced before. In Manchester, the weigh-in would usually be upstairs in a function room at the Midland Hotel with the press and a few fans there. In Vegas, the weigh-in for a Ricky Hatton fight became an event in itself.

For the Urango fight, Dennis Hobson, Paul Speak and the rest of the team went down to the Paris hotel on the morning of the weigh-in. When we get there, we see people setting up the scales in the corner of the casino floor. It's hardly even a stage and it's not even roped off, and there's not a lot of room for spectators with all the gaming tables and fruit machines. By this time, we know there's thousands of Brits in town and they're going to be coming down to see it. It's not like back home where a lot of fans might have other things to do the day before the fight; they're all away on holiday and they want to enjoy every moment of the build-up.

We walk up to the organiser and Dennis says: 'What're you doing?'

'We're putting together the weigh-in, sir.'

'Do you know how many we're bringing?' I say.

'No problem, sir – we've done lots of events here.'

'You don't know what's going to hit you today,' says Dennis.

They tell us it's all under control and not to worry, though, so we leave them to it.

In the afternoon, we go down for the weigh-in. As the lift doors open, I can hear a familiar song and it gets louder as I walk through the casino.

'THERE'S ON-LY ONNNNNNE RICK-Y HATT-ON, ONE RICK-Y HATTON . . .'

There are scenes of carnage all around. The place is rammed. People are hanging off the slot machines and jumping on tables to get a view, and the organiser – who'd been so relaxed in the morning – is running round with a handful of security guys in a panic, trying to keep some sort of order. It's mayhem.

Joe Sharpe:

Three thousand people turned up just for the weigh-in! This was a different thing for Vegas. People could come to the weigh-in, they could meet Ricky, he'd have a chat, sign autographs – it was a whole experience.

Adam Darke:

The people of Vegas, and certainly the hotels and casinos and the TV people, loved having Hatton fights on there because it brought them something they didn't see in America. They don't see thousands of fans following one fighter – they certainly don't hear singing. That's an alien concept in any American sport. So they were to a large degree enchanted and bemused by Hatton's army of supporters. They bought into him. He looked like a choirboy and had this old Anglo-Saxon sense of humour. He gave interviews, unlike the sort of bland press releases you get from a lot of American sports stars. He charmed the pants off them for a while.

Dennis Hobson:

Ricky knew how to milk it. If you look back to when Muhammad Ali transformed boxing, he went to a wrestling match one night and saw a wrestler called Gorgeous George poncing around, shouting, 'I'm the greatest' and thought, I'll have some of that. Ali brought a little bit of theatre and Ricky did the same in Vegas at the weigh-ins.

With 10,000 of my fans in Vegas – and the band flown in by Dennis – the atmosphere for the weigh-in for my next fight against Castillo at Caesars Palace was even more full on. When I went back for the Floyd Mayweather bout, the bosses at the host venue, the MGM Grand, were ready for an invasion, and decided to stage the weigh-in in the actual fight arena.

What they maybe hadn't banked on was the size of the invasion. There were around 35,000 of my supporters in town, and they only opened up a section of the venue, enough room to accommodate 6,000 fans. People started to queue in the early hours of the morning to have a chance to get in – for the many fans who didn't have fight tickets, this might be the nearest they got to seeing the fight live. It was hard enough to get tickets to watch the fight on closed-circuit TV, with many of the casinos along the Strip showing the fight already sold out.

Security had to close off the entrance nearly two hours before the start – if the MGM had realised quite the level of interest in the weigh-in, they would probably have got double the number in the arena that day.

In the dressing room before the weigh-in, I can hear the band playing and all the fans singing. Someone counted up that the 'There's only one Ricky Hatton' song was sung over seventy times before I weighed in.

I can hear cheers – for Lennox Lewis and Joe Calzaghe appearing on stage – and boos – for Bernard Hopkins who is spoiling for a fight against Joe the following year. Even the legendary MC Michael Buffer is struggling to make himself heard. 'The last time this many Brits invaded the USA it was 1812 and you burned down the White House,' he says.

When we walk out onto the stage, the noise is absolutely deafening. I'm on Floyd's home turf, and yet virtually all the people there are on my side. It's an incredible feeling to have that support.

It takes a lot to intimidate Floyd with all his experience, but it must be a bit off-putting for him to have so many people singing, chanting and shouting against him: 'Who are ya? Who are ya? Who the fucking hell are you? You're supposed to be at home, There's only one Ricky Hatton, God save the Queen, Fatty's gonna get ya', and all that. It's like Manchester Town Hall all over again, and Floyd doesn't like it, making throat-slashing gestures in return.

At least he does have some support. Fair play to him, he has a foundation for underprivileged children in Grand Rapids,

Michigan, and he's brought a hundred of the kids out to see the weigh-in. They're all waving handmade placards and cheering for him – of course, my lot start singing, 'You're supposed to be at school' at them.

I'm so pumped up. When I get on the scales, rather than look out at the crowd, I stand side-on and stare at Floyd who's standing nearby ready to get on next. Oscar De La Hoya has to tap me on the shoulder to get me to turn to the front so the photographers can get their pictures.

As soon as Floyd weighs in, I march straight across over the scales for the face-to-face staredown: 'Come on then, you dickhead.'

We're nose to nose and after a few seconds he pushes his head in so I push straight back. Kerry Kayes steps in and breaks us up and I give Floyd a wave as he wanders off.

Then Floyd starts shadow-boxing on the front of the stage as the crowd are singing 'Who the fucking hell are you?' while I make a 'knobhead' gesture at him.

Then Floyd lifts two little Mayweather kids out from the back of the stage with his world championship belts. He's pointing them towards me, telling them to hold the belts up in front of me, so I give them a smile as the crowd break out into a chorus of 'God save the Queen'.

Floyd's still trying to get under my skin, throwing his chin forward and throwing wide hooks in an impression of how he reckons I fight, which I just laugh at.

Then Michael Buffer introduces me to say a few words and hands me the microphone: 'I just want to ask you two questions,' I say. 'Who did ya come to see? Floyd?'

'Nooooooo.'

'Me?'

'Yeaaaaaaahhhh.'

'Who's taking the belts?'

'Youuuuuuuuuu.'

'Let's fucking have him!'

I hand the mic back and march off stage to huge cheers.

The crowd loved it, but Ian Darke, who was in the arena to commentate for Sky, wasn't so sure it was good for me.

Ian Darke:

I worried about Ricky at the weigh-in for the Mayweather fight when he grabbed the microphone and all that. I remember saying to a colleague, 'I don't like this.' It was almost as if he needed those fans as an emotional prop. I thought, you shouldn't be doing this now – you should be in there, getting on the scales, getting out again. All this hoopla's fine on the promotional tour and in the press conferences, not on the eve of the fight.

It's true that normally I had never got in my opponent's face before at a weigh-in. It was easier said than done, though, when I'd spent weeks with Mayweather having a pop at me. I didn't bite, didn't bite, didn't bite . . . but come the weigh-in, with all my fans there, I thought, I've had enough of you, and I gave him some back.

If you watch the weigh-in back on YouTube you'll see that most of the time, I was actually standing still on the stage, waving to my fans, nice and cool. It was actually Floyd who was the one bobbing around all over the place. I wasn't out of control, my pulse wasn't racing. Behind the curtain afterwards, straight away I was laughing and joking about it, saying to Billy Graham: 'Did you see that, Bill?' Floyd hadn't got under my skin. It didn't take anything out of me.

Looking back now, it's just an amazing memory. Nowadays, the big fights in England have followed the American example and weigh-ins for big fights have become more of an occasion. I'd like to think I had a bit to do with that. Everyone's cottoned on to it now.

Steve Lillis:

The whole Vegas weigh-in culture that you see now at Mayweather and Pacquiao fights, that all stemmed from Ricky Hatton. The casinos could see they were onto a good thing – let people in the arena free of charge and that way we get them in our facility on Friday afternoon. Ricky triggered all that.

Jeff Powell:

The scenes at the Hatton–Mayweather weigh-in were unprecedented. They do them in the arena all the time now, but that weigh-in set the pattern for making a big production of the weigh-in and having big coast-to-coast coverage of it. Ricky brought that to Las Vegas, that's for sure.

Steve Bunce:

I'd never seen anything like that Mayweather weigh-in and neither had the people of Vegas – they could have had 18,000 spectators in for that, but they only set it up for 6,000. It's become the standard now, but even though they let 12,000 in for the Mayweather–Saul 'Canelo' Alvarez weigh-in [2013], the atmosphere was better with half that number at Hatton–Mayweather.

Floyd was genuinely in shock and awe and wonder at the

atmosphere. He would have loved that support. To this day, he'd still love it.

Robert Diaz:

The Mayweather weigh-in, I'll never forget. The energy this kid generated . . . I still miss the atmosphere of Ricky's fights, weigh-ins – Ricky Hatton events.

AN AMERICAN VIEW

For my fight against Floyd Mayweather, I allowed American writer Thomas Hauser into my dressing room so he could see everything that was going on behind the scenes before and afterwards. He's written novels and many brilliant books about boxing, and one of those, on 'The Greatest', *Muhammad Ali: His Life and Times*, won the William Hill Sports Book of the Year award back in 1991. In 2005, the Boxing Writers Association of America (BWAA) presented Thomas with the prestigious Nat Fleischer Award for career excellence, the first ever internet writer to receive the honour. That same year, following my wins over Kostya Tszyu and Carlos Maussa, the BWAA also voted me their Boxer of the Year, the first time ever a Brit had won the award, something I'm very proud of.

Thomas followed my Floyd fight, all the way from the first press conference, and he wrote a fantastic article about the whole experience. Thomas also covered my Malignaggi and Pacquiao fights, only on those occasions he was in my opponent's dressing rooms. He was there when I won and lost and saw both sides of the story, so he seems like a great person to ask for an American journalist's view of those times.

Thomas Hauser:

The thing that I took away from it the most was the adoration that British fans have for Ricky. We hear loads of talk about fighters' followings, but it's different for Ricky. Sixty thousand people turn out to see Wladimir Klitschko fight in Germany, but they're not going to travel all the way to the United States to watch him, and there's not the same sort of adoration – they are there for the show.

The people, particularly from Manchester, loved Ricky and he really cared about them – it wasn't an act on his part. Lots of fighters just play the fans card for commercial reasons, but Ricky really wanted to satisfy them.

Manny Pacquiao has certainly bonded with his fans, too, and I think Henry Cooper had fans like that, but it was a different world so they didn't travel. Henry was very much beloved. Lennox was respected, but I don't think he was loved the way Ricky was.

There was a particularly poignant moment during the Mayweather fight where it was obvious that Ricky was in trouble, he was not going to win the fight, and with a combination of defiance and love, the fans sang 'There's only one Ricky Hatton'. That was very moving to me.

Ricky's entrance to 'Blue Moon' is one of the great sports entrances I've ever seen. People really looked forward to that. Ricky's entrance was as much part of the show as Michael Buffer saying, 'Let's get ready to rumble.' It felt genuine. So many of these entrances are always trying to top what they did before with smoke and mirrors, and Ricky would have the smoke and mirrors sometimes, but that song, that pulsating 'Blue Moon', really reached into the soul. It was great.

I think most journalists found Ricky pretty easy to be around. He had no pretensions, he was very accommodating. That was also true with members of his team, too – they were just a nice group of people.

I remember being in Boston for the Collazo fight – the first time I was in Ricky's dressing room – and the afternoon of the fight, Ricky was sitting in the hotel lobby playing a card game with some of the members of his team and saying hello to anyone that passed by.

One of the things I remember most fondly about Ricky from the Malignaggi fight was when he came into Paulie's dressing room after the fight. Paulie felt awful, Paulie did not fight well that night, it was the first time he'd ever been stopped and he was very upset. Ricky came in and could not have been more gracious towards him, while everyone in the Malignaggi camp was saying all along how nice the people in the Hatton camp were to deal with. There were only good feelings between them.

I remember Ricky as a world-class fighter, who fought with honour and I wish him every success in the future.

WALKING IN A HATTON WONDERLAND

FAN OF THE FANS

There were so many things that made my Vegas years memorable for me, but nothing was more special than having the support of the thousands of fans who travelled from Britain.

If there was a time machine, I'd like to jump in it and go back and be with the 35,000 fans who went across for my Mayweather fight and experience it all as a fan: singing in the packed bars, drinking the casinos out of beer, walking down the Strip and bumping into people you know from back home, queuing up at 6am to get into the weigh-in and watching the fight live in the arena (or even on closed-circuit TV in Vegas, which thousands did and created an amazing atmosphere). Everyone I speak to says that they had the time of their lives.

There were planes from Manchester that were chartered for no other reason than to come to the fight. As soon as they'd taken off, the seatbelts were off, they were up singing. It was just incredible. My mates told me they'd never known a long-haul flight pass so quickly.

I wish I had been there to be part of all of that.

It's still hard for me to get my head around how an ordinary lad like me ended up with such a huge army of fans, so I asked a few people who followed my career closely for their opinions.

Glenn McCrory and Ian Darke give my first promoter Frank Warren and Sky Sports a lot of credit for building up my fanbase and rightly so. Frank used the lightly-regarded World Boxing Union belt to build up my profile, and stage bigger and bigger fights in Manchester with the support of Sky, who covered all the build-up so people got to know me as a person.

Glenn McCrory:

It's rare you get a fighter with the crossover appeal Ricky had. Normally, fighters just get fight fans. Ricky, because of his passion for Manchester City, attracted their fans, too, but his passion for the city of Manchester as a whole meant he attracted United fans too – here was a City fan getting Wayne Rooney carrying his belt in. Then he cut across to football fans in general around the country. The type of fans he got were very vocal, boisterous fans.

Ricky is also into darts, and the best darts player of all-time, Phil Taylor, was a big fan of Ricky's, which pulled in more fans too. Sporting icons like Wayne Rooney and Phil Taylor brought all their fans with them.

I've had several nights out with Ricky, but the problem is I don't see much of him because he'll never turn anyone down for a picture or a chat, so you never really have a chance to talk to him. He was almost the property of the fans at his peak – he knew that, and he was okay with that.

Ian Darke:

He was the first fighter who became a household name purely from fighting on satellite television. Everybody else we had – Lennox Lewis, Steve Collins, Nigel Benn, Chris Eubank – had already featured on terrestrial TV, but Ricky Hatton was a Sky Sports-made fighter from day one.

Adam Smith thinks that it was a mixture of my fighting style and personality that drew in different types of fans.

Adam Smith:

He had this exciting come-forward style and he got cut which made him a bit more human. Then he'd grab the mic at the end of each fight and say, 'This is for you, Manchester'.

Johnny Nelson is the only sportsman I've ever met who has absolutely no ego at all, but Ricky was pretty close to that. He had a bit of ego in the ring where he was devastating. There was a switch. I'd go and see him in the dressing room, give him a hug as if you were meeting him down the pub, and then he'd turn it on in the ring. As well as being likable, he was a winner.

My wife isn't a big boxing fan, but she was a massive Ricky Hatton fan. She used to come to all his fights at the M.E.N., she used to love it because afterwards she'd meet a couple of the Corrie stars and Ricky would come and chat to us. She loved the story rather than the fights. My mum was the same – she used to come to all the Hatton fights.

Ricky would train like a monk for twelve weeks, but as soon as the fight was over, it was, 'I'm off for a Guinness, who's coming?' That made him normal. He sold out 22,000 tickets at the M.E.N. and I bet 15,000 have had a pint with him. They felt they knew him.

Steve Bunce and Mike Costello put Adam's theory to the test before the Mayweather fight with a challenge live on air on BBC Radio 5 Live. There were thousands of people queuing up for the weigh-in and Buncey bet Mike that if they picked ten people at random, as long as they were British or Irish, they'd all have a story about meeting me personally.

Steve Bunce:

I said to Mike, 'Go on – you choose the ten' and he tried as hard as possible to find people who looked the least likely to have ever met Ricky personally. He'd find a pregnant British-Asian woman and lo and behold she'd met Ricky when he was down in Kent. He'd find a seventy-year-old man from Norwich, and he'd had a drink with Ricky when he was in Great Yarmouth one day. By the time it got to 8–0, Mike was looking for someone that stood no chance, but all ten we spoke to had met Ricky, and every story was different. Unbelievable.

There was a real personal connection with Ricky. He came along when social networking was still in its infancy. He didn't have to go online and tell people how much he loved them; it was still very much a people thing. All the hours our boxers spend online nowadays, if they spent some of that going to a pub, a working man's club, going to amateur boxing, they might meet 500 people instead of just communicating online with them.

Dennis Hobson and Joe Sharpe, who got the ball rolling for me in Vegas, say that I was a bit like the Pied Piper.

Dennis Hobson:

Everyone wanted to follow Rick because they knew there was going to be some drama because of the way he fought, and they knew it would be fun because after the fight he wanted to socialise. He'd always meet and greet and tell a few funnies. He gathered troops wherever he went and it snowballed. When Ricky was fighting in Vegas, I'd walk into the bar at Caesars Palace and it was just like going into a working men's club back home.

Joe Sharpe:

Ricky always called me after the fights to come meet him. He loved being around the people. We'd go out to a nightclub and the music would be drowned out by fans singing 'There's only one Ricky Hatton'. The fans loved him and he loved people being around him. People who didn't even know who he was, or weren't into boxing, also wanted to have their picture with him. There's never been support like that for any British fighter over here. Ever.

He's special. Very unusual. There's no fighter like that today. I'm an avid fight fan and I'm always looking, but I don't think there's another Ricky Hatton. No disrespect to anyone else I've ever worked with, but they don't have the confidence to have a personality. They think they have to be mean to each other, and Ricky's not that kind of person; he was nice to everybody outside the ring.

Fighters these days think they are businessmen, want to be tough, but what they're missing is the fans who are paying for the show. They don't have fans that say, 'I'm going to catch this guy and he's going to brighten my day.' Ricky would brighten your day.

I remember when Ricky came over for a press conference to announce the Paulie Malignaggi fight. We get together with Mike

Tyson – who loves Ricky – and go out. Wherever we go in Vegas there are always Brits around who recognise him and mob him. Ricky invites the fans he meets along with us and they follow us like he's the Pied Piper. We end up going from club to club till 5am and Ricky has such a good time he misses the press conference!

Ricky's the number one fan of people I've ever met. He's a fan of the fans.

'A fan of the fans' – I'm happy with that description. It's true. I was so grateful, proud and humbled to have had such great support in my career.

THE MISSUS

Throughout my Vegas years, I was very lucky to have the love and support of Jennifer, my partner and wonderful mother to two of my children, Millie and Fearne. She was there with me to enjoy all the great times in Vegas and to pick me up whenever things went wrong. Jennifer even quit her job as a lecturer in Business at Manchester College of Art and Technology when they wouldn't allow her time off to come and see my fight against Floyd Mayweather.

Amazing to think then that just a couple of years before that, Jen had only knew of me because we'd been at the same primary school . . . and she didn't approve of boxing, let alone follow it.

Jennifer Dooley:

I met Ricky in 2005 through my friend Jenna. When she told me she was dating a guy called Matthew Hatton I knew who he was because he'd been in my class at Mottram Primary School and Rick was a couple of years above.

She explained to me that they were both boxers and Ricky had this big fight against Kostya Tszyu fight coming up, but it didn't mean anything to me. I didn't follow any sports and none of my family were particularly into sport either.

Jenna said I should watch one of his fights and I said, 'No, absolutely not.' I was quite against boxing. I thought it was brutal and absolutely ridiculous that two men would have a fight for no reason.

We didn't have Sky Sports at home so I didn't see any of the build-up to the Kostya Tszyu fight and I didn't read the sports pages. I was completely oblivious to this massive event in Manchester, but a week later Jenna invited me to come with her to a Hatton family party for one of Ricky's cousins who was going travelling round Australia for a year. Jenna had had a fall-out with Matthew and he wasn't going, so I said, 'Look, Jenna, I'll go with you, but I'm only staying for an hour because I'm going to meet the girls later.'

Ricky traditionally went to Marbella for a few days after his fights, but he was back in time for the party and we got introduced. He sort of remembered my name and we were laughing about old school stories, some of the teachers who were still there – his son Campbell was starting at the same school that September. I left the party to meet my friends, but then Rick arrived at the bar we were in an hour or so later and we spent the evening together as a big group and that's where it all started for us.

I think he liked it that he'd met a girl who didn't know anything about boxing. I knew who he was, but I didn't understand how successful he was at it. When we first went out, I couldn't believe people were asking for autographs and photos. I thought, 'Bloody hell, what have I got involved in here?'

One night, I stayed at Rick's house and my friend Liz had stayed too. The next morning, Rick said to me he'd got to go downstairs to have an interview with Jim Rosenthal.

I didn't know who Jim Rosenthal was, but when I told Liz, she was, like, 'Oh my God, you know who that is?'

'No.'

'He's a famous TV presenter.'

I didn't have a clue.

Ricky didn't seem like a boxer when I met him, because he wasn't in the boxing zone. But then he got back in training for his next fight against Carlos Maussa. I'd call in at Kerry Kayes' gym and watch him doing the padwork and body belt with Billy Graham. I never watched the sparring though and I kept out of the way whenever I knew TV cameras would be there.

I'd never known anyone whose weight went up and down so much as Rick. When I first saw the photo on his mantelpiece of him at his heaviest with Campbell, wearing matching shirts, I asked him who the bloke with Campbell was.

'That's me, you cheeky cow,' he replied. 'And if you play your cards right and we're still together in a few weeks, that's what you've got to put up with.'

When I first met him, he had the six pack, the shadow of a bruise under his eye – a woman's dream! Then the weight went on, but by that point I'd fallen in love with him and it didn't matter.

Once he got in the gym it was like the weight just melted off him, but I saw all the graft he put in and how little he ate. I used to say to him, 'Do you want one Haribo sweet?' 'No, I won't even have one.'

I'd sneak off into the kitchen to have a square of Dairy Milk chocolate rather than eat it in front of him.

It was my first experience of the trash-talking before a big fight and I hated Maussa because he was saying he was going to cut Ricky up which really upset me.

Rick got badly cut in the fight. Watching from ringside was quite a horrendous experience. It wasn't just the blood, it was the sound of the punches landing – I'd never heard anything like it before. I found it very brutal. I didn't like the crowd's reaction to someone being hurt. Whereas a boxing fan saw someone performing well, I saw the opponent getting hurt. I saw the complete flipside of what a boxing fan would see. Jenna wasn't there, but Kerry Kayes' wife Jan was sat next to me and she comforted me through the whole thing – I will never forget her support.

It was horrible and I can't believe I ever went again, but of course I went to all of Ricky's fights to support him – as much as I hated watching it.

I have a cousin who lived in Vegas, so I'd been there with my family three times before Ricky's first fight there. But those visits were before I was twenty-one, and Vegas is a completely different experience when you can go in the nightclubs and to the shows, and going there for a big fight was something different again.

We were looked after very well at Caesars Palace for the first couple of fights; when Ricky got on board with Golden Boy and the MGM Grand [for the third, fourth and fifth fights], the red carpet was really rolled out.

They gave us an incredible Skyloft at the MGM – a two-level duplex apartment, bigger than a normal house. It had a huge hallway, pool table, big dining room, floor-to-ceiling windows, glass staircase, two massive bedrooms with huge en-suite bathrooms, and a music system with speakers in every room. It even had its own Starbucks machine – not that I could operate the damn thing.

The second time we stayed there, we were walking back to the suite with Liam Gallagher and the walls of the corridor leading to it were covered with this luxurious padded fabric. He was running his hands along the walls, 'Oh my God, I've never seen anything like this,' and with Oasis he'd stayed in some of the best hotels in the world.

For Rick's fight against Pacquiao we also stayed some of the time at the Hard Rock who comp'd us another incredible suite. The luxury of it all was mind-blowing.

Win or lose, we always had a great time afterwards, but before the fights I was in a state of sheer panic. From the point Ricky left for Vegas to train – which got earlier and earlier with each fight – I really struggled. I've always shied away from media coverage but I got tricked into doing interviews a couple of times and I found that very stressful.

Then flying over there with Rick's family and fans, everyone was drinking and having fun but I could never get involved in that because my mind was so focused on the fight.

Jenna used to like going to the weigh-ins, but I didn't go to any.

There was too much exposure. Usually in my day-to-day life I don't get recognised, but fans out there knew I was Ricky's girlfriend, and I was a little bit intimidated by it. Every time I got in a taxi, when they heard my accent, the driver would ask, 'Are you here for the Hatton fight? Do you know this guy?'

I just used to say: 'I've heard he's a really good boxer.'

Ricky takes having loads of people around in his stride, but I didn't really know how to deal with it. Since meeting him, it has helped me open up a bit, get rid of some of my shyness. I'd be hopeless being famous – I couldn't deal with it at all. I used to just keep my head down, go shopping, have early nights and prepare myself.

Jenna would stay in the suite with me leading up to the fight, which helped – it meant that I wasn't rattling around in this massive room on my own. Matthew and Rick would come up to the suite after the weigh-in and the day of the fight, Jenna and I would always go and get our hair done.

Of course, we had other extended family and friends around too and we were taken out for some lovely meals by Golden Boy. We had this lovely meal one night with Oscar and Shane Mosley who was so nice. Rick's mum always had a jokey flirtation with Richard Schaeffer, who was Golden Boy CEO at the time – she called him 'Dick'.

It was surreal at times. A lot of the celebrities you were expecting to meet because someone had said so-and-so is coming to the fight or is over there. But when Brad Pitt made a beeline for me in the Green Room before the Pacquiao fight and introduced himself, saying, 'You must be Ricky's partner,' I was thinking, oh my God! Angelina came to see us afterwards too.

So I don't want to give the wrong impression that it was all doom and gloom – we did have some lovely times – but I couldn't really relax until the fight was over. The fights were torture for me and never more than the last Vegas one against Manny Pacquiao. I hardly watched any of it. During all of Rick's fights – maybe because it's the man that I love in the ring – I only used to see the punches that landed on him. In my mind, I thought Rick lost every round of every fight I ever watched!

The first round of Pacquiao, things didn't go Ricky's way and I couldn't really watch the fight after the first knockdown. I literally shut my eyes tight and stuck my fingers in my ears so I could hear less of the crowd. At the end of the round, I said to Jenna, sitting next to me, 'Tell me what happens.' It was only when Jenna nudged me that I took my fingers out of my ears and she said, 'It's all over.'

When I opened my eyes I saw Rick lying flat on his back on the canvas. No exaggeration, I thought he was dead. That's when I must have let out a scream although I don't remember doing that.

In seconds the ring filled up with people so I couldn't see Ricky and that made it even worse. All I could see were legs. It had gone deathly silent around us and the whole atmosphere was one of panic. I was crying and I'm not going to be as dramatic as to say I collapsed, but my legs kept going from under me when I tried to stand. Of course, I always had a camera stuck in my face after the fight. Matthew went up to one of the cameramen and shoved the camera away and said, 'You've got your shot, now give her some breathing space.'

One of the paramedics came over and he said, 'Jennifer' – I remember he used my name – 'Jennifer, he's okay.' When I heard that, I ran out of the arena and when I got to the curtained off area, I crouched down on the floor and just sobbed.

Jenna and one of the security guys who worked with Ricky on fight night, this massive American called Tyler, came after me. Tyler, who is seven feet tall and as broad as he is tall, scooped me up off the floor as if I was a child – and I'm not a small girl – and carried me into the changing room.

There was a little TV monitor in there and we could see the live stream. Tyler said, 'He's coming now.' I wiped the tears off my face and stood up because I didn't want Ricky to see me like that. I thought that seeing me upset is the last thing he needs right now. I don't believe Ricky ever saw me cry after a fight. I used to wait till he fell asleep and then look at the bruises on his face and cry then.

It was only when we got home and he saw a recording of the fight and saw how I'd reacted – that piercing scream and crying – and I know it upset him. That was a massive thing in his mind when he had that Senchenko redemption fight. He said to me: 'I don't want to put you through that again, but this is something I have to do.' Of course, I always supported him.

It was really hard when he lost, because I could see how much he was hurting behind closed doors – he took defeat harder than anyone. I felt it was my job to keep him as up as possible and I also knew how important it was for him to get out there. He needed to be around his fans.

As the fights went on, we worked our way up from staying a couple of days after the fight to staying a week or so and making a holiday of it. Of course, when Rick lost, those times were tinged with sadness, but they were minimal compared to all the great times we had. [see also Post-fight refuelling, page 267]

I haven't been back to Vegas since Ricky's fights there. We were booked to go when I'd just got pregnant with Fearne and I couldn't leave Millie at that point, so the night before, I said, 'You know what, I can't come.' I would like to go back and experience a fight weekend there without the worry of Ricky fighting. I do look back at those days and wish I could have been there as a fan rather than as his girlfriend and really enjoy it because I did miss out on a lot of things – the weigh-in etc. Obviously, I wouldn't swap the amazing times I had, but I'd love to also rewind and experience it as a fan as well. Unfortunately, I'll probably never experience anything like the atmosphere surrounding Ricky's Mayweather fight, because it's unlikely ever to happen again.

I did feel bad for putting Jen through all that stress. The summer after the Mayweather fight, I said I'd treat her to a holiday wherever she wanted to get away from it all, because I'd been busy all through 2007 with Vegas fights and all the training and promotion that goes with them.

She says: 'Do you know what, I'd like to go Vegas without shitting myself because you're fighting.'

So after I beat Juan Lazcano, we jet off to Vegas and for once boxing takes a back seat (well, most of the time – this was the trip when I slipped away to meet Floyd Sr. for the first time).

We have a lovely, relaxing break, and one day we're sipping champagne together in our cabana by the pool at the MGM Grand, getting happily drunk in the sunshine. I've seen adverts around and about for a Tom Jones show and ask Jen if she fancies going tonight. A few drinks later we weave our way to reception and buy two tickets.

After a bite to eat, we go back to our room to get changed for the gig. An envelope has been pushed under the door. I open it and inside there is a note saying: *Please phone Mr Stern, Entertainments Manager,* and his mobile phone number.

I ring him: 'Oh, hiya Mr Stern. Ricky Hatton here – got your note. What's up?'

'Hey Ricky. Look, the MGM has never made more money in a weekend as they did when you fought here against Floyd Mayweather. Your money is no good here. The tickets for the concert are on us and your bar bill's taken care of as well.'

Jesus Christ. Me and Jennifer are already pissed.

But we head down to the concert and have a few glasses of wine as we watch Tom belt out the songs.

Then Tom says: 'Please give a round of applause for a Brit hero in the audience tonight . . . Ricky Hatton!'

The spotlight beams down on me as I stand up and get a lovely ovation.

'Ricky, are you going to join me for a drink afterwards?'

Who am I to say no, even though me and Jennifer are already two sheets to the wind? I give him the thumbs up.

He finishes off his last song, and a security guard comes to get us and takes us backstage to his dressing room. Tom's having his picture taken with various people and then he asks us: 'Have you two eaten? Would you like to come out for something to eat?'

Me and Jennifer are, like, 'Ooh, lovely, yeah.'

So we go out for dinner with Tom and his agent. I can handle my booze, but by now Jen is really struggling.

'Sorry, Tom, we've been out all day and we started drinking about half eleven this morning.'

'Ah don't worry. You're on holiday – enjoy yourselves.'

Bottles of red wine, white wine and a rosé are lined up in front of us while we eat and Tom tells us stories about Frank Sinatra, Elvis and all the Vegas legends he's known.

Then when we've finished our meal, Tom says: 'Would you like a cognac, Ricky? A little nightcap.'

I don't even know what a cognac is, but who am I to refuse: 'Yeah, go on then.'

When Jennifer starts talking about boxing, which is not her area of expertise, I start to think it's probably time for us to bail out; and when she says to Tom, 'What does your wife think of all the gallivanting that goes with showbusiness?', I know it definitely is.

'IS ELVIS COMING TOO . . . ?'

At the after-party at the Paris hotel following my win over Juan Urango, I'm sat there having a drink when I catch sight of a familiar face across the room. It takes me a few moments to register who it is.

'Fucking hell, is that Frank Gallagher?'

Sure enough, it was the actor David Threlfall who plays the drunken philosopher in the TV series *Shameless*.

The show was a huge hit at the time and I was a big fan, so I was well chuffed to meet him, but that was only the start of celebrities cottoning on to my Vegas fights.

For the second fight, against Castillo in summer 2007, my promoter Dennis Hobson arranged the dates so the footballers could come and watch – and half the Premiership turned up. Wayne Rooney (see *Wayne Rooney, Celine Dion and Me*, page 171), Rio Ferdinand, Wes Brown, John O'Shea and Michael Carrick of United, Joey Barton and Kieron Dyer who were both at Newcastle at the time, David Dunn of Blackburn Rovers – they were all there.

The week of the fight I couldn't walk through a casino without bumping into a Premiership footballer. I saw Rio and Kieron one time and asked them how they were finding it.

'Oh we're loving it. We can just sit at the bar and have a pint.'

I'm sure a few of the fans will have asked them for an autograph or picture, but in comparison to England during the season they could relax.

David Dunn:

I first met Ricky, his brother, dad and a load of his pals in Magaluf when we were both starting out – me as a footballer, him as a boxer. I've always been interested in boxing and we got on straight away.

Then I started going down to Kerry Kayes's gym, Betta Bodies, where Ricky trained in Billy Graham's Phoenix Gym out the back. The first of Ricky's fights I went to was against Jason Rowland at the Manchester Velodrome in 2001 and after that I didn't miss many. People talked about Ricky's fitness and being a pressure fighter, but I always thought that he was very good technically as well.

Once he started fighting in America, it wasn't so easy to go because of the football season, but the timing of the Castillo fight was perfect. I went over with a group of about twenty-five people and had a brilliant time.

One of my pals is quite high up at the MGM and he got us 'The Beatles Boogie Bus', as we called it, to take us to the Thomas And Mack Center. It was just a normal bus covered in adverts for The Beatles show over at the Mirage, but we turned it into a party bus that weekend.

After the fight, we all went to the Piano Bar in New York New York. You normally put down a few dollars to put in a request for the pianist and singers. But everyone was buzzing about the boxing and there for the Hitman, so some of the lads were putting down fifty, hundred dollars at a time to jump the queue and the only song being requested was Blue Moon. *They must have played it six times in a row and Ricky walked in with Jennifer, Wayne Rooney and Coleen as they did.*

It's amazing how many supporters Ricky attracted over to Vegas. There was a good 10,000 there for Castillo and not many teams would take that many with them away from home for a big Champions League match, let alone the 35,000 who went to the Mayweather bout.

People like Robbie Williams, Max Beesley, John Travolta, Bruce Willis, Vinnie Jones, and Bryan Robson came to the fight, too. Dennis also asked Tom Jones to sing the national anthem.

A few days before the fight, I got a call on my mobile.

'Ah, Ricky, it's Tom Jones 'ere,' says this deep Welsh-sounding voice.

I'm sure it's one of my pals messing about.

'Oh, fuck off.'

No, Ricky, it's me, Tom.'

'Yeah, whatever dickhead, I'm tired . . .'

'Ricky, seriously, it's Tom Jones.'

The penny finally drops and I'm well embarrassed: 'Oh, I'm very sorry Tom . . .'

He's rung up because he can't make the fight after all and wants to apologise to me personally.

In the end, Dennis Hobson's fifteen-year-old daughter sings the anthem on the night. One or two asked, 'Why didn't Robbie Williams sing it?', but he just wanted to watch the fight. Robbie was very supportive of Dennis's daughter and she did her dad proud.

Things started to get even more surreal for my next fight against Floyd. The amount of A-listers who turned out to watch that fight was amazing – Will Ferrell, Jude Law, David Beckham, Wesley Snipes, Denzel Washington, Tiger Woods, Brad Pitt and Angelina Jolie and others. Everyone is there. When Tom Jones comes into my dressing room (we'd got Tom this time to sing the national anthem), I look around at him and say: 'Is Elvis coming too?'

David Beckham is at the Mayweather fight as my guest. We'd been introduced a few months before and I'd been out to watch a game at LA Galaxy with him. David was saying then he needed to get me to sign loads of stuff for his kids – I was thinking, you what? Give you my autograph? I wanted him to sign stuff for my family and friends!

My party after the Mayweather fight is at Studio 54 at the MGM Grand, and packed with Brits; in theory, David shouldn't go to places like that because he's just too big a name.

I say to him: 'You don't have to come – it's going to be torture for you.'

'Oh, no, no. I want to come. I'll come for an hour.'

It's strange, though, because when Jennifer and him get out of the lift at the MGM to go across to the club, everyone is mobbing me and ignoring him – I suppose they are in Vegas to see me and just don't expect to see him with me. David turns to me and whispers, 'Don't worry, Ricky, I'll get Jennifer to the party,' and he takes Jen with him before people clock him. I really appreciate that, because Jen doesn't really like the crowds. He's just a class act. I meet Victoria for the first time the next day too and she's lovely as well. The Beckhams get a lot of stick in some circles and I can't for the life of me understand why.

Paul Speak got a taste of what it's normally like to be around someone as famous as Becks, though, when he goes to pick him up at his hotel for the after-party for my next Vegas fight against Malignaggi. When Speaky leads David and his bodyguard out of the entrance at the Hard Rock hotel, there are paparazzi everywhere blocking the way to the car. Speaky is just barging them out of the way, telling one of the photographers: 'If you put that camera any closer, I'll shove it up your arse.'

'Hey, man, you can't do that.'

'Just fuckin' watch me.'

David's bodyguard is looking at Speaky, like, 'What the hell are you doing?'

They'll sue you in America for stepping on their toes.

In the dressing room after the Mayweather fight, a security guard pops his head round the door and says: 'Brad Pitt and Angelina Jolie would like to come in. Is that alright?' Before I can answer, Jennifer, my brother's fiancée Jenna, and my mum all say yes at once.

Brad comes over to me and says, 'There's still only one Ricky Hatton,' which is nice of him, but I'm so upset at losing at the time, I don't say much in return. God knows what Brad and Angelina think of me because I'm even less talkative when they come to see me after the Pacquiao fight. They are so worried by the knockout they want to check on me, but I feel even worse than after the Mayweather loss, so when they catch up with me on the way to the dressing room and Brad asks if I'm alright, I just said, 'Yeah' and carry on walking.

There's a who's who in my dressing room before the Malignaggi fight, too. David Beckham was there, the Oasis lads (See *C'mon Floyd! He's gonna smash his napper in!*, page 158), Jason Statham and Sylvester Stallone with my family and all my mates off the council estate mixed in. As I'm warming up I can see my mates asking for autographs and to get their photos taken with them. The best moment is when The Duck goes up to Sylvester Stallone and says: 'Can I have my picture taken with you please, Rocky.'

I was as starstruck as The Duck to have people like that in the dressing room around me. Even now when I go to Vegas and I bump into Sylvester Stallone at a press conference or a weigh-in, it'll be: 'Hey Ricky, how're you doing?' because he'd been to all my fights. It still amazes me.

Before the Pacquiao fight, Paul Speak spotted a guy wearing a hoodie coming through the dressing room door. The security guards outside have let him in, but Paul doesn't recognise him and thinks it's some chancer, so he rushes over: 'Whoah, where the fuck do you think you're going, mate?'

The guy pulls down his hood: 'Oh, I just wondered if I could watch Ricky warm up . . .'

Speaky has no idea who this fella is and is just about to frogmarch him out again, when I look over and do a double take: 'Fucking hell, Paul. Why are you chucking Denzel Washington out?'

I didn't find it a distraction to have all these famous people around – it spurred me on. But I think it was the mix of people in the dressing room that made the atmosphere special before those fights. My mates always come first for me.

In the run-up to fights, I was always get calls asking me if I had any more tickets for the fight or passes for the after-party.

'What are you on about? You've already had five . . .'

I'm sure my mates were flogging them on, but if I could get spares they could have them as far I was concerned. Probably helped them to pay for the trip which was not cheap.

Sometimes the timing wasn't the best, though. After the Pacquiao fight, I'd been knocked out cold and I was absolutely gutted at losing like that. I was on my way to the after-party after the check-up at hospital, when a pal came up.

'Rick, you haven't got fifty on yer, have you mate? I've done all me money. If you can't lend me fifty quid, I won't be able to get in.'

'Alright, then . . .'

I think the big-name Hollywood celebrities enjoyed meeting some of the characters I know, too. They're used to people sucking up to them, but my mates don't stand on ceremony. Like the time in the Green Room before the Mayweather fight when Jen, my mum and some of the girls want to ask Brad Pitt for a photo, but are too afraid to ask because it's not the done thing. My pal Simon Boot just marches up to him and says: 'C'mon, Brad, cock – you don't mind having your picture taken with the girls, do you?' And he didn't mind at all.

Jack Nicholson might have preferred not to have had quite such a close encounter with my mate Simon Boot, though.

Jack came to the Pacquiao fight (Jay-Z, P-Diddy, Russell Brand and Mariah Carey were also among the spectators that night) and my friend Simon Boot is a massive fan of Jack's. When he sees him standing next to him at a urinal in the gents, he's totally starstruck. They're both standing there, having a wee, and Simon turns to Jack and says: 'Sorry to bother you, Jack, but I'm a big fan of yours. Can I get a picture, please?'

Jack turns to him and replies very politely, in that drawling voice of his: 'Why certainly, sir. Just let me put my cock away first.'

WILL & BILL

Among the people who came to support me in Vegas were the actor Will Mellor and his dad Bill. Will's appeared in loads of popular TV series over the years, including *Hollyoaks*, *Casualty*, *Two Pints of Lager and a Packet of Crisps* and *Broadchurch*. He grew up not far away from me in Bredbury and comes from a fighting family – Bill boxed, his uncle Sid boxed for England and Will himself started boxing at seven years old, and trained in Hyde near me as kid. Even though we're a similar age, I never met him growing up, but we got to know each other well as I was making my way in the pro game. What was fantastic was that, by fulfilling my dream of fighting in Vegas, I helped Will and Bill fulfil their dreams too.

Will Mellor:

Me and my dad watched every kind of boxing – from Europe, America, all over the world. We still do phone each other up in case we might miss a good fight. We always particularly kept an eye out for the young Manchester fighters and we heard of this local kid called Ricky Hatton. At the time he had this pudding bowl basin haircut, but who fought a lot different than he looked – he was like a terrifying choirboy. He was really exciting to watch and we picked him out early as one for the future – definitely a British champion, but with a chance of going on to the bigger stage.

I'm not sure exactly when Rick and me were first introduced, but with my love of boxing I was always around the fighters. I was ringside at most of Rick's fights in Manchester. But I also used to follow all the other fighters from the area – the likes of Jamie Moore, Michael Brodie, Michael Gomez, Steve Foster, who I knew very well and used to train with sometimes. Anyone that was local, we used to go and support. I got behind them all, but Ricky just took it that step further.

I'd go to his fights, the after-fight parties – although I was never free to go to one of his 'Shit Shirt' parties the next day. I've been out for a few drinks with Rick on many occasions and had a great time and he's been back to my house and we'll talk about boxing for hours. Rick and my dad used to have a right good laugh too – he'd call my dad 'Tick-Tock' after the catchphrase of the Early Doors *sitcom character.*

From the word go, Rick got the support of the fans, not just because he was a working-class kid from round here, but the way he fought as well. He came out in round one and did the same thing for as many rounds as it took. His fitness and energy levels were incredible. Everyone called him Ricky Fatton, but when he walked in that ring, that showed how hard he worked in training. Look what he did to Kostya Tszyu – no one had ever outworked, out-manned him like that. To make him retire on his stool at the end of the eleventh round was almost better than knocking him out. He couldn't stand another three minutes of this Manchester kid, this whirlwind. What a proud moment that was. It was an amazing feat for him to get to Vegas, but it was an amazing journey along the way too.

The Vegas fights were a double whammy for me – the fact that Rick was fighting there and the fact that I could go and watch with my dad. The first time he fought there against Urango, I surprised my dad. He opened his Christmas card and his tickets were in there. He was gobsmacked. It was on both our bucket lists, that dream of one day going to Vegas to see a big fight. That dream of one day, 'We'll go to Vegas, dad.' It just happened to be a lad from round the corner that led us there. Maybe we'd have gone to see a Mayweather fight once, but to actually be in Vegas supporting a mate was something special.

We had such a great time that when Rick signed to fight Castillo, I said to my dad, we've got to go again. The Castillo fight was even better. The only way I can describe the weigh-in was like something out of a Rocky film. There was a band playing and it was bouncing in there. My dad was walking round with a sombrero on – I don't know where he got it from.

I think the people of Vegas were shocked at how many people had come over – there was an army of us. I've never seen so many Mancunians in one place in my life and we were on the other side of the world! I was saying hello to people on the Strip and going, 'You only live round the corner from me.' I'm sure it must have given Rick a bit of a lift to feel he was at home even when he was away from home.

The atmosphere was incredible at the fight and I had the perfect view of the best body shot he's ever thrown in his career. To hit someone in the body and make them turn 360 degrees . . . I was diving around hugging my dad, then Jason Statham and Robbie Williams who was there. Then, afterwards, we went backstage to congratulate Ricky, and got on a minibus with Joey Barton singing songs in the back.

At the after-party at the Wynn hotel I found myself standing there with Rick, Wayne Rooney, Rio Ferdinand, my dad and three mates of Ricky's off his council estate, all having a laugh. That was the thing with Ricky – he brought everyone together. There were no airs and graces. It was not about whether we were off the TV or footballers or whoever, we were all just there as one unit to support Ricky. It was strange, surreal, hilarious and it was just great to share that time with my dad.

Unfortunately, in my line of work I have to take jobs when they come, and I wasn't able to make it to Vegas for his last three fights. I was gutted I couldn't go to the Mayweather fight, so I hired a cinema screen and this massive speaker system for my house so it felt like I was ringside. I had my dad with me and a couple of close mates. We had the sound whacked up full volume and we were sat about eight foot from this eight-foot screen.

I don't think the referee did him any favours that night. I was screaming at the screen because Ricky has to fight on the inside and the ref wouldn't let him. I got a bit emotional when Rick got dropped, because he was one of those fighters who seemed like he was made of iron. In the end he got caught, and I thought, well, if he's going to lose, at least he's lost to potentially the best boxer ever.

I watched the whole Pacquiao fight through my fingers. From round one, I thought, he's not right here, he was getting hit and hurt with every punch. He got hit with a jab and wobbled and he was leaping with punches and against a counter-puncher like Pacquiao, I thought, he's going to walk onto one. It was horrible to see the knockout, but thankfully he was alright.

Every boxer wants to achieve as much as they can in the sport and get out without any damage. Thankfully, Ricky has done that and he's got a nice bit of money in the bank. But with him it's more than that – he can look on an amazing career, and the number of people he has touched by his efforts as a boxer and a person is worth more than anything. No other fighter has had the following Ricky had, and I think that was genuinely always more important to him than the money. Fans like me are grateful to him because we wouldn't have had those great experiences in Vegas without him. He can look back and be very proud of himself and what he's achieved.

I got to live a few dreams with my dad, memories that Ricky helped to create, and that will last for the rest of our lives.

'C'MON FLOYD! HE'S GONNA SMASH HIS NAPPER IN!'

I was an Oasis fan from day one. Anyone who follows my retweets of videos of their classic songs on Twitter, or visits the Hatton Gym, will know that I still am. At some point most days, you'll hear Oasis blasting out of the speakers in my gym while I put my fighters through their paces.

Liam and Noel were my absolute idols growing up – I went to see them in concert whenever I could – so it was a dream come true when I finally met them.

My first encounter with Liam was a bit random. That was in June 2005, soon after my epic fight with Kostya Tszyu. After that I need a bit of a break, so I take off for a few days with Simon Hodgkinson in New York, before heading to Atlantic City to see the Floyd Mayweather–Arturo Gatti fight.

So we're wandering around New York looking for an Irish bar where we can get a decent pint of Guinness. Eventually, we find one right up the top near Central Park, and then we move on to see if we could find another one near Times Square. We're walking up and down for a bit, but no luck, so we end up going back to the first place.

This time, there's a load of people wearing Manchester City shirts in there and we're, like, what's going on here? I've got my

City shirt on, too. It's like the local pub before a game at the City of Manchester stadium.

We get talking to a couple of the lads and they tell us Oasis are playing Madison Square Garden and Liam and Noel come down to this bar.

The next day we go back, thinking we might bump into them. We're standing at the bar getting our pints, and I can see a group of lads round a table nearby. Among them, I can see a familiar face.

'Is that Liam, there?' I say to my mate.

The bloke's got his trademark floppy hat on, dark glasses, looking every inch the rock star.

'Yeah, that's him,' replies Simon. 'Go over and introduce yourself.'

'No, no, no . . .'

Liam is a superstar in my eyes, and even though we'd come here hoping to meet him, I'm too much in awe to go and stick my face in. But we can't stop looking over and then Liam happens to get up and swagger towards us at the bar on his way to the gents. As he's walking past, I just say, 'Alright, Liam,' he looks round at me, does a double take, then lifts up the front of his hat.

'Fuckin' Ricky Hatton! Come over here, you fucker. Come here and have a drink.'

So me and my mate trundle over to his table and the next thing we're having a drink with Liam Gallagher. I'm totally starstruck, gobsmacked that he even knows who I am. We spend a few hours with him and have a brilliant time.

Noel Gallagher:

The way Liam tells the story is that he heard someone say to him, 'Alright, Liam.' He looked round and saw this bloke head to toe in

Man City's club shop and thought, 'Who the fucking hell is this idiot in all this gear?' It was only when Ricky took his hat off, Liam realised who it was.

When Liam arrived at the Garden later, he goes, 'I've just met fucking Ricky Hatton in the Irish bar.'

'No way,' I say. 'Is he coming to the gig?'

'No, I don't think he's coming.'

Unfortunately, I can't go to that gig because we have to get to Atlantic City. A month later I also miss Oasis's massive home-coming gig at the City of Manchester Stadium, because I'm away in Tenerife. A few of my mates do go though, and one of them calls me during the gig.

'Fuckin' hell, Rick. You'll never guess what. They just dedicated a song to you.'

He holds his phone up and I can just about make out that it's 'A Bell will Ring' (what else?). I'm absolutely made up – only wish I was there to hear it.

I don't meet Noel till the following year, when we were both guests on Granada's *Soccer Night* TV show – it was me, Noel and Mani of The Stone Roses.

Noel Gallagher:

I just thought he was really fucking lovely lad. Ricky turned up with one of his pals, didn't have any airs or graces about him. He knew a lot about City . . . he's like a lot of lads I grew up with. I think he was preparing for the Collazo fight – so he wasn't up for a night out with Mani and me afterwards . . . fortunately.

I kind of missed seeing the first part of Ricky's career, because I've lived in London for twenty-odd years and we were off travelling around the world and being headcases at the time. Every time he fought, Oasis were out of the country, so I was just reading about him in the papers. I took to him immediately because he came out to Blue Moon *and wore* Man City *boxing shorts and all that.*

But I didn't know that he's an Oasis fanatic until around the time of the Kostya Tszyu fight, which I watched live on the telly somewhere. Ricky thinks Oasis were better than The Beatles . . . Genuinely – Ricky will tell you that with a straight face.

I've kept in touch with Liam and Noel ever since. We bump into each other at various functions, and whenever one or other of them are in Manchester, they'll usually give me a call and we'll meet up. Not both together, though, because as is well known they don't get on these days – to be honest, they never did!

As we're all Man City fans, we'll meet up at the games. I was with Liam at Wembley when we won the FA Cup final against Stoke in 2011 and also at Manchester City when Sergio Aguero scored the last-minute winner that gave us the league title for the first time since 1968. I'll never forget that day, because we ended up at the Town Hall celebrating with the team, and I've got a great photo of me with Liam and City captain Vincent Kompany.

Although I'm now mates with Liam and Noel, I'm still massive fans of theirs, too. So when I fought Paulie Malignaggi, I thought I'd ask them if they'd carry the belts into the ring. For me it would be a huge honour to have two of my idols with me on the ringwalk, and they jumped at the chance.

Noel Gallagher:

We were doing a big gig down in Cardiff at the Millennium Stadium, and Ricky came down with some of his mates. We were having a tear-up in the dressing room when he casually says: 'I'm starting training in the next fortnight – where are you in the world on these dates . . .'

'I dunno,' I said, 'I think we're in America.'

'Would you come and carry my belts out for my next fight?'

I was, like, 'Fuck, yeah. If we can make it work, we'll make it work.'

It turned out we were starting our American tour in Mexico three nights after that, so it was perfect timing. It was a great weekend.

On the night of the bout, I'm in the changing room, warming up, when Liam, Noel and the rest of the band come in.

We give Noel *The Ring* magazine belt and Liam the IBO belt.

Liam says to me: 'What am I supposed to do with this?'

'What do you mean what d'you do with it? When you get in the ring you just hold it up above your head.'

'Right, no problem, Rick.'

A few minutes later, I'm doing my shadow boxing and I look across and there's Liam standing in front of a mirror practising how he's going to hold the belt up. I'm concentrating on the fight ahead, but I can't help but laugh.

We've got Oasis tunes blaring out and Liam is getting more and more hyped up. He gets hold of my iPod and changes the song to *Acquiesce*, one of my favourites of theirs.

'Hitman! This is the song we want on! Whooooo!'

Then he looks at my new coach, Floyd Mayweather, who I think is wondering who this lunatic is.

'C'mon, Floyd! He's going to smash his napper in!' shouts Liam.

'What's a napper?' replies Floyd.

Noel Gallagher:

I've never been backstage at a fight before. We got to the dressing room and there were loads of lads from Manchester, Sylvester Stallone, Jason Statham, David Beckham, the guy that does the 'Let's get ready to rum-ble' – he's in there. Ricky had his iPod on and he was playing loads of Oasis.

There was a good vibe, but then you're getting towards fight time, and I was thinking, 'Wow, this is not my mate anymore – fucking gladiator, this lad.' You saw him change. It went quiet and it was, like, right, 'This is fucking show time now.'

We all march out into the arena, me in my Ricky Fatton suit (see page 240), Liam and Noel proudly holding the belts above their heads. I get in the ring first, then Noel, Liam and the others. Next thing I know, I see Liam strut past me, straight up to Paulie and hold the belt out right in front of Paulie's nose.

I'm looking round at Paul Speak, going, 'Speaky, get him out of here', but Liam's having a great time.

Noel Gallagher:

The atmosphere was great as we walk out – thousands there from England and no one could believe it, seeing me and Liam coming out with him.

We've got in the ring and I was standing in the corner with the belt. Because it's something I've never done, I didn't really know what I was doing. Ricky's gone, 'Walk round the ring with the fucking belt, show the belt.' I felt like a bit of a showgirl. Meanwhile, Liam was over in the other corner trying to intimidate the opposition.

There were a few naughty-looking Italian-Americans at ringside supporting Paulie near his corner. I found out later that Liam and Noel's seats were right in the middle of The Sopranos.

Noel Gallagher:

There was me and Liam with David Beckham sitting in between. Of course as soon as the first bell goes, me and Liam are up and screaming: 'Come on, Ricky – kill him, Rick! Fucking kill him!'

All these Italian-Americans are turning round going: 'Hey, who the fuck are you guys. Hold it down.'

We're like, 'Fuck off, fatty.'

Beckham was sat there with his head in his hands, thinking, 'What am I doing here with these two fucking idiots.'

So Ricky ends up winning the fight and we all shuffle back in the ring to congratulate him. Malignaggi is walking around, looking devastated, and Liam goes up to him, shakes his hand and says, 'Thanks for coming, mate.'

When we get back to the dressing room, I don't think I have ever seen anyone, ever, more desperate to open a can of Guinness as Ricky Hatton was. He was necking it while they were trying to cut the bandages off his hands.

After the fight, I say I'm going to the hotel to have a shower and get changed.

'Go on, we'll come and have a beer with you,' says Noel.

Then David Beckham says he'll join us too.

When we get back to my suite, I can't get showered and changed quick enough. As usual, the MGM have given me an amazing Skyloft duplex suite. I look down from the top level and there's all the members of Oasis, my rock-and-roll heroes, and one of the most famous footballers in the world, all having a laugh together. I'm thinking, 'Jesus Christ, the kid from Hattersley has done alright.'

Paul Speak's down there with them. Liam and Speaky both own dachshunds and they get chatting about their dogs. I think Liam's missus had called the dog 'Fluffy' or something, and Liam is saying how he used to get embarrassed taking it for walks in the park calling its name, but that it's so cute he loves it now.

Noel Gallagher:

We went out afterwards and it all got extremely messy – a fucking great night. And then we all jumped on a flight.

Me and a couple of pals, Mav Crompton and Lee Garvey, fly down with Liam and Noel to Mexico City where they are playing a huge gig as part of their Dig Out Your Soul tour.

The hotel is fantastic but I also want to see downtown Mexico City, the real life too, so after a couple of days of luxury, me and my mates go for a wander. I've been told that Mexico City is the kidnap capital of the world and you shouldn't go outside the hotel; but, as usual, I don't take a blind bit of notice.

So we're tootling down the road, me with my City shirt on, and we see a little Mexican bar. We walk in and it's a real spit-and-sawdust place.

'Three Budweisers, please.'

I look around, and everyone in the bar is looking at us, giving us evils. They're all locals, wondering who these Brits are. Then I see one guy say something to his mate; his mate looks at me, and shakes his head, but the other guy isn't convinced and comes over to us.

'Ricky Hatton?'

'Yeah, yeah.'

'Ahhhhh, Rick-y Hatton!'

Next minute, we're all drinking together. My phone rings. It's my girlfriend who's back home.

'Ricky, alright, where are you?'

'Brilliant – I'm in Mexico City.'

'Are you at the hotel?'

'I've gone down the road to a bar . . .'

'Oh, you idiot, we told you to be careful.'

'Nahhh, we're having a fuckin' great time here. Don't worry, luv. Here y'are – have a word with Fernando . . .'

I hand the phone to one of my new friends and he starts chatting away in broken English then turns to me:

'What is her name?'

'Jennifer.'

'Oh, Jennifer, Jennifer . . .' and on he goes.

Eventually, he hands the phone back to me, and Jennifer's like, 'Oh my God – alright, I'll leave you to it . . .'

After a few beers and tequilas, we wobble back to the hotel to join Liam and Noel.

Their gig is in a huge arena called Palacio de los Deportes and before it starts, they take us from the dressing room to our seats on the side of the stage, just behind the curtain out of sight of the 40,000-odd Mexicans in the audience. Not only have we got the best seats in the house, but a table with four coolers filled with ice, lagers, vodka and Guinness.

'Where did you get Guinness in Mexico City?'

'Imported just for you, mate,' says Noel.

My performance against Paulie had been one of the best of my career. To have Noel and Liam carrying the belt in for me had made it even more special. Then, to top it all off, watching my favourite band play in Mexico City – and with my own personal supply of Guinness – well, it was all a bit of a dream.

Noel Gallagher:

The last I've seen of Ricky was the morning after the gig, by the pool at our hotel because he'd not been to bed. He was just passed out and his mates were going, 'Look at the state of him – the fucking champ.'

Liam and me are shouting at him: 'Ricky! Ricky! We're going now! Ricky! We're off.'

He's like, 'Yeah, yeah, yeah . . .'

RUSSELL CROWE, OASIS AND THE HITMAN ON WHEELS

In December 2008, I went over to watch Manny Pacquiao against Oscar De La Hoya at the MGM Grand. I'd beaten Paulie Malignaggi there just a couple of weeks earlier and there was talk of me fighting the winner.

Funnily enough, for two multiple world champions, there were no titles on the line as Manny hopped two divisions to welterweight for the fight, and Oscar lost his light middleweight title to Floyd Mayweather Jr. the previous year. It's one of those megafights that didn't need belts to capture the public imagination though, and it attracted over $70 million-worth of Pay-Per-View buys.

I'm at the fight with Paul Speak, my dad and a lad called Scully, a mate I got to know through Noel and Liam Gallagher.

Beforehand, we're in the VIP section and there's a few famous names milling about. Scully sees William Shatner and shouts over in his broad Manc accent: 'Hey, T.J.!' – as in T.J. Hooker – 'How you doin'?'

Shatner looks over and half-smiles, obviously thinking, who is this dick?

A few minutes later, we're having a drink when I hear this voice singing: 'There's only one Rick-y Hatt-on, Onnnnne Ricky Hatt-on . . .'

I look round and it's only Russell Crowe.

We have a beer with him and he tells me, 'You broke my fucking heart when you beat Kostya Tszyu in Manchester, mate, but what a great trip that was. What an atmosphere. If Kostya was going to bow out with a defeat, that's how I would have liked him to bow out. The sportsmanship you both showed was great.'

Russell was staying in the Lowry hotel when he was over for the Tszyu fight, and the story was that he went back there afterwards and got absolutely blitzed in the bar. He then flew to New York to promote his new movie, *Cinderella Man*, in which he played the 1920s world heavyweight champion James J. Braddock. But while he was there, he got arrested for allegedly throwing a telephone at a porter of the Mercer Hotel and the photos of him, wearing a distinctive jacket, being led away by a cop were seen around the world. He's wearing the same one tonight, and as we're chatting away, Speaky says: 'Oh, you could have worn a different jacket to the one you had on when you got arrested.' I'm cringing, but Russell takes it on the chin.

Russell's really knowledgeable about boxing and it's not the last time I'll bump into him. After the Pacquiao fight, Jen and me go on holiday to Australia and when we are in Melbourne, we eat at a restaurant on the harbour. The first night we were there, one of the other punters pointed out this beautiful apartment above the harbour and tells us that Russell Crowe lives there.

We think nothing more of it, but keep going back to this strip of restaurants on the harbour each night because the food is so good. One night, a fella comes in with a cap pulled down low over his head and sits down next to me.

'How you doing, Ricky.'

It's Russell Crowe. 'I heard you were here. It'd be rude of me to be round the corner watching TV and not come down and say hello.'

He's only there a matter of a few minutes because, as soon as people in the restaurant realise it's him, they keep coming over, and I can see he's uncomfortable with the attention.

'Ricky, Jennifer, I'm going to get off – but great to see you.'

Anyway, back to De La Hoya–Pacquiao – Manny ends up dominating the fight in a way that no one expected over the naturally bigger man, and Oscar's corner pull him out at the end of the eighth round. Oscar announces his retirement to become a promoter and the wheels are in motion for a fight between me and Manny.

Oasis are playing at the Palms hotel the same night and straight after the fight Speaky, Scully and me shoot straight over to the Palms for the gig. The band have a post-gig party arranged in the Playboy Club in the Palms Fantasy Tower and we're invited to that too. Lovely.

After a cracking gig, we womble up there. There's a queue a mile long outside, but we're supposed to be on the guest list so we go straight up to the entrance, just in time to see Noel's mate Russell Brand go inside.

'Ricky Hatton plus two,' I say to one of the doormen, who flicks through the sheets on his clipboard.

'No, I can't see you here . . .'

'We're meeting Noel and Liam – our names should be on the list?'

'No, no, you're not here, I'm afraid, sir. I can't let you in.'

'Could you go and get them – they invited us personally.'

'No, I'm sorry, sir, we can't do that.'

I look back at the queue and think, 'Shit, we're not going to get in.' If we go to the back of that, we probably won't get in until tomorrow morning. Instead, we go downstairs to the bar to get a pint. We're sitting there feeling dead sorry for ourselves, when Scully notices a wheelchair next to the lift nearby. The next thing, he's got hold of it and is calling me over: 'Sit down in this, Hitman.'

'What?'

'C'mon, get in . . .'

So I sit down in the wheelchair, he pushes me into the lift and we all whizz up to the Playboy Club's floor. I adjust the chair so my legs are sticking out straight in front of me, and when the door's open, Scully pushes me along past the massive queue.

'Watch out . . . coming through . . . coming through.'

We get a different person at the door this time, luckily. I stay quiet while Speaky and Scully go into full bullshit mode: 'Excuse me, our friend won a competition to come to the concert tonight and meet Noel and Liam . . . He was in a car accident a couple of weeks ago, but he's managed to make it anyway . . . He's never met the boys before so it's a dream come true . . .'

'Okay, sir, no problem – please come through, come through.'

Noel Gallagher:

I got in, Russell Brand got in, but we were saying, 'Where's Ricky got to?' Then all of a sudden, I hear his voice: 'Nurse, nurse . . .' and there he is being pushed in on this wheelchair. Honestly, I nearly cried laughing. It was funny as fuck.

He is hilarious. I'll never forget the time he came down with his mates to one of my gigs at the Royal Albert Hall. We're all sat in the dressing room before the gig, and my missus walks in – she's eight-months pregnant.

Ricky's gone: 'Hello, love, how're ya doing? Oh, are you pregnant?'

'*Yeah.*'

'*I hope it's not mine.*'

My missus is looking at him going, 'Really? Really?'

Anybody who's ever made anything of themselves from Manchester is an ordinary person with extraordinary talent. Because in Manchester you're brought up – never mind by your parents – you're brought up by your mates. You're not allowed to be a Flash Harry or step out of line. If you've been blessed to have a talent and seen it through, good for you, but to the lads down the pub, you'll always be a nobhead – I've been in Ricky's box at City and his mates are calling him 'a fat little bastard'.

Ricky is an ordinary lad with an extraordinary gift. The gift was not just the fighting. For him to have the mental fortitude to be one night passed out in a dressing room with Oasis and the next day thinking, right, I'm fighting someone in twelve weeks, I'm living on ice cubes and carrots – that discipline is amazing; that in itself is a gift.

That is why Ricky Hatton will always be genuinely loved in this country, more than, say, Carl Froch, because Carl Froch is a robot. There's a little bit of Ricky in all of us, and there's a little bit of all of us in Ricky.

WAYNE ROONEY, CELINE DION AND ME

Being a huge Manchester City supporter, a lot of people were surprised when I invited Wayne Rooney to carry one of my belts in against José Luis Castillo alongside Marco Antonio Barrera. A few people on Manchester City fan websites had a go at me for that, and there was an article on the official Manchester United website suggesting fans should back Castillo because he's a Red and had been over from Mexico to watch a game at Old Trafford recently. Castillo himself even said he wasn't happy that Wayne was walking to the ring with me not him!

The simple reason why I asked Wayne is that he's a mate. I first met him when I was out to dinner with Jennifer at Lounge 10 in Manchester. He was with his girlfriend/future wife Coleen, we got talking and hit it off straight away. We found we had the same sense of humour and we both love to talk boxing.

I'd sparred with his cousin Ritchie when we both went to Russia with England Schoolboys years ago and Wayne himself had been involved in the sport throughout his childhood. For years when he was coming through the youth ranks at Everton, he did football training on Wednesday and Friday and boxing on Tuesday and Thursday. In the end, Everton made him choose one or the other, and he was such a talented footballer there was only choice to make. He'd never lost his love for boxing, though.

We're very similar characters and we have the same mentality when it came to playing our own sports. On the football pitch, he has very much the same approach as I had as a fighter in the ring – heart on the sleeve, fearless, aggressive and full-on commitment. He had a period where he landed himself in trouble, getting sent off, but he's got that aggression more under control now.

Wayne is someone I've always admired. I see some footballers from a distance, and they seem so full of themselves, but Wayne is not like that. Like me, he doesn't want a big entourage of people around him. He's got a special talent, but not only that, he's got a down-to-earth attitude, and always works hard for his team, even when he's not at his best. It's great that he's gone on to become the captain of England – thoroughly deserved.

Just before I went into training for the Castillo fight, Coleen had a birthday party and I really fancied going. The only problem is that I have previously agreed to do a charity dinner on the same night in Bournemouth, and her party is taking place where they live on the Wirral. I decide to hire a private jet so I can be there, but we have to take off before 10pm or we won't be allowed to fly. At

9.30pm I'm still doing my after-dinner speech, and then it's a mad dash with Paul Speak to get to the airport in time. We make it with literally two minutes to spare. The plane flies into Manchester, we jump into Speaky's car and I get changed in the back on the way to the party.

Wayne can't believe it when we rock up around midnight: 'You really did that? Not many would have done that.'

Later I ask him if he fancies carrying my belt in against Castillo, and he's like: 'Yeah, too right.'

When he comes out to watch me train in Vegas, I can soon tell that he has the boxing bug. As I'm doing my warm-up stretches, I can hear 'thud, thud, thud', and when I look round it's Wayne leathering the heavy bag.

He loves being part of my team on the night – being in the dressing room, meeting boxing legends like Marco, carrying the belt, having a ringside seat for the fight and then celebrating with us in the ring afterwards.

The following day Wayne and I spend the day with the girls sharing a cabana by the pool at the MGM Grand, and in the evening we all go to see Celine Dion in concert at Caesars Palace. We have front-row seats, and have to get our drinks in before the show starts because we can't keep nipping to the bar when Celine's trying to hit her high notes. Jen and Coleen take their seats, while we go to the bar to stock up for the night; just as we're coming back into the arena, we can hear a voice over the PA: 'Ladies and gentleman, please take your seats now, the show is about to start.'

The lights go down and it's all quiet in the arena except for the sound of me and Wayne coming down the aisle overloaded with wine, beer and glasses – clink, clink, clink, clink. We can see everyone looking over, thinking who are these two? and we only just about rattle back to our seats in time for Celine's walk on stage.

DO YOU KNOW WHO I AM? ER, NO . . .

I've never been one to give it the big I am or flash the cash, unlike some people I've fought – no names (Floyd). Even though I got pretty well known in Vegas, had my handsome face plastered across massive billboards around town when I fought there, some of the locals still didn't have a Scooby Doo who I was. Including a couple of the croupiers.

One night I'm with Jen in Caesars Palace on the way back to our hotel room. I stop at a Blackjack table, pull out a $50 note and say: 'Here y'are, Jen, let's have a bet here. Me last fifty dollars.' I hand the note to the croupier to get some chips, but he won't take it. 'No, no, sir. I'm not taking that off you.'

They are supposed to accept all bets, but this guy is genuinely worried for me.

'No, man, you keep that. Have you got kids?'

'Er, yeah.'

'You have? You need that.'

'No, no, it's okay, mate,' I say. 'I've got money. I was only pissing about.'

But he just won't have it. He's really nice about it and I don't want to argue with him so that's the end of my gambling for the night.

Another time, after the Mayweather fight, me and Jen head down to the MGM to have a gamble and relax. I sit down at a Blackjack table and say, 'Can I change two hundred dollars please.'

The croupier says, 'May I see your ID please, sir.'

I rummage around in my pockets and realise I've left my driver's licence back at the apartment. 'Oh, no, I haven't got it with me, luv, sorry.'

Maybe I should be flattered that she thinks I look so young and fresh-faced that I might be under the legal age of twenty-one, but I think it's more a matter that they want to see ID to cover themselves legally. Sometimes they don't ask, but this croupier is insistent. I don't want to have to go all the way back to the apartment to get it, though.

I look down at the table. The poster for my fight with Mayweather had been reproduced on the felt, complete with close-up head shots of me and Floyd.

'That's me!' I say, pointing at the image of my face.

'Nah, man. Go and get your ID, then you can gamble.'

There's some other Brits at the table and a few more standing around watching. 'Honestly, it is him. We came over here to watch him fight.'

She looked at the picture on the table, looked back at me: 'Nah, that's not him. Go and get your ID, come back and then you can play.'

Everyone's looking at her like she's crazy: 'You're joking! He was fighting for the world title on Saturday. In this bloody hotel . . .'

The more people protest, the more she shakes her head: 'Nah, not him.' She isn't having it. In the end, I give up and go looking for another table where the croupier either doesn't ask for ID or knows their boxing.

MIXING WITH BOXING LEGENDS

DURAN, DURAN: SINGING FOR ROBERTO

The first time I saw Roberto Duran in Vegas was at the aborted José Luis Castillo–Diego Corrales III fight in 2006. The fight itself was called off because my future opponent, Castillo, didn't make the weight, but the rest of the show went ahead anyway.

I'm sat at ringside with my brother Matthew when I hear this voice calling my name: 'Ricky! Ricky! Ricky!'

I look around and see a very overweight and scruffily dressed bloke a few rows back, waving at me and smiling. It takes me a second to register who it is. Bloody hell, it's Roberto Duran. When I became a student of boxing history growing up, he was my favourite fighter. I go over, say hello and give him a hug.

'Ah, Ricky, I remember you,' he says.

I had met him once before at a sportsman's dinner in Newcastle long before I was world champion – think I might have been British champ at the time – so I was really surprised he remembered. I was chuffed, but I was also upset to see him in a bad way – I think he had some money troubles at the time.

He had been such a great fighter. Of all the great middleweights of the Hagler/Hearns/Leonard/Duran era, he was the one I related to most. First of all it was down to his aggressive style, especially in his younger days. He had this no-fear attitude where he took on all-comers and wasn't afraid to move up and down in weight to do so. When you think Duran was mixing with the likes of Marvin Hagler at middleweight and Hearns at light middleweight at their best, when his own prime years were as a lightweight, it's incredible. I found it really hard to move up just one division.

Like me in my career, he enjoyed a fight, and like me, I don't think he got enough credit for his boxing ability. But it was not just about his boxing ability, it was the way he always came across as a normal bloke. Once top sportsmen get to the level he did, mixing in celebrity circles, they can get above themselves, but he seemed unaffected. He was just like the people that supported him. I used to watch the old fight videos of him, read stories about him and think, he's Jack the Lad – rough and ready – not got his head up his own arse. That appealed to me and I always wanted to be like that when I became a fighter and had some success.

A few years after bumping into him that time in Vegas, I went to a World Boxing Association convention in Panama with my matchmaker Philippe Fondu. Before we fly out, my agent Paul Speak gets a phone call. He passes on the message to me claiming it was a guy saying that Roberto Duran wants to pick you up from the airport with his brother. I think Paul's on the wind-up, I've not seen Duran since the Castillo non-show and it just seems far too good to be true.

When our plane lands in Panama City, I remain unconvinced until Philippe and I walk into the terminal building and there he is, before we even get to passport control.

'Hey, Ricky!'

He comes over and gives me a hug. He looks slim, healthy, in really good shape – a totally different man to the last time I saw him. Great to see.

There's a queue a mile long at passport control, but Roberto just leads us past everyone to the front: 'Come on, come on . . .'

He's not stopping there. Philippe and I are scrambling to get our passports out of our pockets, but Roberto just walks us straight past the bemused official in the booth. The fella's shouting, 'Roberto, Roberto, passport, passport', but Roberto just gives him the finger and keeps walking. I look back and the official throws his arms out and shrugs his shoulders in surrender, as if this has happened before.

How famous have you got to be in your country that you don't even get stopped at passport control?

He invites us to join him at his pub the following evening. He's got a karaoke machine and I get up there and give the locals a blast of Elvis.

The most famous local of all is not impressed though.

'You barred!' shouts Roberto Duran.

IRON MIKE, 'HURRICANE' PETE AND ME GRAN

I always tended to prefer watching boxing in the lighter divisions – between the welters and middles – but Mike Tyson was an exception to that rule. I enjoy watching all styles of boxing, but my favourite fighters are the ones who don't take a backward step and have it out, so Tyson was right up my street.

He had some of his most memorable fights in Vegas, too, including winning his first world title – the WBC belt – against Trevor Berbick at the age of just twenty to surpass Floyd Patterson as the youngest-ever world champion. The fight was at the Las Vegas Hilton Hotel, it seemed a foregone conclusion that he'd win. Tyson himself said beforehand, 'I'll win the title as surely as

Tuesday follows Monday.' Then he went in the ring and did it in style, 'rubberising' Berbick with a huge left hook in the second round. It was the third knockdown of the fight but it was two for the price of one – as the big Jamaican tried to get up, his legs were misbehaving like he'd just downed a couple of pints of Captain Morgan, and he toppled over again before bravely trying to get up again only to fall into referee Mills Lane's arms.

Within three more fights, Tyson had cleaned up the division, unifying the WBC, WBA and IBF titles when he beat Tony Tucker, and went on to dominate the heavyweight scene for a couple of years until his shock defeat by Buster Douglas.

Then in his second career, after he came out of prison in 1995, promoter Don King got him a six-fight deal with MGM Grand; six of his first seven fights back were staged there. There were some bizarre ones among them, not least his infamous rematch against Evander Holyfield, which ended with him being disqualified for biting a chunk out of Holyfield's right ear. An MGM employee actually found the missing bit of ear lying in the ring afterwards and took it to Holyfield's dressing room where it was placed in an ice bucket. The plan was to go to hospital and hopefully get it reattached, but when the plastic surgeon and one of Holyfield's team dug through the ice pack, it had gone.

A couple of years ago, Mike and Evander made a joke of the incident for a Foot Locker advert, with Mike turning up at Evander's house and presenting him with a small box. 'I'm sorry, Evander,' he says. 'It's your ear. I kept it in formaldehyde.'

Tyson's first fight back after prison was probably one of the most widely anticipated boxing matches of all-time, even though it was a total mismatch. Everyone wanted to see whether Tyson was still the same fighter after four years out of the ring, and every journeyman heavyweight in the world was queuing up for the privilege of being knocked out by him and getting paid a small fortune for their troubles. Twenty-six year old Peter 'Hurricane' McNeeley hit the jackpot, manoeuvred into prime position by his 'colourful' manager Vinnie Vecchione (who was said to have Mafia connections) and promoter Don King (who else?).

At first glance, McNeeley's record looked impressive – 37 wins including 30 knockouts and just one defeat – but it was more padded than a baby's nappy. Only four of his opponents had more wins than losses and fourteen of his wins were against boxers who had never won a fight between them. One of his victims, Ron Drinkwater, had been in retirement for fifteen years (yes, *years*) before McNeeley stopped him inside a round. But, as Don King put it, 'Few boxers have fought lesser fighters with greater skill.'

McNeeley was obviously a tough guy and a half-decent fighter, just nowhere near Tyson's class, and the whole thing was a bit of a circus – with King as ringmaster. At the final pre-fight press conference, he was in full-on bullshit mode, saying, 'The leprechauns will be dancing from glen to glen, the chaps will be singing Irish lullabies and the shamrocks will be shining,' at the prospect of Irish-American McNeeley taking on the former champ. McNeeley himself came up with a belting line, telling Tyson: 'I'm going to wrap you in a cocoon of horror.' I don't know about horror, but Mike nearly split his sides laughing at that one.

To be fair, McNeeley did actually try to deliver on his promise, charging at Tyson from the opening bell like a lunatic, winging in haymakers. The Hurricane's only chance was to blow his ring-rusty opponent away, and he was doing well . . . well, for the eight seconds before Tyson dropped him. McNeeley jumped up straight away, and before the referee – Mills Lane again – could give him a standing count, he was jogging round the ring towards Tyson. Lane had to drag him away to give him the count and tell him to calm down. To be fair, he kept on throwing bombs, before being knocked down again halfway through the round. McNeeley got up and still looked like he wanted to continue, but his manager Vecchione had other ideas, jumping in the ring, meaning his man had to be disqualified.

An estimated two billion people watched the fight, generating $67 million in global pay-per-view sales and $14 million in ticket sales. Tyson had made a reported $25 million for 89 seconds' work, McNeeley around $550,000. Don King, who no doubt made a few million himself, was thrilled, claiming afterwards: 'Tonight I gave you sensation! Spectacle . . . No one has ever gone for Mike like that. It was the most terrific altercation mankind could wish to see.' I'm more of the opinion of the crowd at the MGM, who chanted 'bullshit'.

I used to see Mike out and about in Vegas a lot when I was fighting over there. This was a couple of years after his retirement; he was very overweight at the time and had a vacant look on his face. Mike and I have a lot in common, in that we've both suffered from severe depression, but this was before I got to my bad stage, so I didn't quite understand what he was going through then. I just found it sad to see him like that.

In winter 2013, I was asked to do an interview together with him for *The Clare Balding Show* on BT Sport, but then he was refused entry to the UK. I was gutted, because I was really looking forward to having a proper chat with him. But the producers said they were going to fly him to France instead and would I fancy being flown to France to interview him? Go to France to see Mike Tyson? Yeah, too right I would. I'm so glad I did – I had a brilliant time. Mike looked in great shape and much happier in himself. He's promoting fights and has got a successful theatre show that he's taken all over North America where he talks about his life . . . or lives – he's had about five lives, that fella.

Clare's a brilliant interviewer and had us talking about our fight careers, our problems out of the ring and all sorts of random stuff.

Among other things, Mike revealed he loved *Downton Abbey* ('awesome show') and that Evander Holyfield's ear 'tasted like shit'. He obviously doesn't know his football, though, because he asked me: 'What's the difference between Man United and Man City? I've been in Manchester for long periods of time and I've never heard of Manchester City.' The funny thing was I knew he had actually been to the City of Manchester Stadium before, because I invited him to my fight against Juan Lazcano there in 2008. My after-fight party that night was at Vermilion, a Thai restaurant down the road, and Mike came along to that.

I'm sitting there in the VIP section chatting to him about the fight, and this and that. Then all of a sudden, my grandma, who's sitting nearby, gets her cigarettes out of her handbag and lights one up. Mike leans over and says to her quietly: 'Scuse me, Mrs Hatton, I don't think you're allowed to smoke in here.'

She takes another puff and replies: 'Listen, my grandson's Ricky Hatton and has just topped the bill. You're Mike Tyson. Now, who the hell is going to tell me to stop smoking?'

Can't argue with that logic. Mike shrugs and smiles: 'Okay, give us one too, then,' and joins her for a smoke. I can see the doorman looking over, but my gran was right. There's no way he's going to come over and tell Mike Tyson to put his ciggie out.

THE MANCHESTER MEXICAN

I grew up watching Marco Antonio Barrera fight. He's only four-and-a-half years older than me, but he turned pro in Mexico when he was just fifteen years old. He was Mexican super-flyweight champion five years before I turned pro, and in 1995 at the age of just twenty-one he won his first WBO world title, at super-bantamweight, still two years before I'd had a paid bout.

He was a prodigy, a phenomenal talent who lived up to

his 'Baby-Faced Assassin' nickname. Once his fights started being shown on telly over here, I always tuned in because I loved his aggressive, pressure-fighting style, and learnt a lot from watching him.

Then in 1998, during my second year as a pro, I was lucky enough to fight on the same bill as Marco in Atlantic City as he regained the WBO super-bantamweight title, beating Liverpudlian Richie Wenton in three rounds. I won my fight that night, knocking out a guy from North Carolina called Kevin Carter in the first round, but I didn't think Marco noticed because I was way down the undercard.

Marco Antonio Barrera:

I did notice! I remember that Ricky finished him with body shots and I was impressed at how composed he was and how he hunted and chose his targets. I knew then he would be great.

It would be another four years before I actually spoke to him, and that came about on one of my first trips to Vegas. I went there purely as a fan of his to see his second fight against his great Mexican rival, Érik 'El Terrible' Morales at the MGM Grand. Their first fight in 2000 had been an all-time classic (see *Ricky's top ten Vegas tear-ups*, page 192), with Morales edging a controversial split decision, and I wanted to be there to see the rematch.

I turn up a couple of days before with my mate Simon and we go to a few bars where we mix in with all the Mexican fans who have come to see the fight, which this time is being fought at featherweight. Everyone's excited to see what is being billed as 'The Ultimate Feud' between their country's two best fighters since the heyday of the legendary Julio César Chávez. Although

I've made a bit of a name for myself back in England as the WBU light welterweight champion, I'm surprised that most of the Mexican fans recognise me, which shows how fanatical they are about their boxing. They're telling me they like how I fight, that I fight like a Mexican.

When I rock up to watch the weigh-in at the MGM Grand a Mexican lady comes up to me. 'Ah, Ricky Hatton, Ricky Hatton,' she says. 'Picture, picture . . .'

So I have my photo taken with her and a bit later I get recognised again as I'm walking through the casino. 'Oh my God, Ricky Hatton!' says a guy wearing a 'Team Barrera' tracksuit.

'Hiya, nice to meet you.'

'Are you over for the fight?'

'Yeah, I'm a massive Barrera fan.'

'I work with Marco,' he replies. 'He's a massive fan of yours too!'

'Get to fuck.'

'Seriously.'

He introduces himself. His name is Robert Diaz (yes, the same Robert Diaz who went on to become Golden Boy's matchmaker) and he insists that he really does work with Barrera. 'Please come and see him. Marco would love to meet you.'

'Really? Alright, then. What, now?'

'Yeah, come on.'

So we go up to Marco's suite and there he is with his whole family, which surprises me because I didn't like to be around my family during the week of the fight – that was when I felt I had to get a bit nasty. When Marco sees me, a big smile crosses his face and he comes over and shakes my hand. 'Oh, Ricky Hatton! I love the way you fight! Love the body punching!'

Here's one of my heroes telling me how much he enjoyed watching me fight. It's surreal. Incredible.

Marco Antonio Barrera:

Ricky was becoming a force to be reckoned with in the boxing world and I had seen a few of his fights. They were always action-packed and he applied non-stop pressure on opponents. As Floyd Mayweather Jr. would later say about Ricky after fighting him, 'Ricky Hatton came to fight,' whereas most of Floyd's opponents were just trying to go the distance with him. Ricky always came to fight.

As people, we got along from the day we met. He's a man's man. He's also a very funny guy – he has a great sense of humour and tells a great story. We are both professional fighters and belong to a sort of fraternity – we are the only people who really understand one another.

Marco introduces me and Simon to everyone in the room, his wife, kids, grandparents – and someone I recognise. It turns out that the woman who asked me for a photo at the weigh-in was Marco's mum.

Marco Antonio Barrera:

My mother is a real boxing fan and, yes, she was a fan of Ricky's! Ricky always had exciting fights, and that's why boxing fans like my mum supported him.

They're all off to have a meal and Marco invites us along to join them.

'Do you like sushi?'

'Yeah, yeah.'

Fucking hate it. Not really my idea of a post weigh-in meal, but we're just saying yes to everything because we're so happy to be there in Marco's company. At the restaurant, they're bringing out little plates of sushi, one after the other. Marco and his crew are all digging in. Me and Simon are forcing it down, because we don't want to be impolite.

'You enjoying the sushi?'

'Ah, it's lovely this.'

Afterwards, Marco has to go back to his room to rest, so we say our goodbyes. As we wave to him, I turn to Simon: 'Come on, let's go for a steak . . .'

The fight itself is another absorbing contest, but I'm delighted that this time my new mate Marco comes out on top, taking a close but unanimous decision. In theory, Morales's WBC featherweight belt was on the line, but Marco didn't accept it, instead opting to take *The Ring* magazine's vacant title belt instead.

It's my first live experience of a Vegas fight night and the Mexicans certainly created a lively atmosphere. But, without wishing to sound disrespectful, the audience of 16,000 is fewer than the 20,000 people already coming to see me at the M.E.N. Arena back in Manchester, and it's nothing like the football match-style atmosphere of those occasions. I'm looking around thinking, 'Wait till I get my lot over here – they'll take the roof off this place.' I meet a couple of Nevada Boxing Commission officials at the fight who seem keen on the prospect too: 'Hey, Ricky, can't wait until you come and fight here.'

It would be four and a half years before I achieved that ambition, but I made two great friends in Marco and Robert Diaz that week.

Marco and me would support each other whenever we were fighting. I invited him over for the Kostya Tszyu fight, but he couldn't make it. Then Marco found that he couldn't get the fight on TV back home, so instead he was on the phone to Robert, who was watching it on telly in America, for updates every few minutes:

'How's he doing, how's he doing?' They were both very nervous because they knew how good Kostya was and they were thrilled for me when I won.

The following year, Marco invited me to carry his belt to the ring with him at the MGM Grand for his WBC world super-featherweight title rematch against Rocky Juarez. That was a great privilege, and having won their first bout on a split decision, Marco came out on top again, this time getting the nod from all three judges.

The first fight of mine Robert came to in the States was my Vegas debut against Juan Urango. That was at the Paris hotel, a relatively small venue compared to where I'd end up, but he couldn't believe how many Brits came out to support me. He'd grown up watching mega fights involving Mexican legends like Chávez, Barrera and Oscar De La Hoya – fights that united two countries, America and Mexico – but even he was blown away by the atmosphere that my fans generated.

Robert Diaz:

I had never experienced anything like the weigh-in, for example. I didn't know anything about English football culture at the time, so when I heard his supporters singing 'There's only one Ricky Hatton', I thought, this guy has his own song! When I came over to Britain and saw George Groves fighting in an amateur show and heard fans singing 'There's only one George Groves', I thought they'd copied Ricky's song. It was only years after the Castillo fight when I attended a Man United game and heard the whole crowd singing 'There's only one Wayne Rooney' that I realised. I still think the song flows better with Ricky's name in it, though.

Marco Antonio Barrera:

I think most fighters would be envious of what Ricky had and still has with his fans. It was amazing to watch – the British fans are the best! I was always more popular and recognised outside of my home country of Mexico. I fought so much in the US and at that time few fights were broadcast in Mexico, especially the pay-per-view events. I think Ricky is a very fortunate person to have so many people who admire and support him.

I was present at both the Mayweather and Pacquiao fights and the crowd was amazing; the energy was amazing. I also travelled to Sheffield in the UK for his fight with Carlos Maussa. The Brits are very passionate about boxing and it was a very unique atmosphere, like he had the whole country behind him.

It was great to have Marco and Robert pulling for me, and never more so than my big Vegas fight against José Luis Castillo, because Castillo had his own Mexican legend in his corner – the amazing Julio César Chávez. Chávez had been Castillo's childhood hero and become one of his closest friends. They first met in 1996, introduced by mutual friends when Chávez was looking for sparring partners. By then Chávez was past his absolute peak, no longer regarded as the best boxer pound-for-pound in the world, but he was still involved in some huge fights. Indeed, that year he took on Oscar De La Hoya, then young and undefeated, at Caesars Palace in Las Vegas. Even though Chávez was the defending WBC light welterweight champ, Oscar was already a two-weight world champion and a 2–1 bookies favourite to become champion in a third weight class in only his twenty-first fight. Chávez's cause wasn't helped either when he got cut over his left eye in training just five days before the fight. Chávez didn't want the fight postponed so he'd kept quiet about the injury – and somehow the doctor from the Nevada State Athletic Commission didn't notice it in the pre-fight medical – but sure enough the scar opened up in the first round. By the fourth round blood was pouring down his face and the bout had to be stopped. Chávez kept fighting for another seven years and for four and a half of those, Castillo was his main sparring partner and built up his own reputation fighting on Chávez's undercards.

To spar regularly with an all-time great must have been a great education for Castillo and it helped him to go from being an unknown to a world champion himself, when he beat Stevie Johnston to win the WBC world lightweight title. For that fight, Chávez played the sparring partner role, even turning southpaw to mimic Johnston's left-handed style.

Castillo's Mexican promoter had apparently told Bob Arum (Johnston's promoter) that Castillo was a crude boxer who would give Johnston a decent fight – but not enough to beat him. Castillo proved he was a lot better than that, winning a gruelling fight on a split decision. The bout was nominated as *The Ring* magazine Upset of the Year.

Bob Arum himself promoted Castillo in the US after that, and Chávez continued to help him as his career went from strength to strength. He fought Floyd Mayweather twice for the lightweight world title, and lost by unanimous decision both times, but the first fight was very close – much closer than the judges scored it – and I thought Castillo actually did enough to win.

Apparently, Castillo and Chávez got on so well because they had a very similar sense of humour and they both enjoyed partying, eating, drinking between fights and consequently putting on lots of weight . . . remind you of anyone?

Even after they became friends, though, Castillo still regarded Chávez as a hero, so much so that he took to wearing a red headband to the ring, the way Chávez did, as a tribute. But before he did so, he travelled all the way to Chávez's home in Culiacan to ask for permission first. He thought Chávez might be upset if he copied him, but Chávez was happy for him to carry on the tradition.

I'm in a similar situation with Marco before my fight against Castillo. While we're good friends by this time, I still also think of him as one of my boxing heroes. I've carried his belt in before the Juarez fight and I really want to invite him to do the same for me. But when I ask him, I half-expect him to say no, as I am fighting against one of his fellow Mexicans.

'I'd love to,' he says.

Marco Antonio Barrera:

It was an honour to be there with Ricky for that fight. I did speak to Castillo beforehand and I explained my friendship with Ricky and he understood. He was gracious and thanked me for being honest.

Billy Graham and me always plan our fight tactics together and don't really listen to anyone else. But Marco does give me some good advice that sticks with me.

'Do your body punching which you're good at, but Castillo throws a lot of hooks so don't forget the punches down the middle,' he says. 'Remember, Ricky – a good straight left jab will get there first.'

As well as walking to the ring with Marco, I also want to wear a sombrero, but again I'm worried how that will go down with the Mexican fans. When Floyd Mayweather fought Castillo he wore a sombrero on his ringwalk but I think he did it just to wind up Castillo and his supporters. With me, I love the Mexican style of boxing and it was more about showing that, but would they think I was being disrespectful? I ask Robert for his opinion.

'By all means, do it,' he replies. 'They'd be offended if you didn't fight like a Mexican. If you danced, boxed and held and played it safe, they'd boo. But they'll be honoured and proud and accept you because you actually fight like a Mexican.'

Robert is so into the idea, he even goes as far as getting an authentic sombrero made for me in Mexico. Authentic, with 'El Matador' sewn into the brim . . . and in the Man City colours, of course.

So come fight night, there's Castillo coming to the ring wearing his red headband, with Julio César Chávez by his side. Then when it's my turn to enter the arena, I've got my own Mexican boxing legend, Marco Antonio Barrera, carrying one of my belts. As well as the sombrero, I'm wearing a poncho with 'Manchester Mexican' embroidered on the front.

It's a bit like an all-Mexican boxing event . . . well, apart from the thousands of Brits in the audience, the Winston Churchill 'Fight them on the beaches' speech and then 'Blue Moon' played as I walk into the arena.

Manchester Mexican? Yes, I like to think that I lived up to the nickname that night, beating a top-class Mexican fighter at his own game.

Marco Antonio Barrera:

Ricky was a great fighter – intense and relentless. He only had two defeats in his career (I don't count his last fight as a pro as a real loss because he wasn't really in the game at that point) and when you are fighting at the top level, it's so hard to win them all. When Ricky was on he was on – those were the days to remember.

In my opinion, Ricky lost nothing in those fights with Mayweather and Pacquiao – he fought and gave his best against two elite fighters, two of the greatest of all time.

Ricky fully deserved the 'Manchester Mexican' nickname – when I spent some time with him while he was in training camp for Pacquiao, I even gave him some lessons in Mexican dancing. In the ring, I loved the way Ricky attacked the body – just like a great Mexican warrior.

He's a true Brit with a touch of Mexican!

RICKY'S TOP TEN VEGAS TEAR-UPS

Here's my selection of the most memorable Las Vegas scraps of all time, ranked from ten to one. There's been so many great fights in Vegas down the years that I'm sure I've missed out a few belters, but these ones all have significance to me in one way or the other, either because I was there in person or because of the great boxers involved. In the words of Michael Buffer (and Ant and Dec), let's get ready to rumble . . .

10
Kostya Tszyu vs. Zab Judah
3 November 2001
MGM Grand

This one might not feature in many people's top ten Vegas tear-ups, but it was an explosive fight and a significant one for me personally, because it was the first Vegas boxing show I ever went to. I'd knocked out American Freddie Pendleton inside two rounds to retain my WBU light welterweight title the previous week, and me and Billy Graham decided last-minute to fly to Vegas and combine a much needed post-fight jolly with checking out the two top guys in the division – and my possible future opponents.

We just pitched up there, no hotel booked, nothing, and had a great time. Adam Smith and a Sky TV crew came out there too to cover the fight and do a bit of filming with us on the Strip. I was a bright-eyed twenty-three-year-old enjoying the dazzling lights of Vegas, and a big unification fight.

Zab 'Super' Judah came to the ring with a perfect 27–0 record. At just twenty-four years old, he had already made five successful defences of his IBF light welterweight title, including a landslide points win over Sheffield's Junior Witter at Hampden Park. A fast, flamboyant southpaw, Judah made Floyd Mayweather sound modest. He was already claiming to be 'the best pound-for-pound fighter in the world, the best that ever did it, number one for ever'. Like Mike Tyson, Judah is from Brooklyn, New York, and Mike is a mate of his – Mike could even be seen among his entourage on the night, chanting 'Ju-dah, Ju-dah' in the dressing room.

'The Thunder from Down Under', Kostya Tszyu, was eight years older and more my kind of fighter. Born and raised in the old Soviet Union, winning 259 amateur fights and the amateur world championship, before migrating to Australia with his girlfriend, he fought more like a Mexican. His bone-crunching body shots had seen him compared to the great Julio César Chávez, and he also had one-punch KO power. He'd won the IBF light welterweight world title in only his fourteenth fight, back in 1995, and, like Judah, he now had twenty-seven wins under his belt, including a successful world title defence against someone I'd go up against years later – trainer, 'Uncle' Roger Mayweather. The only blemish on Tszyu's record was an upset defeat in his sixth defence of that IBF title by Vince Phillips (another future opponent of mine), but he bounced back to win both the WBC and WBA versions of the title, demolishing an ageing Julio Cesár Chávez along the way.

Tszyu was totally the opposite of Judah out of the ring – a quiet, modest family man. 'I want to be remembered not only as a champion, but as a good person,' he said before the fight.

The prize on the line for Tszyu and Judah on the night was to become the first man in thirty-three years to unify the three major belts in the 140-pound division.

Judah makes a confident start, nailing Tszyu on the chin with a big left uppercut halfway through the first round and dancing in and out of range to dominate the action with his lightning speed. But in the second round, Tszyu stalks him down and started to connect with a stiff-looking jab. Then with seconds to go, boom! Tszyu levels him with a perfectly timed right hand. Judah jumps up straight away, but his legs are doing a river dance and he topples over face first again. By the time he gets up a second time, the referee has already waved the fight off. Takes some doing to knock someone down twice with one punch, but that's the power Tszyu had.

While Tszyu celebrates, Judah goes berserk, chucking his corner stool across the ring and sticking his left glove under the ref's chin (later, he gets banned for six months and fined $75,000 for his shenanigans).

One journalist asked me after the fight whether I still fancied fighting Kostya after seeing that devastating knockout. I was, like: 'Yeah, of course, I'd love to fight him one day, I'll beat him.' I don't think anyone really took me that seriously, and I don't blame them, but I think my self-belief was the main reason I achieved what I did in my career. It wasn't so much the talent I had as the belief and I wasn't scared of taking on anyone.

After an exciting night of boxing, Billy and me go out and get blind drunk, so we're not in the best state when we check out of the MGM the following morning. But through bleary eyes I spot a huddle of people wearing 'TEAM TSZYU' tracksuits across the reception, including the man himself.

'I'm going to congratulate him on knocking that loudmouth out,' I say to Billy and wander over.

'Hey, Kostya. Well done last night. Congratulations.'

'Thank you.'

'My name's Ricky Hatton, I'm from Manchester in England.'

'Nice to meet you, do you want a picture?'

'Yeah, if you don't mind. I'm a light welterweight, I've just got into the top ten. I'm going to fight you one day.'

'Yeah, alright. Nice one.'

Three and a half years on, at the press conference to announce our fight, Kostya leans over and says to me:

'You said you would fight me, didn't you?'

I was amazed and absolutely made up that he'd remembered the half-cut Brit coming up to him.

In November 2014, I was in Melbourne where my Belarussian fighter Sergey Rabchenko was taking on the Aussie veteran Anthony Mundine. While we were Down Under, I saw Kostya for the first time since our 2005 fight, when he came along to the press conference. I had the privilege of spending an evening with him at an Australian Boxing Hall of Fame dinner.

It was fantastic to see him again and, as I said to the press out there, it was certainly a lot less painful than when we boxed. He is such a genuinely nice fella, a gentleman, and we had a great time chatting about old times and taking selfies. It was like I'd only seen him last week, not nine years ago – we had such a laugh together.

To beat such a great champion was the greatest win of my career. Winning the world title is one thing, but to beat someone who was in the top three pound-for-pound fighters at the time, one of the greatest light-welters of all-time, was extra special.

Kostya was the hardest puncher I ever faced, it was just that I was prepared to walk through walls that night and his punches just bounced off me. It was the same earlier in my career when I fought Vince Phillips – I'd won almost every round, went in to finish him off and walked onto a huge right uppercut. I didn't know where I was for about half a minute, but somehow recovered. Mayweather and Pacquiao knocked me out later in my career, but I think that by then my punch resistance was nowhere near as good as it was back then. I'd had over forty fights, and with my come-forward style of fighting – taking one or two punches to land a hurtful one – there were a lot of miles on the clock. When you're younger and fresher, you can take the punishment, but as you get older, training hard for fight after fight, taking more punches, the wear and tear does catch up with you. Kostya faced me at my absolute peak.

Just as important as the fight itself was the way we both conducted ourselves afterwards. It couldn't have been a more physically demanding fight, but once it was over we were mates. That's how it should be, but it's not always the case when you get to top level and there's so much on the line. He was a winner almost all the way through his career, he wasn't used to losing, but he still showed a lot of class in defeat and that says everything about his character.

Kostya said that he could still remember every detail of that night and had great memories of it despite the defeat. He was actually grateful to me for making him realise that he had other things in his life other than boxing and it was time to do something different. He promised his mum that he wouldn't get back in the ring again, and he's been as good as his word; but he still dabbles in boxing. He's based in Moscow nowadays where he is a businessman with interests in the water industry, but he has kept his gym in Sydney – his son Nikita is a good amateur. Kostya started training at nine years old, so he's been involved in the boxing game for thirty-six years and he says he'll always be involved in one way or another. We'll always have a special bond from that epic fight in Manchester.

9
Barry McGuigan vs. Steve Cruz
23 June 1986
Caesars Palace, Outdoor Arena

Barry McGuigan was one of my heroes as a little boy growing up in the Eighties. At that time, I was too young to know much about boxing, but I loved his all-action style, as it meant he was never in a boring fight. As I got older and became more and more interested in boxing and its history, he was someone I looked up to and wanted to emulate. Barry was a great inside fighter with a wicked left hook to the body, but also was a really decent bloke who was loved by boxing fans and the general public alike.

He was brought up close to the border of Northern Ireland during the Troubles, but the whole of the UK and Ireland seemed to unite behind 'The Clones Cyclone' whenever he fought. Barry, a Roman Catholic, married a Protestant; he just refused to take sides. People admired him for that and wherever he fought, from Belfast to Dublin to London, he packed out venues, while millions watched him on TV and cheered him on. The King's Hall in Belfast was reopened purely because they needed a venue suitable to host Barry's fights.

Seeing that incredible atmosphere when he ripped the WBA world featherweight title from Panama's Eusebio Pedroza at Loftus Road in front of 27,000 fans inspired me. Pedroza was regarded as one of the best featherweights of the twentieth century and yet Barry knocked him down in the eighth and won a landslide decision which shows just how good he was too.

His fights were huge events and drew in people beyond hardcore boxing fans. Twenty million BBC1 viewers watched that fight, and when Barry talks about all the celebrities who came to his dressing room that night, it reminds me of my biggest nights in Vegas. The likes of George Best, Pat Jennings, Alex 'Hurricane' Higgins and even Lucian Freud, Britain's greatest artist and a huge boxing fan, turned up to support him. Incredible.

Because Barry had such a huge fanbase in the UK and Ireland, he hadn't needed to fight in America before, apart from a bout in Chicago fairly early in his career. Like me, it was only when he'd won the world title that he decided to break America. After defending his title in Belfast and then Dublin, his Vegas fight in June 1986 against a little-known Texan called Steve 'Super Kid' Cruz was supposed to be the start of superstardom for him in the States.

Cruz had stepped in when Barry's original opponent, a stocky Argentinian called Fernando Sosa, had pulled out with a detached retina. Cruz was lanky, and a totally different style to Sosa, but no one expected Barry to lose. Boxing fans were all looking ahead to a proposed unification match against the great Ghanaian boxer Azumah Nelson. What they hadn't factored in was that the fight was to take place outdoors in the car park at Caesars Palace in the middle of a Nevada summer. Pale Irishman against a Texan in a fifteen-rounder in temperatures approaching 125-degrees – what could possibly go wrong?

The brutal conditions sapped Barry of his normally incredible stamina. It didn't help that Cruz, a 9–1 underdog, produced the fight of his life. There's a famous photo of Barry in his corner between rounds, looking glassy-eyed and exhausted, and it says everything about his fighting heart that he made it through the fifteen rounds and nearly retained his title. The three-knockdown rule was in effect, and when Barry was knocked down for a second time with half a minute to go in the final round, it was a miracle he managed to get up and see out the fight on rubber legs. The 10–7 round was decisive on two judges' cards, though, as Cruz took a close but unanimous decision by scores of 143–142, 143–139 and 142–141.

Credit to Cruz, he was working as a $6.50-an-hour plumber's assistant and training for a $4,000 fight when he got the call to fight Barry. He took his chance of a lifetime and the $70,000 purse he earned more than paid for his planned wedding and honeymoon. After the fight he said that he was going back to his job as a plumber, though, adding: 'I think I'm going to ask for a raise.'

Meanwhile, Barry was so badly dehydrated, he had to be put on an IV drip and hospitalised after an almost life-or-death battle. Thankfully, he was okay. He didn't box for a couple of years after the defeat and he never regained the world title. But even though his Vegas experience had been hellish, the courage Barry had shown in a fight named as *The Ring*'s 'Fight of the Year' will never be forgotten.

I can't imagine fighting in brutally hot conditions like that. The nearest I got to that was training in the legendary Kronk Gym in Detroit, when I went out there back in 2000 to defend my WBO Inter-Continental light welterweight title against Costa Rican Gilbert 'Animal' Quiros.

The gym was in the basement and the late Emmanuel Steward, who was in charge, always kept the radiators turned up as high as they'd go so it was over a hundred degrees in there. It was horrific – hotter than a sauna, sweat pouring down the walls.

If anyone ever got a cold virus in that gym, everyone must have got it. You can't argue with results, though, and so many top fighters came from there – Tommy Hearns, of course, then the likes of two-time WBA welterweight champ Mark Breland and the brothers Milton and Steve McCrory who both won world titles. The gold and red colours of Kronk became world-famous and it was a dream come true for me to train there, despite the hellish conditions. As a pro boxer I wanted to go there at least once in my life and I'm glad I had the chance before it closed in 2006. Luckily for me, it was the week of the fight so my training was tapering down.

Everyone in there is black, and I walk in, like a milk bottle, and I can feel all eyes on me as I'm warming up. Then when I go on the heavy bag, the other boxers in the gym are taking the piss out of the way I grunt as I throw punches, mimicking me: 'Uhhh, uhhh, uhhh.' I do look very young for my age and they're probably thinking, 'Who is this little shit?'

Then Billy Graham puts on the body belt and we get in the ring and do a few rounds. I'm throwing my combinations, power punches – bang, bang, b-bang, bang, bang, bang. Soon everyone's standing round the ring watching me. When I get out, one guy goes: 'How many fights have you had, man?'

'Nineteen, unbeaten.'

'Wow, man.'

Now they've seen what I can do, I've got their respect.

That was a great experience . . . but I'm glad I never had to actually fight anyone in that sort of heat, unlike Barry. Air-conditioned indoor arenas in Vegas suited me fine, thanks.

8
Nigel Benn vs. Iran Barkley
18 August 1990
Bally's Las Vegas

Watching Nigel Benn was what first made me want to become a boxer myself. When I reached the age of eleven or twelve, that great British middleweight era of Benn, Chris Eubank, and Michael Watson was just beginning, and those fights were being shown live on TV. Everyone had their favourite among them; Benn was always mine. He was hugely exciting to watch, and never took a backward step. I wanted to be like him. It was only as I started to look into boxing history that Roberto Duran took over as my favourite, but Benn was my first boxing hero.

It was a great thrill for me to meet Nigel years later as I made my way in the pro game. He was in Manchester the day of my WBU title defence against Aldo Rios in 2003 and came and had lunch with me. We've since worked together on various sportsman's dinners before he emigrated to Australia. Most recently, I bumped into Nigel at the WBC convention in Vegas in December 2014. While we were out there, Sky Sports interviewed him for a *Ringside Special* programme on my life and career and he told them, 'Ricky's one of my heroes.' I couldn't believe that coming from the man who was the reason I started boxing. He also spoke to me about possibly training his son Conor, a promising light welterweight. Nigel reckons Conor is more talented than he was, so he must be good.

After Michael Watson had beaten him in 1989 and taken his Commonwealth title belt, Nigel went to America to rebuild his career, and after four fights within a year he'd beaten Doug De Witt to claim the World Boxing Organisation world middleweight title. The WBO had only just been created, but Nigel and then Chris Eubank helped to establish it as a major belt.

He didn't pick an easy first defence, taking on Iran 'The Blade' Barkley. Barkley was coming off two successive losses, but they were both agonisingly close defeats in world title matches against top-class opposition – Roberto Duran on a split decision and (then) undefeated Michael Nunn on a majority vote. Before that he'd caused a massive upset in a war at the Las Vegas Hilton, stopping Tommy Hearns in the third round after being beaten up for two rounds and cut above both eyes.

Barkley was from the Bronx and tougher than old boots. The story behind 'The Blade' nickname was that he'd been part of a street gang whose initiation ceremony involved walking between two lines of gang members who smacked you with bike chains and baseball bats. Barkley made it through that . . . and Benn only had his fists and boxing gloves to hit him with. Not that 'The Dark Destroyer' was one to be intimidated – he'd been in the army and had plenty of street fights in his time.

The fight could actually have been Benn's homecoming, but the British Boxing Board of Control wouldn't allow it because Barkley had needed eye surgery on a detached retina after the Nunn fight. It went ahead at Bally's in Vegas instead, and Benn went for Barkley from the opening bell, knocking him down in his own corner, catching him again as he jumped straight up before the referee had a chance to give the count. Looking for the finish, Benn then got caught by two left hooks by Barkley and suddenly was on the ropes himself. Then both men were just loading up throwing huge bombs, until Benn had Barkley toppling over again with about half a minute left in the round. He was lucky not to get disqualified for hitting him again with a right while he was down, but the ref only warned him. When Barkley touched down again a few seconds later, it was all over on the three-knockdown rule.

Two minutes and fifty-seven seconds of total mayhem.

7
Sugar Ray Leonard vs. Thomas Hearns I
16 September 1981
Caesars Palace, Outdoor Arena

This welterweight unification war in September 1981 saw two special boxers in the same weight class fighting each other at their absolute peak. Staged outside at Caesars Palace, it was one of the mega fights that established Las Vegas as the new Mecca of boxing in America. I love watching the old footage of the build-up and the fight.

At the first press conference, Leonard claimed, 'You're in store for what I consider the greatest fight in history,' and it was a massive promotion even by today's standards. WBC champ Leonard got paid $11 million and WBA champ Hearns $5.1 million, and both fighters did three weeks of media promotion before they went into serious training. Not that it was a fight that needed any hype.

The young Larry Merchant called it as 'Sugar Ray, a master boxer and puncher, against Tommy Hearns, a devastating puncher and boxer'. Leonard had just one loss on his thirty-one fight record – to Roberto Duran, which he had since avenged when Roberto said '*No Más*' in the rematch. The six-foot-one-inch tall Hearns came to the ring with a four-and-a-half-inch reach advantage, an unblemished record of thirty-two wins in thirty-two fights, and thirty KOs courtesy of his atomic right-hand.

I admired both of them – Hearns for his explosiveness, punching power and because he always went for the knockout, very exciting; Leonard because he could box, punch, fight . . . he could do it all – one of the most naturally gifted boxers in history.

The fight started as expected with Ray boxing and moving and Hearns stalking him and trying to cut off the ring. Hearns was getting the upper hand and Ray's left eye was swelling up, which caused him to change tactics and, as he put it, 'Go to work'. In the sixth and seventh rounds, Ray battered him and nearly knocked him out, only for Hearns to show his heart too, and win the ninth to twelfth rounds on all judges' cards.

That's when Ray's legendary trainer, Angelo Dundee, famously told his man in the corner: 'You've only got nine minutes. You're blowing it now, son. You're blowing it . . . You gotta fire. You're not firing. Separate the men from the boys now, we're blowing it.'

Leonard was well behind on all the scorecards, partly because his big sixth and seventh rounds had only been scored 10–9 rather than 10–8, so Dundee had reason to be worried. Although afterwards he denied that he actually thought Leonard was losing, saying that he just 'wanted to give him a little zest'.

At the time, one of the HBO co-commentators said it was a bad thing to tell a fighter because it makes them worry too much. How a commentator can say that against a trainer who spends every day with his fighter, I don't know. As a trainer myself now, I think it was perfect advice in the circumstances – the fight was slipping away from Leonard. Sometimes you need to be told.

A good trainer has the right word to say at the right time. Billy Graham was great at that with me. He knew exactly what I needed at different times. He gave me a Dundee-style dressing-down – only with more swear words – when I fought Gilbert Quiros in Detroit. Quiros cut me over the left eye with the first punch he threw and, to make matters worse, by the end of the round the eye was almost closed. The doctor examined the eye and I was told that they'd give me one more round. At that moment, I did think I've lost this and Billy sensed that.

'You've fucking given in, haven't you?'

'No, no I haven't.'

'The first time your back's been up against the wall, you've crumbled. World champion? I tell you, you're going fucking nowhere, son.'

I didn't like it, but Billy was right – it was the first time in my career I'd sat on my stool and almost resigned myself to defeat – and his words had the desired effect. I was fuming and, even though I was half-blind, I went out and stopped Quiros in the next round.

Dundee's kick up the arse did the same trick for Leonard. With his left eye closing fast, he smashed Hearns through the ropes with a furious combination in the next round and had him sitting on the rope again taking a standing (well, half-standing) count at the bell.

Hearns bravely kept going into the fourteenth round, but the fight had turned on its head, with Hearns on his bike and Ray chasing round the ring until the ref stopped it.

Ray paid tribute to his opponent straight afterwards: 'I said earlier that he didn't have brains in the ring, but he proved to me that he had enough natural ability to outmanoeuvre me . . . it ended up a matter of conditioning and stamina.' He only just had enough; Hearns had pushed him so hard, Ray nearly collapsed after that interview.

There were nearly 24,000 spectators at Caesars and 300 million watching on TV that night and they'd seen an all-time classic. In an interview a couple of years ago, Ray recalled the battle saying: 'Tommy Hearns brought out the best in me, and I brought out the best in him. Did I want to quit? No. But it was close. It's one of those things where I was like, I don't need this shit. But the part of me that's the fighter was like, hey, you've got to kill me, baby.'

He also claimed that both he and Hearns as they were then in their prime would beat Floyd Mayweather Jr. by a knockout. I'm not so sure. There were some great fighters around in the era that Leonard and Hearns fought, like Marvin Hagler, Roberto Duran and even the likes of Pipino Cuevas. But Floyd has beaten all-comers, including great fighters like Oscar de la Hoya and bigger men like Saul Alvarez. I'll get splinters in my arse and say that if Sugar Ray at his peak fought Floyd six times, they'd probably win three each!

Fighting Tommy Hearns would have been a tough task for anyone at welterweight because of his physique. He was six-foot-one and had a seventy-eight-inch reach, which is fourteen inches greater than mine! But it's not just the reach that is important, it's the timing of when you throw the shot. All my opponents had a reach advantage over me and that's how I overcame that, and that's how Mike Tyson (who was just five-foot-ten) was able to outjab much taller heavyweights when he was at his best. It would certainly have been interesting to see how Floyd could have dealt with Hearns.

Eighteen years after that great fight with Ray Leonard, Hearns boxed in Manchester at the M.E.N. Arena against Nate Miller for the IBO cruiserweight title in 1999. He was forty by then and some way past his best. Beforehand, everyone was excited to see Tommy Hearns fight in the flesh, but when the fight got underway it was clear he just didn't have it anymore. He actually won the fight by unanimous decision, but people were walking out before the final bell. It was heartbreaking to see that happen to someone who was once arguably the most exciting boxer in the world and got people on the edge of their seats.

He came to train at Billy Graham's gym in Salford for that fight, along with his trainer Manny Steward. I was a twenty-year-old novice then, with only eleven pro fights under my belt, so to have this iconic boxer in our gym was massive for us.

Tommy was in the ring working with Manny, and when they had a break, Billy introduced me: 'This is Ricky Hatton – he's called "The Hitman" as well'.

'Ah right, Ricky, come in here . . .'

So I got in the ring and Tommy showed me a few moves. It was great. I still see Tommy nowadays at WBC annual conventions. One time, I was waiting at the bar for my matchmaker, and he walked past.

'Hey, Ricky, how're you doing?'

He's the original 'Hitman', an absolute legend of the sport, but he was chatting to me like his mate. It's something else.

I was also really flattered when Sugar Ray said some lovely things about me on the 2005 BBC Sports Personality of the Year show, following my win over Kostya Tszyu. He said, 'One thing I admire and respect about Ricky Hatton is that he has maintained perspective. He has not become a prima donna, he's become a world champion but a champion to his people. If boxing had more Ricky Hattons, it would be a better sport.'

Coming from him that meant a lot.

6
Riddick Bowe vs. Evander Holyfield II
6 November 1993
Caesars Palace, Outdoor Arena

These two fought a great heavyweight trilogy in Las Vegas. In truth, the first fight at the Thomas & Mack Center the previous year was the best of the lot, but this second fight will always stick in my mind because of 'The Fan Man' landing in the ring.

Already an all-time great at cruiserweight, Holyfield had moved up to the heavyweight division and become the unified champ. But he'd won the belts against a massively unfit James 'Buster' Douglas, who looked like he'd been eating McDonalds every day since his shock win over Mike Tyson. His first three defences were against two old-timers George Foreman and Larry Holmes, and the journeyman Bert Cooper in between, so 'Big Daddy' Bowe was seen as his first major test.

Holyfield went into the first fight as a 7–5 favourite, but some critics suspected that he wasn't naturally big enough to beat the giants of the division like Bowe. Holyfield fought like the true warrior he is, especially in a classic tenth round where Bowe hurt him early with a peach of an uppercut and he battled back bravely. But the size and power of Bowe told, as he dropped Holyfield in the eleventh and won a clear unanimous decision.

By the time of this rematch a year later outdoors at Caesars, Bowe had infamously chucked the WBC belt in the bin after negotiations to fight Lennox Lewis had broken down, so only the WBA and IBF belts were on the line.

Both men came into the ring nearly a stone heavier than for the last fight – Bowe weighing 246 pounds to Holyfield's 217 – but the extra poundage on Holyfield was muscle, whereas with Bowe it looked like blubber. Holyfield's superior fitness and relentlessness told as he more than matched Bowe both in the boxing and slugging departments to take a close majority decision.

But Holyfield's great performance will be forever overshadowed by what happened early in the seventh round, when James 'The Fan Man' Miller flew in on a motorised paraglider and crash-landed into the ring ropes.

Holyfield and Bowe stopped beating the hell out of each other and stood there in disbelief, as it all kicked off outside the ring. One of Bowe's security guys clocked Miller round the head with one those big old mobile phones, knocking him unconscious. Meanwhile, Bowe's pregnant wife, Judy, fainted and Reverend Jesse Jackson and others helped her out of the arena.

Bowe wanted to leave the ring to be with her, but Jackson came back and told him: 'She's alright – focus on your business.'

Luckily, tests at the local hospital later showed mother and baby were fine.

The two fighters had to sit in their corners in their robes and wrapped in towels for twenty minutes, while The Fan Man's chute was untangled from the ring lights and he was stretchered away.

The Fan Man got off lightly considering it was such reckless stunt. He could have killed someone if he'd landed a couple of rows back, but apart from getting a beating, he was only charged with dangerous flying and released on a $200 bail.

As to how the bizarre incident and delay affected the outcome of the fight, if anything Bowe seemed to benefit more. He'd been showing signs of tiredness before the seventh round, but he came out looking much fresher after the break, so Holyfield deserves all the credit for getting the win.

Before rushing away to see his wife, Bowe told an interviewer: 'Tell Evander I said congratulations. We'll be back. It was unfortunate when that guy came out of the sky – he frightened my wife.'

There was even more drama when Bowe's legendary eighty-two-year-old trainer Eddie Futch said he felt faint and he also had to be taken to hospital as a precaution.

A crazy night.

Riddick Bowe went on to win the rubber match with Holyfield a couple of years later, also at Caesars Palace. What a great fighter he was. Struggled with his weight, but I can relate to that. I finally got to meet him at the 2014 WBC Convention last December, which was a great thrill, but even before then he'd send me tweets every now and again out of the blue.

I've been fortunate to meet Evander a few times in recent years. He came to my gym in 2014, when he was over here to do a sportsman's dinner. I believe he was thinking of making a comeback at the time. For a fifty-one year old, he was still in great physical shape, but I'm glad he's stayed on the safe side of the ropes. He was in enough wars during his brilliant and long career and has nothing left to prove. He's a great guy – lots of fun and a nice character. I'm a patron of the Barnabus charity for the homeless in Manchester and while he was here, we went down there together and took down a load of food for homeless people. They couldn't believe it when the great Evander Holyfield turned up with me and was dishing out food, chatting to them. Top man.

As for the Fan Man incident, I never had anything to compare with that in my career. The only time intruders got in the ring was when I fought Luis Collazo in Boston. When the fight ends, there are loads of people in the ring and there seems to be a lot more security than normal. Among them are these people in suits carrying walkie-talkies who at first I assume are Americans working at the venue. But when the decision is announced in my favour, I see these guys jumping around celebrating, and putting their arms around a confused-looking Don King who's waving his little American flags as he does.

I'm thinking, 'These officials are acting a bit daft.' Turns out they're all Scousers, fans of mine, who've blagged their way into the ring. Fair play to them, great effort. I think it's hilarious, but Speaky, with his ex-copper's head on, is not amused at the security breach. When they try it on again at my next fight, my first in Vegas, Speaky's primed and ready for them. He spots them at the press conference – same suits, same walkie-talkies – and goes over with the real security guards to chuck them out. Which they do, but not before the Scousers pour beer all over Speaky. He's not happy.

5
Meldrick Taylor vs. Julio César Chávez
17 March 1990
Hilton Hotel

One of the most controversial endings ever to a fight anywhere in world, let alone a world title fight in Vegas, with referee Richard Steele stopping the fight with just two seconds left on the clock.

Julio César Chávez was already a legend at twenty-seven years old going into this WBC/IBF light welterweight unification fight; a three-weight world champion, with a perfect 66–0 record and thirteen successful world title defences behind him. The ultimate Mexican fighter, teak tough and durable, he didn't mind taking a couple of punches on the way in to land his own more hurtful punches. My kind of boxer.

Chávez also had an incredible fanbase in Mexico. I've seen old footage of him training in the gym, and it's literally packed with spectators chanting his name. He seemed to have an entire nation behind him and fought not just for himself but his country. He was as proud of being Mexican as I am of being British, and, like me, his supporters followed him everywhere – for the Taylor fight, the Las Vegas Hilton was packed to its 9,200-capacity, and it's estimated at least 7,000 were Mexicans.

Chávez was the undisputed pound-for-pound king at the time, but the twenty-three-year-old IBF champion Taylor was showing signs of greatness himself. A brilliant, flashy boxer, he was in the Sugar Ray Leonard mould, able to throw a six-punch combination before his opponent blinked. But Taylor was from Philadelphia, and wanted to be like legendary Philly champion Joe Frazier and get stuck in and fight too. That attitude ultimately cost him against Chávez.

Even those who fancied Taylor's chances would never have predicted how the first nine rounds of the fight would play out. He was far too fast for Chávez, hitting him two, three, four times to every one back. Chávez's corner resorted to saying to him: 'Come on, do it for your family, Julio.'

However, referee Steele, the man closest to the action, noticed something many others didn't. Steele said later that the punches that Chávez was landing were 'shots that would break bones'. While Chávez was still losing rounds, from midway through the fight Taylor was the one taking the physical beating. By the end of the eleventh round, you could see that all over Taylor's swollen face.

One judge, Chuck Giampa, controversially had Chávez ahead 105–104 at this point, but the other two judges had Taylor a street ahead, as did most people, so he could afford to run away for the entire last round and still win the fight.

He got terrible advice from his corner before the last round, though – his trainer Lou Duva claimed later they told Taylor to dance and move, but when you watch the tape, they were actually telling him the fight was all hanging on the final round.

Then there was Taylor's Philly fighting heart – he probably wouldn't have run away even if his corner had told him to. I know from my own experience that it's hard to go against your fighting instincts even when it might be better for you. Before round ten with Floyd Mayweather, when it was clear I was losing, Billy Graham urged me to jab and move and see the final bell, but I refused. I wanted to win, and my only chance was to knock Floyd out; so I went for it and got knocked out myself.

In this case, Taylor seemed determined not only to win the boxing match, but the fight. That last round turned into a war, Chávez finally knocking the exhausted Taylor to the canvas with seconds remaining. Taylor was up at the count of six. Steele asked him twice: 'Are you okay?' No response from Taylor. Steele waved the fight off with official time of the stoppage given as two minutes fifty-eight seconds of the final round. Taylor had been two seconds from glory.

Richard Steele found himself in the middle of a shitstorm. Lou Duva, who went ballistic in the ring afterwards, had objected to Steele's appointment as referee in the first place, because he was rumoured to be friends with Chávez's promoter Don King, and felt to have favoured King fighters in the past. Steele strongly denied being friends with King or that his decision was biased in any way, saying: 'I don't care about the time. If I see a man's had enough, I stop the fight.'

To my mind, Richard Steele is one of the best referees there's ever been in boxing. He was the only person who could look closely at Taylor and if he felt he was gone, he had to stop the fight no matter how close it was to the final bell.

And Taylor was badly hurt – he had facial fractures and was pissing pure blood afterwards. He was talented enough to come back and win another world title at welterweight, but that Chávez beating was really the start of a slow, painful decline (including a comprehensive eighth round KO defeat by Chávez in their 1994 rematch) which saw him fight on too long and harmed his health. Very sad, because he was a great fighter as he proved that night in defeat against Chávez.

4
Sugar Ray Leonard vs. Marvin Hagler
6 April 1987
Caesars Palace, Outdoor Arena

Sugar Ray Leonard and Tommy Hearns are friends nowadays, but the same can't be said for Ray and another of his great rivals from that era, Marvin Hagler. They still refuse to shake hands. At the World Boxing Council convention in Las Vegas, in 2011, I saw people trying to get them to pose together for a picture, but they weren't having it. Actually, it was more Hagler who didn't want to do it, and his bitterness towards Ray all dates back to their fight in 1987, what proved to be the last fight of Hagler's career.

Ray had come out of retirement to fight him and a lot of people thought he shouldn't have been allowed to. He'd only fought once since 1982 and had had operations on the retinas of both eyes. Meanwhile, ever since he won the undisputed middleweight championship by going through Britain's Alan Minter at Wembley Arena, Hagler had dominated the division, beating the likes of Roberto Duran and Thomas Hearns (see below) in Vegas classics. Marvin was so good he had actually legally changed his name to include his 'Marvelous' nickname – from Marvin Nathaniel Hagler to Marvelous Marvin Hagler.

Like many of the best (and worst) ideas, alcohol was involved in Sugar Ray's decision to take him on. Ray had been sitting at ringside at Caesars Palace having a few beers with actor Michael J. Fox, watching Hagler's twelfth title defence against Ugandan John 'The Beast' Mugabi. Mugabi was known as a murderous puncher (he'd won all twenty-six of his fights up until then by KO) rather than a slick boxer, but Ray reckoned he was outboxing Hagler that night. It might have been the beer goggles making Ray think The Beast was boxing more beautifully than he actually was, because all the judges had Hagler ahead when he stopped Mugabi in the eleventh round. Nevertheless, during the fight Ray tried to convince Michael J. Fox that he could beat Hagler.

Fox replied: 'Do you want another beer?'

'Yes, I do,' said Ray, 'but I can beat Hagler.'

It was a bit like the bloke down the pub who's had a few too many scoops and says, 'Yeah, I could take him . . .' The difference was that this was Sugar Ray Leonard, one of the all-time greats, who could actually back up his boast.

Because of his eye operations and inactivity, though, many people thought that the fight was an accident waiting to happen and shouldn't take place. The brilliant Sheffield boxer Herol Graham wasn't too happy either because he was the WBA's mandatory challenger for Hagler's crown. The WBA stripped Hagler of his title, while the IBF said that if Leonard won the fight the title would be declared vacant, so only the WBC title was on the line.

As it turned out, Leonard showed he still had plenty left in the tank and produced a great performance. Hagler was trying to keep him on the ropes, but as part of the deal that saw Hagler guaranteed the larger purse ($12 million to $11 million), Leonard had been given the choice of the size of the ring, and the twenty-foot ring helped his trainer Angelo Dundee's box-and-move strategy.

But Leonard couldn't resist going to war with Hagler at times – as in a fantastic ninth round when 190 punches were thrown – and that made for a thriller. In the last few rounds, every time Hagler seemed to be wearing him down, he'd produce a lightning flurry of punches.

Another pre-fight trade in return for a bigger slice of the money that Hagler might have regretted was agreeing to twelve rounds instead of fifteen. Later, Leonard admitted that his legs started to go in the sixth round and it was only his heart and ring intelligence that got him through the last three rounds.

Leonard also went into the fight with the plan to frustrate Hagler and get him angry, by doing the Ali shuffle and throwing bolo punches etc, but also to 'steal rounds' – he had his corner shout out 'one minute' in each round and he'd then unload eye-catching combinations. In a very close fight, that perhaps just swung the judges. Hagler had thrown more punches (792 to 629), but they landed a similar amount (306 for Leonard to 291 for Hagler) so Leonard was more accurate. Personally, I think Hagler just edged it through twelve rounds of relentless pressure and harder punching, but Leonard's round-stealing tactics swayed the judges.

Both fighters thought they won decisively, but two judges had it about right at 115–113 either way. The controversy was over Mexican judge José Guerra's card who had it 118–110 in favour of Leonard to give him the split decision. The funny thing – well, not funny for Hagler – was that Guerra had only been called up when the Hagler camp had objected to English judge Harry Gibbs, thinking that a Mexican judge would appreciate Hagler's style more. Even worse, Harry, watching a tape of the fight back home in England, said that he scored the fight for Hagler. No wonder Marvin has been pissed off about it for the last three decades.

3
Marvin Hagler vs. Tommy Hearns
15 April 1985
Caesars Palace, Outdoor Arena

Billed simply as 'The Fight', this was massive, and particularly so for Marvin Hagler, who still felt that he wasn't getting the respect he was due as someone making his tenth defence of the WBA and WBC world middleweight titles and fifth defence of the IBF version.

Hagler was an all-time great. A very, very hard man, a strong, no-nonsense pressure fighter, he could also box southpaw as well as orthodox – a lot of fighters can switch nowadays, but back in the day most didn't and that gave Marvin an edge.

After losing to Sugar Ray Leonard in '81, Hearns had moved up to light middle and shown that his punching power could be just as destructive at the higher weight, knocking out Roberto Duran in two rounds in defence of his WBC title the year before. Duran had taken Hagler the full fifteen rounds, the first challenger for his titles ever to do so.

This fight actually should have happened back in 1982, but was postponed because Hearns hurt his little finger. Hagler accused him of being afraid to fight him, saying: 'He was going to make two million dollars, but started complaining about his little baby pinkie. You know how many people would give that little baby pinkie for two million dollars? They'd cut that thing off.' But after demolishing Duran, Hearns claimed that Hagler 'must be shaking like a leaf in a tree', and when their 1985 bout was confirmed predicted he'd knock Hagler out in three. Hagler, who wore a cap with one word – 'WAR' – written on the front in the days leading up to the fight, promised to 'come out smokin' . . . and when the smoke clears, it'll my hand that's being raised'.

This was another of those huge open-air boxing events that Caesars Palace was renowned for in the Eighties. There were loads of boxing legends present, including Sugar Ray Robinson, Carmen Basilio and Jake LaMotta. To add to the sense of occasion, during the playing of the national anthem the biggest American flag in the world was unfurled from the top of a Caesars' Fantasy Tower.

The Fight exceeded all the hype with a wild first round. Hearns went head-hunting straight away, while Hagler marched forward and battered Hearns to the body. In the first minute, Hearns hurt Hagler with a monster uppercut and opened a cut on Hagler's forehead, then Hagler shook him with a couple of left hooks on the chin. Soon it was just a case of the two men exchanging huge bombs, Hagler pinning Hearns to the ropes, but Hearns firing back. I've seen less action in a few twelve-round championship fights.

Hagler switched to orthodox at the start of the second round without much success as Hearns slipped and moved. For a minute or so it was almost like a normal boxing match, then Hagler reverted back to southpaw and it was back to trench warfare. By the end of the round Hearns's lanky legs were starting to look a bit rubbery. Hearns's trainer Emmanuel Steward later said that without his permission a member of Hearns's entourage had given the fighter a pre-fight leg massage while he was out of the dressing room, which hadn't helped. Getting punched by Marvin Hagler probably didn't help much either.

In the corner before round three, Steward pleaded with Hearns to box and move and he did that with some success, but Hagler just kept coming. The only break in the action came when referee Richard Steele asked the ringside doctor to check the cut on Hagler's forehead, which was leaking blood all down his face. When the doc asked him if it was affecting his vision, Hagler just replied: 'I ain't missing him, am I?' Soon after the restart, Hagler certainly didn't miss him with a huge right hook out of a southpaw stance that turned Hearns sideways. Another big right and left hook and it was all over. Hearns's third-round KO prediction had been right, except he was the one who ended up being counted out.

Hagler had won an all-time great fight and his battle for respect as one of the all-time great middleweights.

2
Diego Corrales vs. José Luis Castillo I
7 May 2005
Mandalay Bay Resort and Casino

This was one of those match-ups where there wasn't any personal needle between the two fighters. There was a lot of mutual respect, but they both desperately wanted to win this WBC/WBO unification bout to prove who was top dog in the lightweight division – and that desire made for a great fight.

Castillo was regarded as the tougher man physically – he'd never been knocked down in fifty-nine pro fights, whereas Californian Diego 'Chico' Corrales had visited the canvas three times in the previous two years (in two fights against Joel Casamayor) and five times against Floyd Mayweather Jr. in their 2001 bout. Despite that, Corrales told everyone beforehand he was going to make it a fight and was prepared to go through hell to beat Castillo.

Reportedly, Corrales had been doing sparring sessions of sixteen rounds with four different partners. The amount of sparring you do is a personal thing, really; I never did as much as that – my maximum was usually eight rounds in a session. The exception to that rule came at the end of my career when Floyd Mayweather Sr. had me doing twelve-round sessions with three different sparring partners for the Pacquiao fight.

My view was, if you did too much sparring, you'd end up having a fight before the fight, and you could get timing and sharpness in other ways instead, like by doing the pads. I'd sometimes hear fighters say they'd done hundreds of rounds of sparring for a fight, and I'd think, 'What the fuck for? What are you trying to prove?' For me, the question is can you do the rounds? Can you maintain the quality of punching throughout the rounds?

With Billy Graham, we used the body belt to test the stamina side. If I could do fifteen rounds of constant punching on the body belt, I knew I was more than fit enough for the twelve rounds, but doing it that way, I built that stamina without the wear and tear of sparring. Floyd Sr. didn't use the body belt so he put more emphasis on the sparring.

But it's a case of whatever works for the individual fighter, and you could see from the way he fought that Corrales's way was right for him. He was in tip-top condition and, true to his word, he went to war with Castillo. The Mexican was known for using his head and elbows inside, but Corrales showed he wasn't going to be bullied from the start, hitting low and landing a rabbit punch in the first round.

Aside from the odd foul, though, the fight was a master class in the art of in-fighting, with both fighters working the body and head and delivering flurries of powerful punches. Just as one man appeared to be getting the upper hand, the other would fight back furiously.

The ring might as well have been six-feet square for most of the fight as they pummelled away at each other in the centre, and ref Tony Weeks deserves a lot of credit for letting them get on with it.

Castillo was cut above the left eyebrow in the fourth – ruled as an accidental clash of heads by the referee, but replays seemed to indicate a punch had caused the damage – and Corrales almost put him down for the first time ever, with a great left hook at the end of the seventh.

After the fight, Corrales would say: 'We were throwing some hard shots all night . . . we were bound to hurt each other eventually.' That happened in round ten, with the fight too close to call.

Corrales's left eye was puffed up and almost closed, and half a minute into the round, Castillo nailed him with a peach of a left hook. Corrales went down and his gumshield fell out. He was up at eight and got a little extra time to recover while his mouthpiece was cleaned and replaced, but it wasn't enough as Castillo sent him to the canvas with another left hook soon after. Corrales only just beat the count, and he was deducted a point this time for excessive spitting of the gumshield. But the extra time that bought him may have saved him.

His trainer Joe Goossen could be heard telling Corrales, 'You gotta fucking get a sign on him now,' and despite being hurt and exhausted, he somehow found the strength to fight back. Then, amazingly, he caught Castillo with a short left hook coming in which stopped him in his tracks. Suddenly it was Castillo who was all over the place – he'd put so much effort into trying to finish the fight that he had nothing left. Seizing his chance, Corrales pinned the Mexican on the ropes connecting with what Castillo later admitted was 'a perfect right hand' among other powerful shots. With Castillo swaying like a palm tree in a storm and not defending himself, the ref stepped in to end the fight. It was the right call – Castillo was gone.

I've never seen a turnaround like that in one round in my life. What a comeback. What an incredible fight.

Castillo had still never been put on the canvas, though. He'd have to wait a couple more years for a Mancunian to do that to him.

1
Érik Morales vs. Marco Antonio Barrera I
19 February 2000
Mandalay Bay Resort and Casino

I've gone for Morales–Barrera I as my number one, because it was just round after round of relentless, high-quality action. Their fierce rivalry added an edge too, because for them it was just as important to prove themselves as the number one in Mexico as the best in the world. The first of three contests between two Mexican legends, this was the only one of the three that my future mate Marco lost, but I have to pick it as it was just an incredible fight.

Érik 'El Terrible' Morales was defending the WBC super bantamweight title for the ninth time, while Marco was making his third defence of the WBO version. They were two fighters in their absolute prime. Pre-fight, promoter Bob Arum hyped this match-up as 'the Mexican equivalent of Hagler vs. Hearns'. It turned out Bob was right – except it lasted twelve ferocious rounds, instead of just three.

Morales had a bit more stand-up style. Usually when you see boxers as aggressive as him, they use a bit more head movement, but Morales was happy to stand there and trade. That made for an incredible fight because Marco was ultra-aggressive at the time too. In true Mexican boxing tradition, Marco loved to have a scrap, but he could box brilliantly too (as Naseem Hamed found out a year later), and I think he had the slight edge over Morales in terms of skill.

The action never let up with Morales throwing by far the most punches – 868, landing 319 – but Marco the more accurate, nailing his opponent with 299 of 618 punches thrown.

Named *The Ring*'s Fight of the Year, the phenomenal fifth round, where Morales dominated before Marco caught him and fought back, was the magazine's Round of the Year and must be one of the greatest rounds of boxing ever. The only round I've seen that bettered it for action was round ten of Corrales–Castillo I, and that was only because there were knockdowns and a stoppage. This was two evenly-matched fighters desperately going toe-to-toe, with the pendulum swinging in favour of Marco, then Morales. Neither fighter would give an inch, and both showed incredible stamina, heart and desire. When a standing count was wrongly given against Morales who slipped in the final round, he got up and, fearing the lost point could have cost him, literally ran at

Marco and slugged it out until the final bell. He needn't have worried, though, because the split decision went in his favour – 114–113, 113–114, 115–112.

Afterwards, Marco said through a translator, 'What does a man have to do to win a decision in Las Vegas?'

'Morales got the decision, but Barrera won the fight,' was the verdict of the TV commentator, and I agree, but then again Marco was possibly a bit fortunate to get the decision when they fought again two years later, and he ended up winning the rubber match in 2004 on a majority decision.

After three fights, the combined punch stats were unbelievable. A total of 4,266 punches had been thrown, Marco connecting with 796 of 1,982 (40 per cent) and Morales 757 of 2,284 (33 per cent). Between them they landed 1,219 power shots in total, which says a lot for both men's punch resistance, because both could bang a bit.

The bitter rivalry between the two has continued since retirement, although Marco has tried to make peace. A couple of years ago, Marco was on a TV show with Morales and said to the interviewer that they could be friends now their careers were over; but Morales turned to him and said, 'No, you'll never be my friend.' It's a shame really, because they made each other boxing legends by battering the living daylights out of each other.

In terms of personal dislike, the only person I had similar feelings towards throughout my career was Junior Witter. He fought out of the Ingle Gym in Sheffield and was always calling me out. At the time I hated him, but we never actually shared the ring. Junior wanted to fight me and I wanted to fight him, but my promoter at the time, Frank Warren, didn't want me to because he wasn't a great ticket seller. By then, I was in a position to fight the likes of Kostya Tszyu and Junior wasn't on my list of priorities.

Funnily enough, unlike Morales and Marco, Junior and me get on well now. It all changed when I called up my matchmaker

Richard Poxon, who is from Sheffield, to get some sparring partners for the Upton brothers. A few days later, Junior walks through the door at my gym.

'Fucking hell – when Richard said he was going to send some sparring down from Sheffield, I didn't think he'd send you!'

We have a good laugh and I discover he's actually a really nice lad. At the end of the session, as he's about to leave, I call after him: 'Junior, do you mind going out the fire exit in case anyone sees you in my gym.'

He's been back a few times and it's been great experience for my young fighters to spar with a former world champion like him. I've got a lot of time for Junior.

TBE OR NOT TBE?

When I fought Floyd Mayweather Jr., he was going by the nickname of 'Pretty Boy', which he'd been given early in his career because he came out of fights without a mark on his face. Very similar to me, then . . .

But even Floyd realised that a man in his thirties couldn't keep calling himself 'Pretty Boy' so he became 'Money' Mayweather instead. The 'Money' nickname came from his habit of flashing bundles of cash in front of the camera.

He's still 'Money', but in more recent times, he has also taken to calling himself 'TBE' – The Best Ever. He's even got his own range of clothing with TBE written all over it.

From my experience in the ring with him, I have to say that when it comes to technical boxing skills, there can't have been anyone much better than Floyd. His defence was ridiculously good. At times, it felt like I could have chucked a handful of confetti at him and still not hit him. Plenty of other opponents down the years have had the same problem.

If you look at the punch stats for our fight, I only connected with 63 out of 372 punches, 17 per cent. That percentage would have been a lot higher if the referee had allowed us to fight inside, but it shows how difficult he was to catch.

Whatever you try to do against Floyd, there's a price to pay. He knew body-punching was my strength, but whenever I came in with a body shot, he would counter and catch me with a right uppercut. He was always setting traps and had the lightning speed to punish any mistakes.

He had this uncanny ability to measure distance and pull just out of range of punches. Even if you do connect, because of the way he dips and rolls, he takes the sting out the shot. I managed to land one good hard jab, which wobbled him, but that was partly because he was slightly off-balance for once. It's so hard to hit him flush on the chin, and very few have in his entire career. The only time I've seen him in trouble was against Shane Mosley who nailed him in the second round of their fight, but Floyd recovered and won the fight easily, so he's obviously got a decent chin.

He was so frustrating to fight. At times he bent the rules by ducking below the waist and using his forearm to keep me at arm's distance, but I'd never complain about that. If someone caught me with a forearm – I just thought, fair enough, I'll get you with one back in a minute. Floyd was so smart in the ring.

He has the sort of boxing intelligence that you can't teach. He controls the pace of the action, and knows just when it's the right time to step on the gas. He wasn't as concussive a puncher as, say, Kostya Tszyu, but he doesn't need to be. He hits hard enough and, more importantly, he's accurate and knows exactly the time to throw. With Floyd, it's all about timing. He sapped my strength by making me miss, and as I got frustrated and more ragged in the second half of the fight, he stepped it up and closed the show.

I never had a rematch in my entire pro career, but if I could have had just one it would have been against Floyd. That might sound strange because he was the best opponent I ever faced, but I loved the challenge of fighting him.

The following summer there was actually serious talk about staging a rematch at Wembley Stadium. Richard Schaefer, the then Golden Boy's chief executive, told the press in May 2008: 'It's very likely that Floyd will come over. Floyd and his manager Al Haymon are very serious about it. Floyd realises Hatton is the most beloved fighter in the world and he would make history by coming over to Wembley Stadium. For Ricky it's about challenges and it's the same for Floyd. Fighting in front of 100,000 fans would be huge motivation. Floyd knows Ricky felt cheated in the first fight. He wants to show the victory was no fluke – and that's his motivation.'

Floyd was supposedly 'retired' at the time, but Richard was talking about Floyd taking on Oscar in a rematch first in late 2008, and that if I got past Juan Lazcano and then Paulie Malignaggi, the Wembley fight could happen in spring 2009. As it happened, Floyd didn't fight again until September 2009 against Juan Manuel Marquez, and by then I'd lost to Manny Pacquiao, so our potential rematch never materialised.

Aside from hoping that the referee would let us work on the inside, my tactics second time around against Floyd would have been to throw a lot more straight punches. In his commentary on our Vegas fight, Manny Steward commented on how my foot speed was faster than his previous opponents, including Oscar De La Hoya. That helped me cut off the ring and close him down, but Floyd's hand speed was something else.

I threw too many hooks in that fight, and he's too fast to do that – straight punches get there quicker. It made it easy for him to pick me off. If you look at the exchange of punches that proved to be the start of the end for me in the tenth round, I started to throw a left hook first, but his left hook counter hit my chin before mine arrived on his!

So is Floyd really TBE? Before our fight, he was already claiming he was, saying: 'I am the greatest and this is my time. I'm not disrespecting Muhammad Ali and Sugar Ray Robinson. I've accomplished something no other fighter has. I've reigned for a decade and lost to nobody.' Which is a fair point.

His uncle/coach Roger Mayweather was also telling anyone who would listen that Floyd and Sugar Ray Robinson are the two greatest fighters who ever lived, with Henry Armstrong running a close third.

And seven years on, he's still unbeaten 47–0. Some people have criticised him for ducking opponents, but I don't think that's true. He called out Ronald 'Winky' Wright in 2005, who was in the higher light middleweight division and could boast two wins over Shane Mosley and a recent win over Felix Trinidad at middleweight. Wright was technically gifted, in his prime and it could have been a tough fight for Floyd, but negotiations broke down and the fight never happened.

At the time of writing, the only other big name of his era – and the biggest name of all – that's missing from his CV is Manny Pacquiao. A Mayweather–Pacquiao bout should have happened years ago, but in February 2015 they finally agreed terms and signed to fight on 2 May 2015 at the MGM Grand.

I wasn't at my best when I fought Pacquiao so it's tricky to rate him against Floyd, but to win world titles at seven different weights is unheard of. Like everyone else, I wonder how the hell you can do that – I found it tough to go up just one division. Some, like Floyd and Paulie Malignaggi, have suggested he must have been taking something to help him retain that power and speed in higher weight classes, but Pacquiao has passed every test, so only he can know that.

Floyd has said that the reason a fight with Manny fell through in the past is that the Pacquiao camp refused to agree to random drug testing – Floyd claims that they wanted to be notified when USADA [the US Anti-Doping Agency] were coming to test him. That doesn't look good on Manny, but then again no fighter likes his biggest rival telling him what to do, like he's the boss.

By the time you read this, barring injuries, they will have faced each other in the ring. My pick is Floyd to win, although I don't say that with any great confidence. Floyd hasn't looked as convincing in the last couple of years, but the same could be said for Manny. I wish they'd fought a few years back when they seemed to be absolutely in their prime. Now, whatever the result, people may say one or both of them are past their best. It's still the best fight in boxing; I just think it could have been a little bit better a few years ago.

Whatever happens, for me, Floyd certainly has to be in the top three of the best fighters of all time. It's very difficult to compare fighters in different eras, but when you look through the history of boxing, at the brilliant fighters who've moved up through the weight divisions and beaten other world champions, and consider how Floyd has done that unbeaten – and barely even getting hit in a lot of those fights – you have to put him up there.

RICKY'S DREAM VEGAS FIGHT CARD

Imagine staging the ultimate night of boxing at the MGM Grand Arena featuring your pick of the greatest fighters of all-time at their peak, who would you choose? Well, this is my dream Vegas fight card. The cheapest tickets for the Mayweather–Pacquiao fight were $1,500 each, so how much would it set you back to watch this lot? You wouldn't want to arrive late and miss the undercard bouts, that's for sure . . .

Mickey Rourke vs. Rocky Balboa (I did say it was a 'dream' fight card . . .)

What a fight to begin the evening – a legendary film actor who became a professional fighter against a legendary film character played by an actor. Both Mickey and Sylvester Stallone a.k.a. Rocky came to see me fight in Vegas, and have said they were Ricky Hatton fans. If this was real life, Mickey – who was once trained by Freddie Roach – would probably beat Sly up . . . but we're talking Rocky Balboa here (and, as you know, my mate The Duck actually thinks Sylvester is Rocky), so he's bound to pull out a fairytale win. Hadriiiiiiiiiaaaaaannnn . . .

Ricky Hatton vs. Roberto Duran

I think this would be a great fight, but you don't often beat your heroes, so I reckon I might lose on points after twelve rounds of action in the trenches. Then if his 'Hands of Stone' haven't done too much damage, I'd sing a bit of karaoke for Roberto at the after-fight party – I know how much he loves my singing voice.

Floyd Mayweather Jr. vs. Julio César Chávez

A nice clash of styles here between my old foe Floyd, the master boxer, and the greatest Mexican fighter ever. Chávez would probably adopt similar tactics to the ones I used against Floyd – cutting off the ring, looking to get inside and make Floyd work. He'd need a ref who'd allow him to do that, though, so he might not want Joe Cortez in charge. A peak Chávez would give Floyd the fight of his life, but I think Floyd would still find a way to nick the win on a split decision.

Sugar Ray Leonard vs. Sugar Ray Robinson

One for the purists, with two of the finest boxing technicians of all-time facing off. After a dazzling display of boxing, I'll go for

Sugar Ray Robinson to shade the fight on points by the narrowest of margins.

Mike Tyson vs. Muhammad Ali

Finally, to the main event of the evening, an epic heavyweight contest and I'm picking Mike Tyson to shock the world and win by a KO.

Muhammad Ali will always be 'The Greatest' because he was about more than just boxing, he was an iconic figure who transcended the sport. In Tyson's era, the quality of opposition wasn't a patch on that Muhammad Ali faced, but as a boxer I watch the way someone moves and fights, and in those couple of years when he was in his prime, I just think Tyson was the best heavyweight of all time. He was lightning fast – I would say even faster than Ali – he was ferocious and possessed one-punch knockout power. Even though he wasn't the tallest, he was able to get his shots in against heavyweights that out-reached him. I don't think we've seen a more destructive heavyweight before or since – he looked unbeatable at the time.

IN AND OUT OF THE RING

THE FIGHTS THAT GOT AWAY...

Looking back, I'm happy with the five fights I took on in Vegas even though I suffered a couple of defeats. The Urango and Castillo fights got me into position to fight Mayweather. Then, after fighting Lazcano in Manchester and Malignaggi back out in Vegas, I felt I was ready for another mega fight, this time against Pacquiao.

However, both Dennis Hobson and Joe Sharpe who kickstarted my Vegas journey, would have taken me a different route if they'd had their way. They would have preferred me to take a couple more fights before Floyd.

In the run-up to the Castillo fight, Dennis was actually in the process of signing Diego Corrales when he tragically died in a motorcycle accident. Dennis's idea was to create another little semi-final/final tournament after my Castillo fight.

Dennis Hobson:

I didn't want Rick to fight Floyd Mayweather when he did. I'd have avoided that one for another year, eighteen months. In my eyes – and Bob Arum's eyes – we didn't feel there was any need to fight Floyd at that time.

That's why I signed Corrales. I would have put Corrales on the next Ricky fight bill, and then after they could call each other out, and the fight would be easy to make. Continue in that vein and Ricky's brand would have got bigger and bigger.

Joe Sharpe:

At that time, Ricky could have gone a lot of ways. I have a lot of dear friends who were fighting in Ricky's weight division or willing to move up into it at that time. I thought Ricky had a great opportunity to secure fights with people like Érik Morales, Miguel Cotto and Acelino Freitas. I was looking at a series of fights for Ricky. He could have made a lot more money in his career if he had listened to what I was trying to tell him.

Ricky wanted the Mayweather fight so bad, but you had two superstars who were very marketable. They should have had a couple more fights each before they fought each other. And I think they rushed him into the Pacquiao fight – they could have given him more of a break before going into that fight. There were other marketable fights out there like Juan Manuel Marquez. With his style, Ricky could have given fight fans more spectacular victories in Vegas, especially against Mexican fighters.

Dennis Hobson:

After Castillo, we could have matched Ricky with Barrera – although I know they were big mates – or Morales, Freitas . . . There were some marquee names and Rick would have beaten them.

He'd have made the same sort of money as he did for Mayweather over two or three fights, and then his stock would have been massive to make even more money when he fought Mayweather.

I also had good relations with Club Wembley and was looking at possibly staging a Hatton–De La Hoya fight at Wembley Stadium.

I can see what Dennis and Joe are saying, but I didn't miss fighting too many and I can have no complaints about the money I made in my career. I wouldn't have liked to fight Marco Barrera anyway, because of our friendship.

Marco Antonio Barrera:

Would I have liked to fight Ricky? Well, I used to have crazy wars in the gym with my brother Jorge (a fighter too) – since we were kids we would beat the crap out of each other and it never affected our relationship. I had never really thought about fighting Ricky because we were separated by several divisions, but towards the end of my career the idea was around. I did even speak to Dennis Hobson about a possible bout between us. It was mentioned once while Ricky and I were together and Ricky said, 'Sure, we can do it at heavyweight.' If we had fought it would not have affected my feelings for him, but I can tell you that the fans would have loved it!

I wanted to fight for world titles by then. Corrales didn't have a world title, neither did Morales or Marco – Kostya Tszyu, Carlos

Maussa, Luis Collazo and Juan Urango all did. I was fighting world champions. You have to bear in mind that HBO had approval on opponents so they would have had something to say on this.

Oscar would have been a massive fight and tricky for me because of his natural size advantage; although, when he fought Pacquiao at catchweight, he looked half the fighter because he was weight-drained so he might have had the same problem against me. I would have liked to fight Cotto and Arturo Gatti and they would have been crowd-pleasing bouts. Cotto was better as he went up the weights. When I beat Kostya Tszyu, Cotto was at light-welter and I think I would definitely have beaten him around that time.

But I have no regrets about the route I took. I had fancied fighting Floyd Mayweather and Manny Pacquiao for a while, so when those opportunities came along I grabbed them. Both of them were considered the world's number one pound-for-pound boxers at the times I fought them, and I wanted to test myself against the absolute best.

RICKY'S FIGHT NIGHT PLAYLIST

My dressing room before a fight was always a lively, noisy place, and I had to have the right music to get me in the mood. If you'd been in the dressing room at the MGM Grand a couple of hours before the Floyd Mayweather fight, you'd have seen me busy connecting up the stereo system I'd brought with me, making sure the speakers were positioned just right.

I tended to listen to rock music with a heavy, aggressive beat, stuff that fitted with my mentality in the ring. When I was warming up and shadow boxing, I'd often be singing along. Before the Floyd fight, the Rolling Stones's 'I Can't Get No Satisfaction' came on, I started singing the chorus and soon everyone in the room was belting it out.

The last two songs I listened to before I walked out were 'We Will Rock You' by Queen and then, finally, KISS's 'Crazy Crazy Nights' which added a bit of glam to the rock. The KISS song just summed up the dressing room in Vegas before those big fights because it was madhouse, full of all sorts of people from all over the world, from Hattersley to Hollywood.

Here's ten of the tracks I used to get me in the mood for fighting:

Oasis – 'Cigarettes and Alcohol'
Red Hot Chili Peppers – 'Give it Away'
Stone Roses – 'I Wanna Be Adored'
James – 'Sometimes'
Nickelback – 'Burn it to the Ground'
Aerosmith – 'Livin' on the Edge'
Whitesnake – 'Here I Go Again'
Rolling Stones – 'I Can't Get No Satisfaction'
Queen – 'We Will Rock You'
KISS – 'Crazy Crazy Nights'

THE FINAL MOMENTS

Some boxers like a little bit of quiet time and clear their dressing room of everyone, apart from their cornermen, before they head to the arena. Not me. In Vegas, I preferred my dressing room to be full of people and buzzing right up until the moment when I was called. I'd like to go straight out from the madness into the mayhem.

After leaving the changing room, there was always a few minutes' gap waiting backstage before I actually entered the arena, though. It was not exactly quiet time, because I could hear my fans singing and chanting for me, but that was my little time to shut out all distractions and focus on my tactics for the fight, and everything I'd worked on in the gym.

With the atmosphere at a big fight – especially with the support I had – it's easy to get carried away and go out there throwing eight-punch combinations from the opening bell. With experience, you learn to keep it under control.

It's about trying to hold your nerve – because you are nervous and there's no point pretending you're not. The trick is to put that nervous energy to positive use in the ring and not waste it before you even get there.

Billy Graham very rarely used to say too much to me on the night of a fight. By then, we knew the game plan and he didn't want to overload my mind – we'd been talking about the fight for so long, that it was all ingrained in my brain anyway. He'd just give me little reminders here and there – 'Don't forget this, don't forget that.' Floyd Sr. was the same in that respect. Too much information fired at you on the night can confuse you.

Of the Vegas fights, I think I was most confident as I waited to walk out to face José Luis Castillo, because my preparation had gone perfectly. I was absolutely bang on, physically and mentally. I was always of the opinion that I would stop anyone who got into a fight with me, even the top boys, like I did with Kostya Tszyu; and Castillo's style was tailor-made for me. If an opponent jabbed and moved, I was always confident that I'd catch up with them in the end, but I expected it to be a bit more difficult.

Robert Diaz:

Before the Castillo fight, I remember going to Ricky's room prior to the weigh-in and seeing this tiny kid. He looked so small and fragile. I knew Castillo was a big, physical fighter and I was like, oh my God.

But the next day, in the dressing room before the fight, the energy was amazing. The music was at full volume, Barrera was there, Rooney and other friends and celebrities, all watching Ricky hitting the pads, grunting with each punch – rahh, rahh, rahhh. And he looked like a beast. He had recuperated, the weight was back, and my opinion completely changed. There was no way that Castillo was going to hold back this bull. When he knocked Castillo out, I was not surprised. He looked in incredible shape.

Previously, against Juan Urango, I went into the ring as a stronger favourite, but I was a little less confident than I was for Castillo, because I had flu and it was still preying on my mind that I hadn't done my usual fifteen rounds on the body-bag. As I was waiting in the wings to walk out for my first Vegas fight, I did think, Jesus, I hope this is going to be okay. Once I got out there, I felt alright at first, picking him off, but he got close to me in the middle rounds. I honestly don't think he'd have got near me if I had been a hundred per cent, but the illness made it hard work.

I felt very confident against Floyd Mayweather too, even though he was the pound-for-pound king. My preparation had been spot on and I believed I had the tools and the tactics to beat him. Commentator Ian Darke wasn't so sure though when he saw me earlier.

Ian Darke:

On our monitor at the ringside we saw Ricky arrive at the MGM with the rest of the team. I remember thinking – and I may have said it on air – that I'd not seen him look like that. He was less jaunty and he had a look of a guy for whom the reality was crowding in of the size of the task ahead of him. Like, Jesus, I'm in with Floyd

Mayweather here – what am I going to do with this guy?

Maybe one or two doubts were starting to creep in. Rick's a very good analyser of fights and in one or two off-guard comments, I thought he started to doubt his own ability as to whether he was quite in this type of league. I think that did creep up on him a bit that night.

I can honestly say that wasn't the case. I was certain I was going to win – if I hadn't been I don't think I would have taken the defeat so hard.

Yes, I was moving up a weight to fight Floyd, but I wasn't overly concerned, because he was more of a boxer than a powerhouse. I thought I'd still be physically stronger than him. My previous move up to welterweight to fight Luis Collazo had not been a pleasant experience – then I'd really noticed the difference in size and strength – and that was in the back of my mind, but I still had no doubt I'd win against Floyd. As it happened, the extra weight wasn't an issue in the fight – I could match him for strength – but he was so clever, so slick, so smart on the inside, and those were the decisive factors.

After losing to Floyd, I was down in the dumps, and after my next fight against Lazcano, which wasn't impressive, I was asking myself whether I was past it? Had the hard fights caught up with me? But my first training camp with Floyd Mayweather Sr. refreshed me and gave me renewed confidence, so as I prepared to walk out at the MGM Grand against Paulie Malignaggi, I was very confident.

When you've faced an all-time great at welterweight, taking on Paulie in my proper weight division held no fears. I felt that I should beat Paulie. I didn't think Paulie had the punching power to trouble me at all, but I did underestimate his speed and toughness. When he caught me with a right cross in the first round, I was shocked – the speed was incredible, as quick as Floyd. The difference was that he didn't have Floyd's power. His punches didn't hurt me, so I knew that if I kept the pressure on I'd gradually wear him down. Again, though, Paulie exceeded my expectations – he doesn't look the strongest, but he proved to be a very tough individual and never gave up. It was only his trainer Buddy McGirt throwing the towel in the eleventh round that ended the fight.

By far the worst I felt in the final moments before a Vegas fight – or any fight for that matter – was my last one against Manny Pacquiao of course. For all the reasons I've talked about, I knew I wasn't right, but at that stage, I was just trying to convince myself that I could do it. I was saying to myself, if I can just get one big shot in downstairs, then it'll all be over. That's not me, and should never be your mentality as a boxer – to rely on one shot. That's a last resort, but that's the stage I was at. I always took risks in fights to get my shots in, but I was more reckless than usual against Manny and everyone saw the result.

So a lot of thoughts and emotions do run through your mind in those last few moments before you walk into the arena. Then the music kicks in, the crowd roar and it's all on . . .

MAKING AN ENTRANCE

I always enjoyed sitting around over a drink with my team coming up with ideas for my ringwalks. There were a couple of crackers that made the shortlist for Vegas, but unfortunately never came off; I was talking about going into the ring with seven dwarves and 'Hi-ho, hi-ho, it's off to work we go . . .' playing in the background. The idea was that each dwarf would carry one of my belts. I'd picked up a few over the years on my way up including those I'd won for the Central Area, British, WBA and WBU Inter-Continental and WBU titles – and if we were one short, one could always carry a flag. It would have been a good one against Floyd who called me 'that little midget' in the build-up – even with his reflexes, he might have struggled if me and seven other 'midgets' had come flying at him from the opposite corner.

I'm a massive *Only Fools and Horses* fan, and another time I wanted to come to the ring in my Trotters Independent Traders van. I would have loved to come in wearing the full Del Boy gear, with sheepskin coat, red roll-neck, medallion and cap at the MGM. God knows what the American fans would have made of that.

I wasn't flamboyant like Floyd Mayweather Jr., but I always took a great pride in trying to entertain the fans – whether it was by making myself accessible to them, the way I fought or the ring-walk. Floyd's performances didn't always match his flashy ringwalks – before the Urango fight, I took the piss out of him coming into his last fight against Carlos Baldomir dressed like a gladiator, saying: 'He came in dressed like Russell Crowe, but fought like Sheryl Crow.'

I always wanted to do stuff my fans could relate to. Working-class people are not bothered about expensive bling – like me, they just want to have a laugh and joke on their nights out. Boxing is a serious business, but it's also a show and I enjoyed that side of it in my own way.

I'll never forget the look of Floyd Mayweather Sr.'s face in the dressing room at the MGM Grand before my fight with Paulie Malignaggi when I put on my Ricky Fatton suit.

We've just been working on the pads, and he says: 'You alright – had enough pads now, Ricky?'

'Yeah, cheers Floyd.'

Next thing, the TV man pops his head round the door: 'Five minutes, Ricky.'

Then Speaky walks over with my Fatton suit and helps me put it on.

'Whoah, whoah, whoah – what the hell are you doing, man?' says Floyd.

'Just putting my fat suit on . . .'

'What for, man?'

'Er, for a laugh.'

'You're fuckin' crazy.'

I'd worn it before my previous fight against Juan Lazcano at the City of Manchester Stadium, so Floyd obviously hadn't seen that walk-on.

As we leave the changing room, he is still shaking his head in disbelief: 'Man, you fuckin' crazy . . .'

Then, as we wait in the wings, they crank up the *Hi-Ho Ricky Fatton* song – which had also debuted at the Lazcano fight. As I walk out into the arena, you can easily tell the Americans in the audience, because their jaws are on the floor. Meanwhile, the Brits are singing along happily to my new song and then 'Blue Moon'.

The Americans have never seen anything like that. I've never thought of myself as a celebrity, but in this world where famous people can disappear up their own arses, I think people found it refreshing that I didn't take myself too seriously. I guess some people might feel insulted or embarrassed to be called fat, but I really didn't care.

No wonder Floyd Sr. was so shocked, especially when he was used to his son, who's the complete opposite to me – obsessed with money and his image. All of a sudden, he's training a fighter who's waddling out for a world championship bout in a fat suit.

I'd had the 'Ricky Fatton' nickname for a few years, but I can't quite remember what came first out, the suit or the song – they sort of evolved around the same time.

My Fatton suit was made by Suzi Wong Creations, a company in Adlington, Lancashire, producers of custom-made boxing ring wear. It's a business started by John and Susan Angelsea in 2000, and it's grown purely from word of mouth; since then they have made ring wear for lots of the best-known British boxers, including Amir Khan, Carl Froch, James De Gale, Anthony Joshua, Kell Brook and Chris Eubank Jr. Their daughter Melissa, who studied at the London College of Fashion and has designed clothes for the Ministry of Defence, is a designer at the company so it's a real family business. The well-known sports artist Brian Meadows introduced Paul Speak to John Angelsea and they started making my robes and shorts for fights from very early in my career, through all my championship fights. If you visit their workshop you'll see lots of pairs of shorts signed by famous boxers, because they're all boxing fans and often make an extra pair to keep themselves.

Normally, the brief I gave them was pretty simple – I want Man City colours – and then they designed all the badges, frills and tassels. The Fatton suit was more of a challenge for them because it had to look bulky, but still be really lightweight so I wasn't knackered by the time I got to the ring. It also had to be easy to take it off – would have been a bit embarrassing if the ref was calling me to the centre of the ring and my cornermen were wrestling to release the fighting-fit boxer inside the blubber.

We wanted to keep it secret from everyone, so rather than John and co coming to my gym for me to try it on, Paul and me would drive to them late at night for fittings. You'd think we were on a secret operation for the government, not trying on a fat suit. It was a right laugh and great to see the suit taking shape.

It took a week to make and get it just right. They did a brilliant job, matching the look of the fat suit to my satin shorts underneath, but lining it with lightweight foam to get the fatness. The suit was two-piece – with a zip down the back of the top so that it slipped off easily and braces, which I could flick off, so the fat shorts would fall down. Brilliant.

I've got my old friend Joey Blower to thank for coming up with the Ricky Fatton song. Joey is a comedian who has been a headline act at the Merrie England Bar on the North Pier in Blackpool for over twenty years. When I was in my late teens, our family used to go in and watch his shows and thought he was hilarious.

A couple of years later when I still wasn't that well known, I was doing an after-dinner speech at a hotel in Blackpool. What I didn't know was that Joey was at the dinner.

After I've done my bit, he comes up to me and says: 'I'm a comedian and I thought what you did there was fantastic.'

'Fuckin' hell, Joey Blower!' I reply.

'Yeah, Joey Blower,' he says, dead cool.

I'm so excited, I'm calling my dad over: 'Look, dad, it's Joey Blower.'

A few weekends later when I was up in Blackpool again, we met up again and after that we became really good friends.

Joey Blower:

After my father died of cancer, I introduced a section in my show where we'd shave someone's hair off to raise money for Cancer Research. I shaved my hair off, and the next week Ricky came down and had his head shaved too.

If he can do something for you, and showing his face helps, he'll do it for you. I used to have a bar-restaurant in Cleveley – a very small town. One year, he came down at Christmas, did a dinner and turned the Christmas lights on – and when I say Christmas lights, I'm talking six trees and a fairy. He buys into the spirit of things.

I've never known Ricky say no to anything if he could do it. When he comes to Blackpool, I do try and get a private area where he can spend an hour or so just to chat, otherwise he'd just never stop signing autographs.

IN AND OUT OF THE RING

With many celebrities, it's normally very difficult to get close to them. With Rick, he didn't need a PR man, because he'd just go and do it. I've never once heard him say, 'Get me out of here, I'm sick of it'.

Joey wasn't a huge boxing fan when we first met, but he's made a lot of friends in boxing since and has ended up getting right into it. He came to all five of my Vegas fights – even the Floyd Mayweather one, which he wasn't planning to attend.

A few weeks before, I haven't heard from him about coming out, so I give him a call to check he's alright for tickets.

'Sorry, I can't make it, mate,' he tells me. 'I've booked to fly to India on the Monday after the fight.'

'Oh no, you've got to get there.'

After a bit of persuasion, he changes his mind and agrees to come. He books his flights for Vegas, but it's really tight for him to get back to England in time to catch his flights to India. On the way back after the fight, his plane makes a stop in Chicago where it's snowing. The plane is delayed for so long, he misses his flight to India. Because it's no one's fault, Joey can't get a refund and he misses out on a six-grand holiday to India. Ouch. He still reminds me that I haven't written the cheque out to reimburse him for that.

In the build-up to my next fight against Juan Lazcano at the City of Manchester Stadium, I was reading the usual stuff about how much weight I put on and take off again between fights, and it gave me an idea for my walk-on.

I ring up Joey and ask him if I can use his song.

The walk-on song – or 'roll-on song' as he calls it – Joey uses for his act is a reworking of Jeff Beck's classic 'Hi Ho Silver Lining', except the title of his version is 'Hi Ho, You Fat Bastard'.

'But it's rude, Ricky,' he replies. 'You can't use it as it is for a family audience. I tell you what I'll do, I'll redo it without the swearing and so it fits for you.'

'Lovely, thanks very much, Joey.'

A few days later, I receive a copy in the post. Joey's rewritten the lyrics and been into the studio to record a new version just for me, and it goes like this:

Hi Ho Ricky Fatton

They say he's never seen a salad,
That's why he's fat.
He's never been on a diet,
And he'll drink to that.
He likes his pies and pasties,
A pint of Guinness or two.
He's the one they call 'Ricky Fatton',
Tonight he's here for you.

Chorus
And it's hi ho, Ricky Hatton,
He ate all the pies, now, baby,
He's never seen a salad,
He ate all the pies, Ricky Hatton.

He eats for all of England,
He eats so fast.
If eating was a competition,
He'd never finish last.
He's even got a pair of man-boobs,
From eating takeaway.
Drinking too much Guinness,
Getting fatter every day.

IN AND OUT OF THE RING

Repeat chorus

Even Gordon Ramsay,
Tried to get him thin.
He made some Chinese noodles,
He spilt them on his double chin.
The only time he diets,
Is for big fight day.
And that's why we love Ricky Hatton,
We'd love him anyway.

Repeat chorus

Rick-y Hatton, Rick-y Hatton, Rick-y Hatton . . . [repeat to fade]

Apparently, Joey thought nothing more about it after sending me the song and didn't think I was actually going to use it at a fight, so when he heard the 'ba-bom-bom' drumbeat at the start of the song booming out of the speakers at the City of Manchester Stadium, he was as surprised as anyone. He was trying to tell anyone who would listen around him that it was his song. All he got in return were people telling him to shut up.

'But it's my song! I wrote it!'

The other spectators might not have given a shit that Joey wrote it, but he was dead proud of the reaction from the crowd. He deliberately writes songs so they are repetitive and easy to latch onto and within one bar of the chorus, everyone was singing along.

With me wearing the fat suit, it just fitted perfectly.

John and Melissa Angelsea were ringside, proudly watching me wear their creation for the first time. I've been told by a few people who were sitting near the back, that at first they genuinely thought

I was out of shape when I wombled in wearing it. 'Fookin' hell, Ricky's looking a bit round . . .'

In the dressing room after the fight, I introduced Joey to Oscar De La Hoya.

'Oscar, this is Joey who wrote the song that I came out to.'

Joey says to Oscar: 'I'll write one for you, if you like.'

'Very kind of you,' Oscar replies. 'But I don't put on as much weight between fights as Ricky tends to.'

Oscar seemed to think that Joey could only write songs for fat boxers.

As the fat suit and the song went down so well in Manchester, I had to take it to Vegas for the Malignaggi bout. By then, a lot of my supporters knew all the words to the song, and it could be heard echoing through the casinos during fight week along with 'Walking in a Hatton Wonderland' and other fan favourites.

Joey has gone on to record a walk-on song for Blackpool boxer Brian 'The Lion' Rose' – a reworking of 'Glad All Over' called *Here Comes The Lion*. As for me, I now play 'Hi Ho Ricky Fatton' to kick off my after-dinner speeches and stand-up shows – Joey reckons I've nicked half his jokes as well.

Meanwhile, the Ricky Fatton suit now takes pride of place in a glass cabinet at the reception of my gym. I think it's a work of art, a daily reminder to me of my most memorable Manchester and Vegas ringwalks . . . and a reminder to the members what will happen if they don't get down to the gym regularly.

Joey Blower:

One of my best memories of Vegas is from after the Urango fight. We discovered we were booked on the same flight back, and there was just him, his brother Matthew and a few mates sitting in the departure lounge chatting away. He'd just won a fight in Vegas, everyone was happy and Ricky was just mixing in with everyone else as he liked to do. This was before the chauffeur-driven limos and private planes, which he never expects or wants – Ricky's happy to carry his own bag. It might seem strange that that memory stays with me out of all the excitement that went on around those fights, but it just summed up to me what Rick's about.

The worst time was after the Pacquiao fight – it was a long journey home. The overriding feeling among people on my plane wasn't, oh we've spent all this money to come out to watch the fight, it was whether Rick was alright. How was he feeling? There was no bitterness. We'd had a great time in Vegas, a great night out before the fight and everyone just felt deflated for Rick. He felt he'd let everybody down, but none of us thought he had.

Ricky had a tremendous career and without those fights, there's tens of thousands of people who otherwise wouldn't have gone to Vegas.

THE PERFECT SHOT

The best punch I ever threw in Vegas – the best body shot I ever threw – was the left hook to the body that knocked out José Luis Castillo. Picture-perfect from a technical point of view, it was the punch that really announced me to a wider American audience. Before that punch, hardcore American boxing fans had seen my fights in England on the Showtime channel. Then my two wins against Luis Collazo and Juan Urango on American soil had got me more exposure, but hadn't been the sort of spectacular performances required to lead me to the mega fights I wanted. I really needed a decisive stoppage victory against top-rated opposition. Castillo fitted the bill as an opponent, having given Floyd Mayweather his toughest fight and, more recently, stopped Diego

Corrales in four in their rematch. A lot of boxing experts would have had him in their top ten pound-for-pound fighters at the time. Not only that, he was known for his toughness, ability to fight on the inside and body-punching, so to beat him at his own game was a big statement.

Body-punching is an art and, when you are working to the body, there are a couple of vulnerable areas you're aiming to hit. The solar plexus or the breastbone, parts that you can't toughen up, so I used to look to put a good straight left up the middle. No matter how much abs work you do, it's a lot harder to toughen up round the side of your ribs, so if you can sink one underneath the elbow, it can do some damage. That's where my left hook to the body came in.

It has been my favourite punch from ever since I started boxing. Throwing it always came very naturally – I'd always be looking to shift and roll my body weight to get my body in position to have the leverage to throw it with full force. But when you are up against such a good in-fighter as Castillo, who would have trained specifically to counter my body shots, the problem my trainer Billy Graham and I faced was how I was going to get it in. We knew that he knew that I'd be looking for that shot, so we had to work out how to disguise it. We worked on touching him somewhere else first – a quick punch but no real force – to distract his attention and create the opening.

This is easier said than done come fight night, though, because Castillo is wise to all the tricks on the inside. Early on, he always gets his elbows down just in time whenever I unload a hook.

The gameplan I'd actually agreed with Billy beforehand was to start off the fight boxing more on the outside and work my way in. 'Like Urango,' he'd told me, 'he's very strong, a good body-puncher, likes to fight on the inside. Not so good at the distance, where you can be. So let's go with similar tactics.'

From what I'd seen of Castillo that seemed like exactly the right approach, but when I got in the ring, it's a different story. Despite his reputation, he just feels so weak in comparison to Urango. From the early exchanges I feel I'm too strong for him, I can bully him.

This leads to a minor row in the corner after round two with Billy who, understandably, is concerned that I've gone rogue.

'You're not in there, Billy,' I tell him. 'Every time I hit him, I hurt him. Every time I nudge him, he feels weak as fuck, Bill. I swear to God. He's not going to last two or three more rounds at this rate.'

'Okay, okay. Bear in mind how tough he is though. Just be smart. Try and leave a bit for the home straight just in case.'

'Trust me, Bill.'

So I just stay in at close-quarters and, ultimately, it actually takes one of Castillo's own punches to set me up for the shot I've been looking for.

In round four, he connects with a left hook to my head and I move to my left to take the sting out of it. That little shift in my body weight puts me in just the right position to throw my left hook. First, just as we've practised, I throw a little short one to the head and in that split second see that – for once – Castillo has left his body exposed, so I whip in the left hook under his elbow.

I know that I'd thrown the punch with my entire body weight from the boots up and hit him exactly where I wanted to, round the side of the rib cage where there's less muscle to protect the bones. As soon as it lands, I know that I've done some damage – when you get them in the right spot, they crumple like a punctured balloon. He immediately turns away in agony, goes down onto one knee and doesn't get back up until long after the count finishes, by which time I'm running round the ring celebrating.

One of the American TV commentators said at the time it

reminded him of the great Roy Jones body shot to KO Virgil Hill in 1998, which was named as *The Ring* magazine Knockout of the Year. Once he'd got his breath back, Castillo said: 'He got me very good with that punch. I have never been caught that way. It was a perfect shot. I couldn't breathe. I couldn't get up.'

In the press conference afterwards, I describe my tactics in the fight as 'educated pressure', adding that's what it takes to outsmart a great in-fighter like Castillo. One reporter isn't impressed though, sticking his hand up and asking whether Castillo getting knocked out by a body shot is just proof that he's a shot fighter.

Bob Arum, Castillo's promoter, answers that one for me, replying: 'It's strange how the press who've never boxed in their lives know so much about boxing. The doctor has just x-rayed Castillo and Ricky has broken four of his ribs with one punch. So would he have taken that body shot better a few years ago? If four of his ribs were broken, my answer is no, he wouldn't have. I've been in boxing for forty-two years and I've probably seen that shot hit perfectly five times. Once you get hit that way the guy can't breathe for thirty seconds and there's nothing he can do, no matter how much he wants to get up. It is more effective than a knockout punch on the chin. Instead of saying Castillo would have taken it a few years ago, you should be praising Ricky for putting Castillo down like that. Castillo doesn't go down like that for no reason.'

Can't argue with someone who has been in boxing as long as Bob, so the journalist has to take his verdict on the chin (or in the ribs).

REFFING HELL

To beat Floyd Mayweather, an all-time great, was always going to be a massive ask. One thing was for certain – with his speed and slickness, I was never going to do it boxing him from a distance for twelve rounds. But I wasn't exactly slow myself, and the plan was to mix it up a bit to start with, and work my way in.

Before the opening bell, Billy Graham says to me: 'Don't be careless. Choose your moments. Ease into it.'

But neither of us have bargained for just how quick Floyd is. I try to ease into it, but within half a minute he throws a lightning-fast lead left hook which catches me. Bang. Later, a lead right hand. Bang. I realise straight away that standing off him isn't going to work and look to get inside for the rest of the round.

When I go back to the corner I say to Billy: 'I can't stand off this fella. I'm not going to beat him by out-boxing him and I ain't going to beat him for speed – he's too quick.'

I have to get on his chest, out-work him, bully him, hope he loses his shape. That's what I try to do from then on, but every time I get inside, the referee Joe Cortez calls 'break'.

Thomas Hauser:

I thought Joe Cortez did a horrible job in that fight. No one knows what would have happened, but it could have evolved very differently if Joe Cortez had refereed the fight better. I was very troubled by that at the time and I ran some numbers on it; the number of times when he broke Ricky when he didn't have to.

These are the numbers Thomas mentioned in his article. He added up that Cortez broke the action eleven times in the first round, thirteen times in round two, fourteen in round three – and noted that often one or both of us were still punching so there was no need to do so. In the fifth round, Cortez only broke us up four times – and guess what? I won the round on all three judges' cards.

Because he's breaking us too early, that means I have to start over and take more shots from Floyd to get back inside again. Then, when I get there, even though I'm supposed to be the roughhousing fighter, Cortez is letting Floyd get away with leading with his head, forearm and elbows and hitting low. When Floyd is holding, I'm the one getting warned.

About a minute into round six, Floyd turns his back, I throw a punch – which misses – and Cortez deducts a point. I can't believe it. Traditionally in boxing you get a warning, not a point lopped off straight away. I'm probably a couple of rounds down already, but I've been working my way into the fight. Now I've had a point taken away for no good reason and I feel like it's not a level playing field. I'm not getting any favours from this fella here. After that things go downhill for me as I try to force matters and leave myself more and more open to Floyd's potshots.

Reflecting on the fight in the dressing room later, I say I've no complaints about Floyd fouling me on the inside – I'm no Mother Theresa in the ring and I'd have done the same given half a chance – but he was allowed to get away with it all the time. Yet when I was in close, in position to throw hurtful punches, the referee made me start all over again.

I'd never had that sort of issue with a referee in my own career before. The only time I'd ever got really upset with a ref was the previous year and I wasn't even fighting. That was when my brother Matthew was fighting Alan Bosworth in a British welterweight title eliminator. Alan fought out of the Ingle gym in Sheffield and I'd always had a bit of rivalry with them because Junior Witter was based there. In this fight, I think Brendan and John Ingle were in the corner, and every time Matthew got anywhere near him, they went up like a Mexican wave: 'Eh, referee!' Alan was known as a good tough journeyman, but he turned into a wet lettuce that night, complaining to the referee Howard Foster all the time himself –

'ooh, that was low', wincing and turning away etc. Howard fell for it and ended up disqualifying Matthew. Matthew's never been a dirty fighter, so I was fuming.

Alan came up to me afterwards: 'Sorry about that, Rick.'

'Don't speak to me, Alan. You've gone down in my estimation, you. You're a fearless journeyman, you fight anybody, and you have them in your corner and you turn into a prima donna. I never thought I'd see the day . . .'

Back to the Floyd fight, it was a very poor display by Cortez and went totally against my expectations of him. Before the referee for the fight was announced, all Billy and me wanted was a ref who would let Floyd and me get on and work on the inside.

'What Ricky does on the inside – and it's perfectly legal – is he tries to rearrange the position of his opponent's arms to create avenues for his punches,' Billy said. 'So let's have a good referee who's going to let the two best fighters on the planet fight. Let the fans see what they've paid for.'

I was delighted when Cortez was named ref, because he'd refereed me and Castillo and let us get on with boxing on the inside. But, looking back, I was actually being quite naive. What I didn't realise is that Joe Cortez lives in Las Vegas. I never even thought about it until a few months after the fight: a Las Vegas fighter being refereed by a Las Vegas referee. It's mad when you think about it. I would've loved to have a Manchester referee for my big fights in Manchester, but that would never have happened. Maybe for a small-hall show, but never for a major fight.

I'd heard a rumour around the Vegas gyms before the fight, that Floyd had problems with his elbow and was having treatment on it. My thinking was, first time I get him in a clinch, I'm going to give him such a fucking yank on the elbow (like I said, I'm no Mother Theresa). With Joe Cortez being from Vegas and Floyd being from Vegas, I wonder if anyone had said to him, 'Whenever this little bulldog gets near Floyd, break 'em, because Floyd's carrying an elbow injury'? Who knows?

What I do know is that Floyd was very confident that no rough stuff would be allowed, saying in the week of the fight: 'You can't use roughhouse tactics in Las Vegas. Over here we have the Nevada Commission and we have a tremendous referee in Joe Cortez, and they're fair and firm. Boxing is an art, a science. This is smart, intelligent boxing over here in the States.'

When Cortez came into my dressing room before the fight, after running through the usual pre-fight instructions, he asked if we had any questions.

'Ricky is an inside fighter,' Billy says. 'He fights clean but he's an aggressive fighter . . .'

'I'll let the fight take its course,' Cortez replies.

Well, most people who watched the fight would say that he didn't. I sometimes wonder if we were right or wrong to make a point of that. Everyone has an ego, and no referee likes to be told their job.

Another theory is that he got the hump when my fans booed the American national anthem and that affected the way he reffed the fight.

In the weeks we spent in Vegas before the fight, what was quite surprising was that most of the American fight fans Billy and me met said they were supporting me, not Floyd. I know from talking to my American mates, that changed after their national anthem was booed.

Joe Sharpe:

The Americans were rooting for Ricky up until they were singing the national anthem and the Brits started booing for no reason.

Then the Americans took a stand saying, 'Well, we're American.'
People weren't rooting for Floyd, but they respected the fact that he
was American.

It's not right, but at international football matches, national anthems often get jeered. Americans aren't used to that at sporting events. As much as Las Vegas loved the Ricky Hatton bandwagon – all the fans, the atmosphere and the football-style singing and chanting – booing their national anthem was a step too far. It's understandable. I'm very proud of my home city and country, and if 35,000 Americans had come over to Manchester, taking over the bars and then booing our national anthem, I would think, 'Who's this Yank coming over to our town?'

The anthems were sung before Floyd and me came to the ring, but Joe Cortez was already in there with the various officials and dignitaries. Then when Floyd walked out to the ring to Bruce Springsteen's *Born in the USA* with the Brits booing him, the patriotism of the American fans in the arena was stoked up even more to defend the honour of the Stars and Stripes. Maybe the atmosphere affected Joe Cortez, too? Do you know what, if I was him in that position, I think it might have affected my performance.

Ian Darke:

A guy from the Nevada Commission turned to me and said: 'I hope
your guy gets his ass whipped after that.' He was steaming angry. Joe
Cortez is American too. I do think that was a factor. In plain
language, there was a bit of 'fuck you' in there that night.

Thomas Hauser doesn't think the booing of the national anthem influenced Cortez, though; he has a different theory on it:

Thomas Hauser:

I did not think Joe acquitted himself well that night – and there are other times when he did not have such a good night, but he had very good nights too. When I took issue with Joe's work in the ring, it appeared to me that he was favouring the house fighter, the money fighter. You saw that several times. That of course is the big problem with boxing – referees and judges want to get the next big assignment, and you get the next big assignment by keeping the money guy happy. I'm not saying Joe sat down with an agenda, but it could have been at the back of his mind that if he let Ricky fight a certain way, he'd be vetoed to referee Floyd's next fight. I don't know that, but it crossed my mind.

Cortez's last words to the boxers in the ring before the start of the fight were: 'I'm fair, but I'm firm.' He has actually legally trademarked the phrase, his website is fairbutfirm.com, his Twitter handle is @mrfairbutfirm. Well, he was firm, but for whatever reason, I don't think he was fair to me in that fight with Floyd.

The week before the fight, Barry McGuigan had been asked for his prediction and he called it just about spot-on. 'Ricky will have to have the fight of his life on Saturday,' he said. 'I just hope referee Cortez allows him to get inside because that will be his best tactic. Mayweather has such brilliant hand speed and I think he'll be just too quick. But I'm worried he will use the referee and pickpocket the fight.'

Afterwards, Barry described Cortez's refereeing of the fight as 'disgraceful'.

Joe Cortez reffed over 170 world title bouts during a long career before retiring in 2012. He's a Hall of Fame referee, maybe he just had one of those bad nights Thomas Hauser talks about, and I was unlucky that it happened in the biggest fight of my career, but what happened didn't sit well with me for a long time. It still doesn't.

Kerry Kayes:

The amount of concentration involved in boxing is unbelievable and Cortez messed up Ricky's concentration and his rhythm. Ricky got a point deducted for a blow to the back of Mayweather's head that did not land, yet Mayweather did a similar blow to the back of Ricky's head in round two and he didn't even get a warning.

I think the referee played a massive part in the outcome of the fight. But having said that, it wasn't the referee who knocked Ricky out; it was Mayweather. Mayweather was a great athlete and he won, he did a few dirty tricks, which we applaud him for, not condemn him, because if we could have got away with them, we would have done the same.

When I went to watch the Floyd Mayweather–Shane Mosley fight a couple of years later, I was ringside shaking hands with all the officials; Kenny Bayless, who refereed my Pacquiao fight, was there, Tony Weekes, too. It was all very friendly: 'Hiya, Ricky, how're you doing?'

Then Joe Cortez came over. Let's just say I couldn't disguise my feelings towards him. The way he reffed the fight with Mayweather and how he was with him afterwards (watch it on YouTube: he was all over Floyd like a cheap suit), I was like, 'No, that's not right. I'm not having that.'

I'm not saying I would have beaten Floyd. I just wanted a fair crack of the whip, and I don't feel that I had one.

MERCHANT HAIR MALFUNCTION

In America, I had the pleasure of being interviewed by legendary TV boxing commentator and analyst Larry Merchant on a number of occasions. Larry joined HBO in 1978, and I remember seeing tapes of him in his younger days presenting the big fights of the Eighties and Nineties, interviewing the great fighters of those times. To have him ask me questions, twenty years on, was just another part of my Vegas dream becoming reality.

Larry would usually come into the dressing room for HBO a couple of hours before the fight to do a quick interview, as would the people from Sky TV. By then, my mind was on the fight rather than interviews so I don't think I made much sense. After weeks of hype and press conferences, everything that could be said had been and I just wanted to get the talking over with and get on with the job in hand.

The interviews in the ring after the fight are a lot more entertaining for viewers. Larry never boxed himself, but he famously never pulled his punches in asking the questions the spectators and people at home would want him to, even if the fighter didn't like it much.

The best one was when he interviewed my old foe Floyd Mayweather Jr. after his win over Victor Ortiz at the MGM Grand in 2011. By then Larry was eighty years old but he showed he still wasn't afraid to mix it with the big boys.

The fight had ended soon after Ortiz was warned by referee Joe Cortez (yes, him again . . .) for headbutting Floyd. Ortiz went over and hugged Floyd in apology, then as Cortez led him round the ring to take off a point, he touched gloves with Floyd. What happened next caused all the controversy, because Cortez gave the hand and arm signal to box on, but didn't actually say 'box'. For some reason, Ortiz walked towards Floyd with his hands down looking like he wanted another hug. Cortez meanwhile was making a point to the officials at ringside. Ortiz and Floyd touched gloves, went into a sort of half-hug, half-clinch, but as Ortiz stepped back, his hands still down at his sides – and with Cortez looking the other way – Floyd clips him with a fast left hook and floors him with a follow-up right hand.

There will be a real 50–50 split in how people view that incident. In boxing, one of the basics is protect yourself at all times, and you can't get away from that. Equally, though, I think there should also be a mutual respect. While Floyd didn't do anything wrong, he was a bit naughty. If I was in that position, I wouldn't have done it, because Ortiz wasn't ready. I want to win by being the best man – creating an opening and knocking someone out – not by sneaking one on him. Floyd would probably have won anyway, but on the night he didn't show he was the better fighter.

Larry – and many people in the crowd, booing – thought it was a cheap shot and told Floyd as much.

As the post-fight interview begins, Floyd's all smiles and got his arm around Larry, but things quickly go downhill: 'You hear the crowd,' says Larry. 'At least a good part of the uproar is that you took shots unfairly at him, after you went together in the ring, made up for the headbutt, and then you poked him. What's your story?'

Floyd starts off by thanking God and his team and then talks about getting 'hit with a dirty shot' and 'protect yourself at all times'.

Larry isn't letting it go easily though and presses him further: 'What do you say to those who say, "What did you do there?" You were winning the fight, you were in charge?'

Floyd completely avoids answering the question and starts thanking everyone who bought the fight on pay-per-view, so Larry interrupts: 'Floyd, we know you're a promoter, but now we're talking to you as a prizefighter. Let's look at what happened . . .'

They watch the replay together and Floyd repeats his side of the story, but the crowd are booing, Floyd hasn't got his arm around Larry anymore and you can see he's getting more and more agitated.

'. . . We're not here to cry about what he did dirty or I did dirty, I was victorious, if he wants a rematch, he can get a rematch.'

Larry tries again to suggest Floyd took advantage when he shouldn't have, but before he can get his full question out, a fuming Floyd cuts in: 'You know what I'm gonna do, because you don't ever give me a fair shake, you know that. So I'm going to let you talk to Victor Ortiz. I'm through . . .'

By now, he's squaring up to Larry, pointing and shouting: '. . . Put somebody else up to give me an interview. You never give me a fair shake . . .'

There's a great a photo of Larry looking towards camera with a shocked look on his face as Floyd is having a go at him. To be fair to old Larry, he stands his ground: 'What're you talking about? What are you talking about?'

'HBO need to fire you. You don't know shit about boxing. You ain't shit.'

As Floyd turns to walk off, Larry puts his hand on his shoulder and says, 'I wish I was fifty years younger and I'd kick your ass!'

Go Larry! I'd have paid to see that fight.

Everyone was looking forward to Mayweather–Merchant II at Floyd's next fight against Miguel Cotto, but to be fair to Floyd, he did the unexpected and apologised to Larry at the weigh-in to defuse the situation.

'He offered an apology in recognition of my ancient mariner status,' joked Larry.

Our interviews were always friendly, and one after I beat Juan Urango sticks in my mind.

Like all TV presenters, I'd often see Larry get his little mirror out of his pocket before the camera started rolling to check his hair and make-up. He usually looked immaculate, but as he's about to interview me in the ring after the Urango fight, I notice that he's having a bit of a hair malfunction. It's all going a bit Don King; a few strands of his normally perfectly backcombed hair are sticking up like he's rubbed his head on a carpet.

As he starts asking me questions, I can't concentrate so I say, 'C'mon, Larry, let's sort this barnet out,' lick my fingers and stroke his hair back down. He's got a very bouncy quiff, but a little bit of Mancunian spit does the trick.

THE PAIN GAME

For all the glamour of a big fight in Vegas, one thing that doesn't change, whether you're boxing at the Spectrum Arena in Warrington or the MGM Grand, is that you are going to get hit. Getting hit hurts. Of course, as professional fighters, we spend years and years toughening up our bodies to deal with that, but the higher the level you go, the more you meet boxers with the skills to nail you and, no matter what you do to prepare yourself, it is painful when you get caught with a good clean shot.

The difference with the best and toughest fighters is that you don't ponder on it. You might think, 'Oof, that hurt,' but you have to put it behind you immediately. The adrenaline pumping through your body helps you ignore the pain in the fight – unless a punch is enough to stop you. That happened to me as an amateur when I got knocked over by a left cross and my corner threw the towel in. I was hurt and didn't have a clue what I was doing for the next few hours. I went back to the dressing room afterwards, took my boots and shorts off, went to the toilet, came back and started putting my boots and shorts back on again, thinking I still had to fight. I had completely forgotten that I'd been knocked out.

It's usually only the next day that you start to really ache, though. You know if you're caught by a specific punch. If you've been caught with a hard body shot in round five, you know all about it the next day. At the time you have to shake the shot off and get on with it. The pain's come and gone before you have time to dwell on it.

If you've had a tough twelve-round fight, it can take a week to recover. I always won when I went twelve rounds, but those were the fights that hurt the most. Even the punches you take on the arms you can feel the next day. Every time an opponent throws a shot, you're tensing your muscles and it puts a lot of pressure on your internal organs. If I went the distance, I'd always be peeing blood the next day.

Cuts can look a bit gory when blood's running down your face, but they aren't really painful. As a fighter, your only worry about cuts is that the referee might stop the fight. That's the worst possible way to lose because it's something that's out of your control.

By the time I got to fight in Vegas, I had learnt not to worry about getting cut. I had the best cutman in the business in my corner in Mick Williamson, and I became very good at shutting out negative thoughts, getting on with my job and letting Mick do his. I have to admit I was panicking a bit more than normal when I got cut over both eyes within three rounds against the tough Colombian Carlos Maussa in one of my last fights before hitting Vegas. But I got through that, knocking Maussa out in the ninth round.

Billy Graham was always concerned that I'd get cut in the Mayweather fight, because of Floyd's fast slashing punches. Sure enough, I was cut in round three, but Mick did a great job as usual and it didn't affect me at all.

I actually went into the Mayweather fight with an unusual little injury. The day of the weigh-in, I was at the spa at Caesars Palace for a sauna, and somehow manage to stub the nail of one of my big toes and split it. With half of it hanging off, I have to stumble to the nearest nail spa to get it sorted. I ended up sitting in the Venus Saloon getting my nail glued back on among all the ladies having their manicures and pedicures – cost me a hundred dollars. My mate Joe Sharpe has a theory that the injury niggle affected me in the fight.

Joe Sharpe:

Ricky's balance was off in the fight. That toenail experience was the preamble to how the fight ended. He was injured but didn't want anyone to know. If you look at that fight, Ricky was doing well up until the seventh/eighth round. Take into consideration the balance of his feet, because his toe must have been bleeding.

I think Joe's being a bit kind there, bless him. It was uncomfortable, but I'm not using it as any excuse at all. David Haye had the piss ripped out of him after losing to Wladimir Klitschko and saying a broken little toe had affected his performance; and I only had a broken toenail. The main thing affecting my balance at the end of the fight was Floyd hitting me round the head.

People who aren't boxers might be surprised to know that losing by a second-round knockout by Manny Pacquiao wasn't as painful for me physically as winning a twelve-round fight.

Ian Darke:

It was horrible when Ricky was knocked out by Pacquiao. I was really worried – he lay there almost like he was in a tomb. I really

263

did think he might be dead, that it might be that bad. I'll never forget that piercing scream from Jennifer. The whole thing was a horror story – there was genuine alarm. I don't think I've ever seen a fighter lay that motionless after being knocked out, not even Duran after being knocked out by Hearns. It was a horrible thing to behold. I wrote in a column soon afterwards that if Ricky ever thinks about fighting again, he needs to get that tape out and watch it. You can't fight on when you've been knocked out like that.

Jeff Powell:

I thought he'd died. He went down on his back and his arms folded over his chest, like he was lying in a coffin. I turned to the other guys and said, 'This could be serious.' Ricky is always pale-faced, but he looked ashen.

Paul Speak:

I rolled into the ring and was one of the first to get to Ricky. I put him in the recovery position because there were no medics about to start with. Rick opened his eyes, looked at me and said: 'Fucking hell, have I been knocked out?'

'Yes,' I said.

'Oh fuck.'

I told him to rest and lie there. So it wasn't quite as bad as it looked to those at ringside – he was conscious. Ricky's got a very hard head!

I know the knockout was brutal and shocking at the time for people to see, but I hadn't sustained a beating over a number of rounds. I was rushed to hospital straight after and, by the time I got there, my blood pressure and pulse rate were already right down to normal. Thankfully, the brain scan came up all-clear too. For a fighter, the damage from a knockout like that is more to your mentality. As I suffer from depression, it was particularly hard for me to get over that Pacquiao knockout. Later at the hospital, there was my dad, Jennifer, Speaky, Kugan and me all sitting there. I had my head in my hands and there was about five minutes of silence. That was mental anguish and there was nothing anyone could say to make me feel better.

Jeff Powell:

The key to that fight was that Freddie Roach had been working with Pacquiao for a while to get his right hand almost as good as the left hand. Ricky came out moving away from the left, which was the correct thing to do because Pacquiao's left hook is one of the biggest weapons in boxing.

But the first big punches of the fight Pacquiao landed were right hooks to the head – and that caused the first knockdown. As soon as Ricky moved the other way, he got knocked out. They'd been improving Pacquiao's right for a while, but that was the first time you saw Pacquiao really damage someone with the right, close to how he damages with the left. It was a nightmare scenario.

The Pacquiao knockout was the beginning of the end for Ricky. He would always come to talk to the British press the morning after the fights in America, but that was the only time he failed to meet us. He'd always face the music, good or bad performance, but that was the only time he didn't. I think the impact of that knockout was profound – it was more than disappointment.

Paul Speak:

In the ambulance on the way to the hospital, Rick turned to me and said: 'I think I've had enough, Paul; I think I'm going to retire.' I told him not to worry about that now. He didn't have to make any big decisions yet.

It was really eerie at the hospital – going from 16,000 people cheering him on at the MGM Grand to being another average Joe at the hospital waiting his turn like everyone else. The silence was deafening. It was horrible to see him suffering like that.

My fight with Luis Collazo in Boston had been much harder physically, the most gruelling fight I ever had. I didn't go to hospital after that and I wish I had done. The doctor checked me in the changing rooms and I was okay, and was okay at the post-fight party, but I felt worse and worse as the night went on. Back in my room, I couldn't sleep for hours. I had the shakes, was feverish and any light or the slightest bit of noise was unbearable. The strange thing was after I finally got some sleep, I felt alright again in the morning. Well, apart from a swollen face and bruises.

Usually, I didn't feel the effects of the fight when I was out partying through the night afterwards. The adrenaline is still flowing, everyone is still buzzing from the fight and the alcohol numbs the pain a bit too. In all seriousness it's very dangerous to drink as much as I did after a fight when you are dehydrated. The worst thing you can do is drink alcohol and dehydrate your body further. The British Boxing Board of Control advise boxers not to do that, and I advise all my fighters not to. I was very, very foolish to drink the way I did . . . but the problem in Vegas is that there's so much fun to be had.

POST-FIGHT REFUELLING

My brother Matthew and I grew up in pubs and were well known for being able to sink a few beers. After being on the wagon for a couple of months in training, we were always ready for a few days of 'refuelling' with our mates and the fans once our Vegas fights were over. When you've not touched a drop for weeks, your mind is making promises your body can't keep so it didn't take long before we were very merry.

After the Mayweather bout, I went back to my room feeling absolutely devastated, but I dragged myself out to the after-fight party. All my mates and the fans are there, saying that I've done them proud and after a couple of beers I start to feel alright – so alright I end up going out on the piss all night!

We go to Noir at the Luxor, a private, invitation-only club for a while, before heading across the road for a gamble at the Mandalay. As we walk in, I get spotted and all of a sudden, literally a hundred people start chasing me across the casino floor. The security guys come running over and are trying to push them away, but I tell them not to worry.

So I'm sat down at the roulette table with all these people watching. I start winning. But the more I win, the more money I'm betting (by this point, I'm hammered so I'm only telling you what I was told later). It's not long before I see my once huge stack of chips disappear so we call it a night/morning.

Jennifer Dooley:

After all the partying, me and Rick went to get something to eat – it must have been eight or nine in the morning. When we sat down we ordered food but at that point Rick suddenly crashed back down to

earth and put his head in his hands at the table. I had to get him
back up to the room. He was devastated.

Back in our room, I say to Jen: 'Oh God, I think I lost a fortune last night. I was up loads at one point . . .'

'No, you didn't,' she replies and pours out a load of chips from her handbag onto the bed. 'You were getting silly with your bets, so I was pinching your chips and sticking them in my bag.'

That's my girl.

We crash out on the bed.

What seems like five minutes later, I can hear a voice saying loudly: 'Ricky! Ricky! Wake up!'

Through bleary eyes I can just about make out Speaky standing over me, and Jennifer sitting at the dressing table putting on her make-up.

'What the hell are you doing?'

'We've got to be over in the arena for the *BBC Sports Personality of the Year* in an hour,' she says. 'Because of the time difference.'

'I can't go, Jennifer. I can't go. I'm pissed, I'll be falling all over the place in the front row.'

'You've got to go, Rick,' says Paul. 'You've been nominated.'

'No, I'm not going.'

'Come on, Rick, have a coffee, you'll be alright.'

'No, Paul, I'm not going, you dickhead – look at the state of me.'

Paul Speak:

I knew that Rick would be out on the piss after the fight and he had
to be up early for SPOTY, so I'd got hold a key for their suite the
night before. When I walked in him and Jen were both fast asleep,
but she was a lot easier to wake up. Every time I thought I'd persuaded

him to get up and get a shower, he kept on running back and jumping back in. It was like trying to get a kid ready for school.

Jen and Paul won't take no for an answer and, after pouring a couple of coffees and Red Bulls down me, we stagger across the MGM Grand Garden Arena.

When I walk in, Joe Calzaghe, who's also been nominated, and Lennox Lewis look at me, like, 'Whoah, what's happened here?'

Somehow I get through the ceremony, propped up in a seat next to Jen at ringside with Joe, Lennox and other guests like Richie Woodhall and Enzo Maccarinelli.

The hardest part is when Gary Lineker interviews me via satellite link.

He starts by saying: 'So Ricky, how did the fight go?'

I'm thinking, are you taking the piss, Gary – how do you think the fight went? but in my pickled state, I'm just concentrating on holding it together and not making a tool of myself. I think I string a sentence or two together that make sense.

Some people back in the studio must have realised I was pissed as a fart, but hopefully they thought, well, who can blame him?

Joe wins the award, I get voted into third place and then I go back to our room for some kip.

Jennifer Dooley:

Ricky describes it in his own way, but I know he didn't want to go to the Sports Personality of the Year awards and not just because he had a hangover. Paul and I had to force him out of the door that day. He felt embarrassed; he didn't want to show his face. But I knew it was the right thing for him to do.

We both just giggled our way through it – we were both still drunk

– and we did have a good time. But whenever we had a moment on our own back in our room, he was beyond upset, he was absolutely heartbroken.

After a couple of hours, I'm up and off out again. Me and Matthew go for a gamble. I'm not a big gambler, but I get on a lucky streak, winning about $2,000 over a few hours, and when you're gambling in Vegas, they bring you free drinks. We've decided that the hair of the dog is the way to deal with our raking hangovers, so by the time we leave the tables, Matthew and me are both pissed as farts again.

In the evening David Beckham has invited me, Jennifer, Matt and Jenna to join him in his private box at the Mandalay Bay Events Center to watch the Spice Girls concert. It's their comeback tour and they were originally going to be on at the MGM Grand Arena the night before, but got shifted down the Strip so Floyd and me could take the date instead.

Matthew and I have got our second wind and are looking forward to the free bar in the VIP box. When we walk in, there's a big sofa at the back of this long room and there's a bloke and a woman sitting on it, him with his feet up on the coffee table in front. As we walk past, Matthew, who's never short of a wisecrack, glances across and says: 'Why don't you relax a little bit, put your fucking feet up.'

It's quite dark in there and it's only when we get to the balcony overlooking the arena, that I look back and do a double take: 'Fucking hell,' I whisper to Matt. 'That's Tom Cruise and Katie Holmes . . . that's Tom Cruise you've just said to take his fucking feet off the table.'

'Is it fuck,' he replies, then looks over his shoulder not very subtly. 'Bloody hell, it is.'

He goes over and offers to get Tom a drink and we end up having a right laugh with them. Katie and him are fascinated by our Manc accents and keep asking us to say things again. Maybe Tom fancied playing me in a film one day – we do look alike . . .

Jennifer Dooley:

That Spice Girls concert was the most surreal experience I had in Vegas. We met all the Spice Girls in the dressing room before the gig and then we walked into this box and there's David Beckham, Tom Cruise and Katie Holmes snuggled up on the couch, and Sarah Ferguson, Duchess of York, with her daughter Princess Beatrice. David hadn't warned us that any of these people would be there and it was quite a dark room so it took a few seconds to register who was who. It was unbelievable. We met sporting royalty, pop royalty, acting royalty and actual royalty all in one night.

Fergie was fabulous – she speaks with a very posh accent but is very down-to-earth. She was saying to Rick about Mayweather, 'Ricky, you should have knocked him out!'

There are still loads of fight fans in town, so when Matt, me and the girls go to Pure Nightclub at Caesars Palace – regarded as one the best clubs in the world – after the gig, the place is heaving with Brits.

We've got a cabana reserved for us and Emma Bunton and Mel B are in the one next to us with their partners. The dance floor is nearby, behind a glass divider, and when my fans see me they all start pushing up against the glass, singing, 'There's only one Ricky Hatton.' The DJ stops the music and pleads for them to step back, but he's getting nowhere, so Mel B gets up and starts shouting, 'Get back! Step back!' only for the fans to chant, 'Who the fucking hell are you?' I feel bad for her, but it is funny.

Jennifer Dooley:

They've this big line of security holding the people back and one of the men says to Ricky, 'Would you mind saying a few words to ask them to get back from the glass?' So Ricky gets up and does that, but then, in typical Rick fashion, he jumps over the glass and is walking through this crush of fans shaking hands with everyone. I'm like, 'Oh my God, this guy.'

It used to upset me when people were pawing at him and grabbing him when he was all battered and bruised, because I'd see him wince when he was in the shower, but he didn't feel it because he was so connected to the fans. That's where he wanted to be.

It was so different to when we first went to Pure after the Urango fight. I remember my feet were killing me because I'd been out for ages with this big group of lads and I was wearing these massive high heels. I could see a little roped-off area – not the VIP section – where there was an empty couch winking at me.

I went over to this security guy and said, 'Excuse me, would it be okay if we just sit down there.'

'Ma'am, that will be $500.'

We're from Manchester not London, and didn't understand you had to pay to sit at a table.

'Oh right, okay, it doesn't matter . . .'

This time, it's like, 'Ah, Ricky Hatton – come this way . . .' Big bed in the VIP area at the back, a couple of Spice Girls on the bed next to us – and they aren't getting any attention, it's all on Rick. Less than a year before I wasn't even allowed to perch my backside on a couch. It all happened so quickly.

That's true – things really did build up after Urango, and we actually had another good jolly up at Pure in between times. The day after my win over Castillo, Joe Sharpe asked me if I wanted to go there to celebrate that evening.

'Yeah, would love to go, Joe,' I reply. 'But there's fifteen of us . . .'

'Who is there, then?'

'Me, me girlfriend and thirteen of my mates.'

The thirteen are all my pals from the council estate back home.

'Alright, no problem. I'll get you a table. Pick up your tickets on the door.'

So we all head down there.

It's a very luxurious club, and when we are shown to our table, there's a huge bottle of vodka waiting for us. It would probably cost hundreds, if not thousands, but we're told the drinks are on the house today. Lovely jubbly.

But with me coming off three months of sobriety, and fourteen other thirsty Mancunians in celebratory mood, it doesn't take us long to go through the whole bottle, though. Bosh. Gone.

'Can we have another one, please?' I ask the waitress.

'Of course, sir.'

She brings another bottle over. That doesn't take any longer to polish off.

'Can we have another one?'

A third mega bottle of vodka duly arrives and we're busy tearing into that when the waitress brings over a phone and says Joe's on the line.

'Hiya, Joe, you alright?'

'Ricky, you having a good time?'

'Yeah, fantastic, thanks, Joe.'

'Good, good . . . now make that your last bottle, you cheeky little bastard.'

EPILOGUE

So those were my Vegas years. I went there as an unbeaten boxer in January 2007 and came away with a couple of losses on my record two and a half years later. I took those defeats very hard, and there's no doubt that they contributed to my subsequent battles with depression. But doing this book has allowed me to relive the whole Vegas adventure in detail. Reading the fight reports, watching the old videos on YouTube and the *24/7* documentaries, hearing the memories of other people who worked with me and supported me – my overriding feeling is one of huge pride.

Topping the bill in Vegas had been my dream growing up and I made it. It wasn't all success in the ring there, but for a while they called me the 'King of Vegas' because of the unprecedented number of fans that followed me from Britain and took over the town in fight week.

I was taken to the best restaurants and most exclusive clubs, flew about on private jets and stayed in some of the best hotel rooms in the world. Denzel Washington coming to my dressing room to watch me warm up, Brad Pitt and Angelina Jolie checking if I'm alright after a fight, being on first-name terms with Sylvester Stallone . . . this is jaw-dropping stuff where I come from. I've been asked if all that was everything I expected it to be, but I can't say it was because I had absolutely no concept of what it would be like in the first place. Sometimes I did look around and think to myself, bloody hell, I'm just a kid from Hattersley – you've done well, son.

It would have been easy to get swept up in that lifestyle, but I was always paranoid about what people would think of me. I have a lot of lovely things in life, but I'm not really in your face about it. The way I was brought up, and my mates who I knock about with, wouldn't allow me to get too carried away. Some fighters today refer to themselves as 'superstars' – I wouldn't have any mates left if I started behaving like that. I just enjoyed it for what it was, and I was glad that I could have my mates with me so they could enjoy the experience too.

One of my great pleasures now is going back to Vegas and meeting people there who tell me what a great time they had when my fights – and my army of fans – were in town. Mind you, for a while I was a bit worried they wouldn't let me back into America again, let alone Vegas. That problem started when the old *News of the World* newspaper ran the infamous story about me taking drugs during a very low point in my life. There are two main reasons why they might stop you coming into America – one is if you've been convicted of a crime, the other is a story printed about you committing a crime. So even though I wasn't arrested or convicted of anything, the fact that I've openly admitted in print what I'd done counted against me.

Not that it seemed to matter for a while. I went to America three times after the story came out – including going to see my brother fight Saul Alvarez for the world title in LA – with no problem. Then, in May 2014, I rock up at Manchester airport on my way to Vegas to watch my pal Amir Khan fight in Vegas on the Floyd Mayweather–Marcos Maidana undercard. I've got my flip-flops on, shorts and a vest, floppy hat – I'm already on holiday in my mind.

There's a load of Amir's fans on the same flight as me, so I'm chatting away with them at the check-in, having my picture taken with them. Then I get to the gate, and the fella says to me, dead apologetic: 'We can't let you in Ricky.'

I have to walk back past all these people I've been talking to excitedly about going out to Vegas. It's so embarrassing. I feel about an inch tall.

The crazy thing is that a few months later when Floyd and Maidana fought a rematch, Amir himself got stopped from going out to watch even though he'd had his visa approved just the week before. Apparently, the US authorities got nervous because Amir travels to Pakistan, which is ridiculous, he's got family and friends there – and his wife is American.

Anyway, I had to apply for another visa and last December I went to the US Embassy in London for an interview, armed with a lovely letter from Richard Sturm, President of MGM Grand Entertainment, saying, among other things, that the MGM had never made more money than in the week of my fight with Floyd Mayweather.

Sitting in the waiting room, I get chatting to a fella who says he's been coming back every six months for years to try and get his visa again. I ask him why they wouldn't give it back to him.

'Well, I've been convicted of drug smuggling.'

Oh.

I don't know how he got on, but thankfully my new visa got approved, and a couple of weeks later, I was on a plane to Vegas for the annual WBC Convention at the Mirage hotel. Every year I'm at that convention not just because I'm a promoter, but because I'm a boxing fan. Look at my Twitter timeline and you'll see that over that week I had my picture taken with Thomas Hearns, Iran Barkley, Sugar Ray Leonard, Mike Tyson, Roberto Duran, Kostya Tszyu, Riddick Bowe . . . the list goes on.

EPILOGUE

Before the big awards dinner, there was a VIP room where you could go for a glass of champagne and I swear that almost every champion of the past thirty, forty years was in there. They're all coming up saying, 'Hiya Rick, how are you doing? How's the family?' – it's like being in The Grapes with my mates. I only see those champions once a year, but it's like another family; my boxing family.

The only notable person who isn't in that VIP room is my greatest Vegas opponent, Floyd Mayweather. He doesn't attend the rest of the week's events and even though he comes to the dinner, he turns up surrounded by about twelve people in 'Money Team' tracksuits.

The event is eBay heaven for people who want to make a few quid on signed memorabilia, and you're always getting asked to sign boxing gloves and photos. Although you know some of them are not really fans, you have to do it anyway.

Later that week, I see this little Mexican fella go up to Floyd to ask for an autograph, and one of his huge bodyguards just pushes him away and sends him flying. Watching that, I think to myself that Floyd has earned all that money and will go down as one of the greatest of all time, but he's not like the other champions at the event. He doesn't want people near him. It's comes across to me like, get away from me, I'm better than you. Get away, don't touch the champ. To me, being a true champion is not just about what you do in the ring, it's also how you conduct yourself outside. If he had come to a few more of the events that week and mixed with the fans and his fellow fighters, everyone would have appreciated it and been happy to see him. I'd have said, 'Fair play, mate, you're still number one pound for pound.' Hopefully, he'll realise that one day.

As for me, the belts are locked away in the trophy cabinet now, but the unforgettable memories of Vegas and the love of the fans always remain. To me, that is more important than any amount of money.

VITAL VEGAS STATISTICS

1

vs. Juan Urango (Colombia, 17-0-1)

For: IBF world light welterweight title; vacant International Boxing Organisation world light welterweight title; and *The Ring* magazine junior welterweight title
Date: 20 January 2007
Venue: Paris Las Vegas
Referee: Tony Weeks
Result: Win after 12 rounds by unanimous decision
Judges' scorecards: Robert Hoyle 119–109; Dave Moretti 119–109; Jerry Roth 119–109

CompuBox punch stats

	Me	Urango
Total punches		
Thrown	755	570
Landed	258	153
% Landed	34%	27%
Jabs		
Thrown	131	98
Landed	22	13
% Landed	17%	13%
Power punches		
Thrown	624	472
Landed	236	140
% Landed	38%	30%

2
vs. José Luis Castillo (Mexico, 55-7-1)

For: International Boxing Organisation world light welterweight title; vacant WBC International light welterweight title; and *The Ring* magazine junior welterweight title
Date: 23 June 2007
Venue: Thomas and Mack Center
Referee: Joe Cortez
Result: Win via KO after 2 minutes 16 seconds of round 4
Judges' scorecards: Clark Sammartino 30–27; Adalaide Byrd 30–27; Duane Ford 29–28

CompuBox punch stats

	Me	Castillo
Total punches		
Thrown	220	192
Landed	81	58
% Landed	37%	30%
Jabs		
Thrown	19	41
Landed	5	11
% Landed	26%	27%
Power punches		
Thrown	201	151
Landed	76	47
% Landed	38%	31%

3
vs. Floyd Mayweather Jr. (USA, 38-0-0)

For: WBC world welterweight title
Date: 8 December 2007
Venue: MGM Grand, Grand Garden Arena
Referee: Joe Cortez
Result: Loss via TKO after 1 minute 35 seconds of round 10
Judges' scorecards: Paul Smith 82–88; Dave Moretti 81–89; Burt A. Clements 81–89

CompuBox punch stats

	Me	Mayweather
Total punches		
Thrown	372	329
Landed	63	129
% Landed	17%	39%
Jabs		
Thrown	63	72
Landed	11	29
% Landed	17%	40%
Power punches		
Thrown	309	257
Landed	52	100
% Landed	17%	39%

4
vs. Paulie Malignaggi (USA, 25-1-0)

For: International Boxing Organisation world light welterweight title; and *The Ring* magazine junior welterweight title
Date: 22 November 2008
Venue: MGM Grand
Referee: Kenny Bayless
Result: Win via TKO after 48 seconds of round 11
Judges' scorecards: Duane Ford 99–91; Jerry Roth 99–91; Glenn Trowbridge 99–91

CompuBox punch stats

	Me	Malignaggi
Total punches		
Thrown	516	342
Landed	124	91
% Landed	24%	27%
Jabs		
Thrown	139	209
Landed	25	66
% Landed	18%	32%

Power punches

Thrown	377	133
Landed	99	25
% Landed	26%	19%

5

vs. Manny Pacquiao (Philippines, 48-3-2)

For: International Boxing Organisation world light welterweight title; and *The Ring* magazine junior welterweight title

Date: 2 May 2009

Venue: MGM Grand, Grand Garden Arena

Referee: Kenny Bayless

Result: Loss via KO after 2 minutes 59 seconds of round 2

Judges' scorecards: Michael Pernick 7–10; C.J. Ross 7–10; Glenn Trowbridge 7–10

CompuBox punch stats

	Me	Pacquiao
Total punches		
Thrown	78	127
Landed	18	73
% Landed	23%	57%
Jabs		
Thrown	22	22
Landed	2	8
% Landed	9%	36%
Power punches		
Thrown	56	105
Landed	16	65
% Landed	29%	62%

INDEX

INDEX

INDEX

INDEX

INDEX